CASSELL STUDIES IN PASTORAL CARE AND PERSONAL
AND SOCIAL EDUCATION

TEACHING ABOUT VALUES
A NEW APPROACH

Graham Haydon

CASSELL

Cassell
Wellington House
125 Strand
London WC2R 0BB

PO Box 605
Herndon
VA 20172

First published in 1997

British Library Cataloguing-in-Publication Data
A catalogue record for this book is available from the British Library.

Library of Congress Cataloging-in-Publication Data
Haydon, Graham.
    Teaching about values: a new approach / Graham Haydon.
        p.   cm. — (Cassell studies in pastoral care and personal and social education)
    Includes bibliographical references and index.
    ISBN 0-304-33559-2. — ISBN 0-304-33560-6
    1. Moral education—Great Britain. 2. Values—Study and teaching—Great Britain. 3. Teaching—Great Britain—Moral and ethical aspects.   I. Title   II. Series.
    LC314.G7H39   1996
    370.11'4—dc20   96–931
                                                                                    CIP

Typeset by Action Typesetting Limited, Gloucester
Printed and bound in Great Britain by Redwood Books, Trowbridge, Wiltshire

CASSELL STUDIES IN PASTORAL CARE AND PERSONAL
AND SOCIAL EDUCATION

WITHDRÁWN

TEACHING ABOUT VALUES

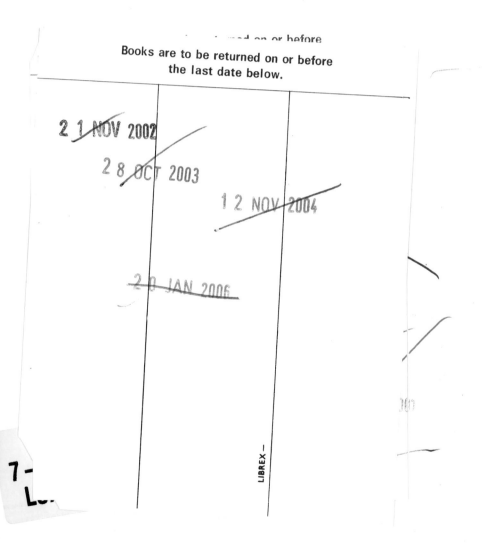

Books are to be returned on or before
the last date below.

2 1 NOV 2002

2 8 OCT 2003

1 2 NOV 2004

2 0 JAN 2006

LIBREX —

7 -
L-.

Books in this series:

R. Best (editor): *Education, Spirituality and the Whole Child*

R. Best, P. Lang, C. Lodge and C. Watkins (editors): *Pastoral Care and PSE: Entitlement and Provision*

P. Lang, R. Best and A. Lichtenberg (editors): *Caring for Children: International Perspectives on Pastoral Care and PSE*

O. Leaman: *Death and Loss: Compassionate Approaches in the Classroom*

J. McGuiness: *Counselling in Schools: New Perspectives*

J. McGuiness: *Teachers, Pupils and Behaviour: A Managerial Approach*

S. Power: *The Pastoral and the Academic: Conflict and Contradiction in the Curriculum*

P. Whitaker: *Managing to Learn: Aspects of Reflective and Experiential Learning in Schools*

Contents

Part VI: Values in the teaching profession

Series Editors' Foreword

It is New Year's Day, 1997.

At the time of writing, the Conservative Government no longer commands a majority in the House of Commons, and a general election is in any case due before the end of this year. The election campaign promises to be one of the most bitterly contested since World War II. The three largest political parties have all identified education as a significant (if not the most significant) issue around which their campaigns will be fought. All three have at one time or another in recent months focussed their comments about schooling upon the expectation that teachers should be contributing more directly to the promotion of moral values appropriate to the creation and maintenance of an orderly and law-abiding society.

As this book shows, there is nothing new in the idea that schooling and social order are intimately connected. However, the relationship between social order and what happens in schools has taken on a very different complexion in recent months. The fatal stabbing of a North London head-teacher, Philip Lawrence, while protecting one of his pupils from attack by a gang of youths, and the massacre of sixteen primary school children and their teacher by a deranged gunman at Dunblane in Scotland, have been seen by many as symptomatic of a society in moral crisis. Ironically, the fact that pupils and their teachers have become the targets of such violence has done something to raise the visibility of the protective and caring work which teachers do. This has compensated somewhat for the otherwise generally bad press which the profession receives, and which all too often follows the pronouncements of politicians, government QUANGOs and their representatives (notably HM Chief Inspector of Schools, the Office for Standards in Education (OFSTED), the School Curriculum and Assessment Authority and the Teacher Training Agency).

In the wake of such tragic events as Dunblane and the murder of Philip Lawrence, emotional and emotive appeals are made both for specific action (e.g. demands for legislation on the sale of combat knives and the ownership of hand-guns), and for a more general raising of moral standards and a greater respect for the rights and duties of all citizens. The debates to which these appeals give rise traverse the whole realm of societal values, moral principles and political responsibilities. Thus, for example, the lobby for continuing the right to own licensed hand-guns has made much of the principle of the individual's freedom to act responsibly in such matters, and has styled proposed legislation as an unwarrented and unjustifiable intrusion by government in the private and lawful business of the individual citizen.

Even without these and similar events to sharpen the debate, the function of education in promoting moral behaviour in the context of social, cultural and spiritual development is high on the political agenda. Of the recent Secretaries of State, John Patten stands out especially for the public and published statements he made on this matter, but the spokespersons for all the major political parties now routinely promise to develop this particular function for schools of the future.

A book specifically about values in education (and education in values!) could not have come at a more appropriate time. In this book, Graham Haydon takes up the challenge of providing a reasoned analysis of the whole perilous territory of morality and education, to argue that teachers, governors, politicians and teacher-trainers need to examine their own values, reflect upon the issues which values raise for classroom practice and debate openly and honestly the many possible responses we might make to demands for moral education in a liberal, multiethnic, multicultural and multifaith society. As he admits, the domain of values and education is too broad to be covered fully in a book of this type and size if, indeed, it could *ever* be covered, but the kind of holistic approach which he adopts is necessary to at least 'flag' its most important parameters.

Graham Haydon's approach is novel precisely because he stands back a little from the practicalities of the classroom in order to focus upon the broader ethical and political issues which underpin teachers' practice. In fact, this sort of reflective distance is (as Haydon himself argues) essential if teachers are to build their practice on firm foundations, and in this sense his book is very practical indeed.

In another sense, the approach Haydon has adopted is by no means new, for its takes us back to fundamental questions about the moral nature of education and the aims of schooling. These are questions which were virtually ubiquitous in courses of initial and award-bearing in-service training for teachers in the 1970s and early 1980s, often informed by the works of such philosophers of education as R. S. Peters and Paul Hirst. As Haydon shows, they are also amongst the questions which are begged by the pronouncements of influential people today. In particular, Haydon shows how a speech by John Patten, when Secretary of State for Education, generated a whole agenda of moral assumptions which demand philosophical scrutiny. Ironically, the Government's enchantment with demonstrable and assessable competencies, and especially those which (it is argued) are most efficiently acquired through school-based training, has squeezed out most of the opportunities for the reasoned debate of such an agenda.

Graham Haydon has done the world of education an important service by reminding us of the value of a philosophical perspective on contemporary issues in education. He has not written an instruction manual for the teaching of values or for the handling of the many controversial and politically charged issues with which he exemplifies his argument throughout the book. Nor has he made his first priority the development of teacher competences in the casework, curriculum and community-building which are the bread-and-butter work of pastoral care and personal/social education. This makes his book rather different from other books in this series, but this is as it should be for his is a different mission.

What this book does provide is an agenda for individual reflection and collaborative analysis of the purposes and values which should inform and justify teachers' practice in pastoral care and personal/social education. It is also a carefully constructed philosophical examination of a range of issues which have particular contemporary significance, and which serve to articulate the relationship between values and education at the most fundamental level.

We believe that books of this type, returning as they do to the 'reason why' of things (to use Peters' term), are an important corrective to the current preoccupation with the development and demonstration of under-theorized technical competence. We are delighted to include it in our series.

Ron Best
Peter Lang

Preface

This book is written in response to two facts: first, that the public tends to expect schools to stand for and promote certain values; and second, that teachers in particular, who are in the front line in responding to these expectations, have very little guidance in how to go about it. So I am writing partly for that broader public, in the hope that what I say will help people to think through just what it is, or is not, reasonable to demand of schools; but more particularly, I am writing for teachers – especially student teachers – who need most of all to be able to reflect as clearly as they can on the nature of their enterprise, the values involved in it and the values they bring to it.

This last point is crucial: teachers do actively bring their own values into teaching. That's why I was tempted to call this book 'Valuing Teachers', by which I hoped to convey two things: that teachers (like all of us) are people who value and care about things; and that society will not value teachers properly if it doesn't recognize this fact, and merely sees teachers as passive repositories or transmitters of society's values. That would have been a lot of meaning to try to pack into two words on the cover, but the title remains for one chapter.

Of course, we are concerned not only with the values that teachers bring into education, but also with the values that pupils[1] take out of it. So a central focus of this book is on values as part of the subject matter of teaching. All teachers, regardless of whether they are specialists in a single curriculum subject or not, are likely to be teaching about values some of the time. But this book sets teaching about values into a broader context, which is also to do with values. Teachers don't grapple with questions of values only when they are concerned about the values their pupils have or will acquire: they arise in almost every educational decision or policy.

Often, though, values are only implicit. Among the day-to-day pressures there is little time for reflection and discussion which is not directly geared to the next decision that has to be made. Unfortunately, this is increasingly the case even for student teachers: the emphasis is more and more on 'how to do it' and less and less on 'what it is all about'. I would like to see all teachers in training, and indeed all teachers in service – not to mention governors and inspectors[2] – having ample time and opportunity to think through and *discuss* amongst themselves the kinds of issues raised in this book. Reading a book is not a substitute for discussion or for anyone's own thinking; but the aim of this book is to help readers – whether teachers, parents, school governors, or politicians – to think about questions of values which a concern for education inevitably raises. That aim, as I see it, is a thoroughly practical one. No book can tell teachers exactly what to do in a given situation in the classroom, and this book doesn't try to. But coming to a clearer understanding of what it is that one is trying to do, and engaging with others in deciding what to do, are activities of direct practical relevance; while trying to forge ahead in the interests of 'doing something practical', without stopping to think, can turn out to be thoroughly impractical!

The book cannot be comprehensive, but I have tried to say something, at least to stimulate further thought, on quite a number of issues about values that are likely to come up for practising teachers. Part I is introductory: it says more about the role of values in education in general, raising questions about the idea of education *in* values, and about aims in education, which will be followed up later in the book. Part II looks at values in general, and begins to ask what is special about moral values. It also looks at the way in which the diversity of values in modern societies can lead to conflict, and at the particular values of tolerance and compromise which may be a response to this diversity. Part III concentrates on the idea of 'morality': what is morality, and why are some people suspicious of it, or of the idea that teachers might impose it on pupils? Part IV, applying some of the lessons of the earlier parts, looks at some particular sources of controversy involving values – controversies that may occur in the staffroom and in the classroom. Part V, drawing together many of these threads, asks how we should understand the ideas of values education and moral education; and what is it that schools are best placed to do in this area? In conclusion, Part VI raises questions and makes some suggestions about the role of values in the professional education of teachers, and in the professional standing of teachers.

Topics are discussed in this book which are relevant to teachers of personal and social education, of citizenship education, of environmental education, and of religious education – but the questions raised in this book are relevant to *all* teachers in primary and secondary schools. Indeed, the public expectations from which I started are on the right lines at least in this: that the approach teachers take to values *is* of significance for the whole society.

Two more points about using the book. First, while the headings of chapters and sections will give an idea of the main topics treated in particular places, where the central themes of the book are concerned – themes such as values, morality, pluralism, tolerance, the relation between morality and religion, the aims of education – there are so many interconnections that what is said in one place will be expanded or sometimes qualified in another place. Many of the interconnections are indicated by cross-referencing in the text or in the notes. Second, the notes at the end of each chapter will indicate further texts in which either particular topics, or sometimes the theme of the chapter as a whole, can be followed up. In this way the book will serve as an introduction to many possible lines of further enquiry.

Remember that this book asks you to do your own thinking – especially if you are responsible for leading pupils into thinking for themselves. Because the questions to be raised about values are far from simple, there is no substitute for serious, careful, hard thinking. The teaching profession needs to recognize this for itself, if it is not to be always responding to a moral agenda set from outside. Above all, teachers can recognize that the fact that someone is doing their own thinking does not mean that any kind of thinking is as good as any other, or that any answer is as valid as any other. It was probably a confusion about this which led a journalist, in a book published just before I revised this preface, to charge me with leading pupils, not merely into moral relativism, but from there into despotism and tyranny. 'Haydon's attitude ... opened the way for ... pupils to say that racial prejudice was no less right than tolerance; or that it was permissible to kill people because they were genetically imperfect.'[3] I think the author of that sentence had not read my arguments carefully enough. My reply is this book; read it carefully, and judge for yourself.

NOTES

1. I need a term throughout for the people whom teachers teach and, in general, it is not adult education I'm concerned with. 'Children' is inappropriate for many of the people whom secondary teachers teach, and 'students' sounds inappropriate (to English ears) for many of the people whom primary teachers teach. So I shall use 'pupils' without intending any connotation of didacticism.
2. Where I refer in this book to a specific political, legislative and administrative context, it is Britain, and sometimes more specifically England and Wales, that I have in mind. But, since the book is about values in education, most of it will be of much broader relevance, and the reader outside Britain can take the specific references merely as examples.
3. Phillips (1996) p. 222. (There is an error in Phillips's reference to my own work; her quotation is from an article in the *Times Educational Supplement*, 19 March 1993, not from a letter in the *Guardian* the following week.)

Acknowledgements

In writing this book I have drawn quite extensively on various pieces I have written in recent years, though this has rarely involved quoting more than a few sentences at a time from other work already published. The main exception is that part of Chapter 1 is a version of a piece called 'John Patten on Values Education – more questions than answers' published (by St Martin's College, Lancaster) in *Values Education: The Magazine for Personal and Social Education* **1** 3, 1994. My thanks to the editor, and also to the editors of *Journal of Philosophy of Education* and *Journal of Moral Education* for permission to reprint extracts from articles on secular society and secular schools, and on the cognitive content of moral education, respectively. There are also echoes of, and some minor recyclings from, several of the other pieces listed in the Bibliography under my name.

The largest self-borrowings have come from a report on conflict of values and values education written for the Oxford Project for Peace Studies (unpublished). Though the links with peace education play a much smaller role in this book, the reader will gather that I do think values education has a role to play in reducing conflict in society. The Project has sadly ceased to exist. I am glad to have this opportunity to publish some parts of that report, and to thank the Director and Trustees for their support during a term's study leave. Thanks also go to the Institute of Education, University of London, for allowing the leave.

Acknowledgements are due to the publishers who have granted permission for the use of quotations from other authors: Harvard University Press, Oxford University Press, and Rowman & Littlefield, for quotations from Gilligan, C., Ward J. & Taylor J. (eds) *Mapping the Moral Domain*; Thomas Nagel *Equality and Partiality*; and Kittay E. & Meyers D. (eds) *Women and Moral Theory* respectively.

Thanks, too, to all the students with whom I've talked about the issues contained in this book over the years – both students in initial teacher education and experienced teachers pursuing Masters' courses on values in education or their own research. It is largely their concerns and interests which I am responding to here.

Part I
The wider context

This part is introductory, and sets the agenda for the rest of the book. In Chapter 1, I show how questions about values cannot be avoided by teachers, or, indeed, by anyone involved in education; and in order to show that the questions don't have easy answers, I refer (not uncritically) to a speech made by one English politician on the subject.

In Chapter 2, I discuss educational aims; not only because questions about educational aims are themselves questions about values but also because I want later in the book to ask precisely what the aims of teachers and schools should be where values are concerned. I suggest that, in thinking about aims in education, we need to examine those outcomes where schools are well placed to make a distinctive contribution.

CHAPTER 1

Teachers and values – and one politician

WHAT PLACE DO VALUES HAVE IN EDUCATION?

A superficial reading of educational reporting and debate in the mid 1990s might suggest that the role of values is rather limited. The talk often seems all to be of management and funding, of competences and skills, of targets and testing. Certainly, from time to time there is explicit talk of values – perhaps in a school's prospectus, or in a politician's exhortations; or in the media when, in response to some particular event, there is a flurry of concern about the responsibility of schools for the moral state of the nation. But this talk will often come across as rather detached from the main day-to-day business of schools.

So, the impression might be that, while there is evidence of concern about values in education, it is generally fairly low-key and rarely dom-inant. But this would be a superficial impression, and one that is partly created by the language we use: though much of the language of education in the 1990s is not explicitly about values, it does not follow that the discussions which go on are value-free. Take an issue that was in the news when I started to draft this chapter: in the spring of 1995, with the threat of budget cuts looming, many schools in England and Wales were faced with cutting their number of teachers, and therefore increasing the size of classes. Teachers, and many parents and governors, protested; but govern-ment ministers responded with the claim that larger classes did not necessarily mean worse education. Indeed, research was cited which had found that larger classes produced, on average, slightly better results. The language employed by these politicians was, as so often in the 1980s and 1990s, the language of efficiency. The end was not in doubt, only the means necessary to achieve it; and if a larger ratio of teachers to pupils would not improve efficiency, then some teachers were being employed unnecessarily.

On first sight, this kind of talk may not seem to be about values (other than value for money), but it is by no means value-free. Even the concern for efficiency represents one of our values, and one that is rarely now questioned; if we think it better that things be done efficiently rather than inefficiently, then we value efficiency. But, of course, this should not be considered in isolation: we also need to take into account *what* is being done (if someone is propagating racism, for instance, you may think it would be much better that it be done inefficiently). The language of efficiency tends to neglect the question of the worthwhileness of the achievement. Talk of better results assumes that we know what constitutes such results: in other words, it depends on what it is in teaching that is valued.

This is not just a quibble. The educational language of recent years has emphasized the attainment of targets, determined by nationally set levels, examination passes and grades. If measurable results of this kind are the only criteria, then it may indeed turn out (though the evidence is far from conclusive) that children in large classes tend to achieve better results. This would almost certainly have something to do with the fact that large classes require either quite formal teaching methods or else an approach highly targeted at individuals (through individual worksheets, for instance). Teachers in smaller classes may be more willing to try out and persevere with alternative approaches involving more group interaction and discussion.

However, what would be the point of adopting such methods if they apparently are not more effective in producing intended results? Well, one might think that people co-operating in some task and talking to each other is worthwhile in its own right, even if it is not the most effective way of producing a given result; or, it might be that the interaction does produce beneficial results, but ones which are less easily measurable. If, for instance, as I shall suggest later (see Chapter 12), a crucial element of education in values is discussion between pupils and between pupils and teachers, then limitations on class size might be worthwhile for the sake of facilitating such discussion, even if it doesn't produce examinable outcomes.

The example of class size illustrates, then, that the question of what we really value in education is never far below the surface. We may at times want to put a lot of weight on the values that are represented by a school and the values that we hope pupils will take with them when they leave; but when we begin to wonder what the school can do in this area, we may easily slip back into concentrating on more measurable factors.

We do have to ask, then, what we suppose education is all about, and why we think it matters. What we may label as teaching about values, values education or moral education, may certainly be an important aspect, but it's not the whole story. We must also consider how this concern fits into some wider set of aims for education – which will be the subject of Chapter 2.

TEACHERS AND VALUES

Another question that needs to be addressed is the expectation that teachers themselves must stand for and transmit certain values on behalf of the wider society. This expectation still exists, alongside the talk of teachers as, in effect, competent skilled technicians. Teachers are still regarded as moral guides and exemplars, whose standards are perhaps just a little above the level of the rest of society. That is why in some minds the idea of teachers going on strike arouses a sense of betrayal only exceeded when nurses or midwives take similar action.

This balance – between the idea of teachers as moral exemplars on the one hand and skilled technicians on the other – could still swing either way; probably both expectations will continue to co-exist. Certainly in England there was ample evidence in the first half of the 1990s of the demand that all teachers be moral educators: increasingly frequent references to the requirements of the Education Reform Act 1988 that schools promote moral and spiritual development; articles and speeches by politicians; a consultative document from the National Curriculum Council (NCC) on spiritual and moral development in 1993; the attempt by OFSTED (Office for Standards in Education) to draw up guidelines for the inspection of a school's contribution to the spiritual, moral, social and cultural development of its pupils; and a speech by the Chief Executive of the School Curriculum and Assessment Authority (SCAA) in January 1996 proposing a national forum to reach a consensus on the values to be taught in schools.

Teachers, of course, find themselves on the receiving end of these varied expectations from the public and the media. But they may have their own ambivalence too, either individually or collectively. Many teachers will claim, with good reason, that they have been playing the role of moral educators for years, even if they have not expressed it in quite those words. Others, in particular many young people entering the profession, do not identify with that role at all, but rather see themselves as teachers of a specific subject, or as developing children's mental capacities. This book is for teachers and student teachers of both persuasions.

Even teachers who agree in principle with the idea of moral education may still feel they are not prepared, in practice, to take on that role. In a literal sense that is quite true: they have received no specific training in this area. When various aspects of educational theory were taught, little time and attention was given to any reflection on how teachers should handle the inevitable influence they would have in the development of young people's values. In the mid 1990s there is increasingly a move away from teacher 'education' towards training in specified competences. The language of competences *could* be used to try to formulate some practical guidelines for teachers in handling matters of values, but there is not much sign of that happening either.[1]

Of course, the picture is more mixed than this might imply. Student teachers within certain subject areas will have given some attention to questions of values: this will be generally true for religious education and, to some extent, often depending on the personal concerns of tutors, for history, English, geography or technology. And some – often very limited – attention may have been given to the role that a teacher could be expected to play in what, in very many schools now, is labelled 'personal and social education'. But the idea that all teachers should undergo a systematic preparation for their role in respect to values as a fundamental part of their professional education hardly exists.

Part of the reason why it doesn't exist is that there is no consensus – either outside the profession or within it – about what the job description should be for this aspect of a teacher's role. Some people – usually outside schools rather than within them – don't see any problem: certain basic values exist to be transmitted, and teachers should just get on with the job. (In Chapter 11 I shall question the idea that teachers should, or could, function just as transmitters where values are concerned.) Teachers would be quite right to express unhappiness with that role, which is not a viable one within our society. And they should be suspicious of any rhetoric which asks them to endorse and pass on certain values without thinking through the issues for themselves.

Actually there is, within the profession, and perhaps especially in the institutions of higher education, a strong strand of recognition that teachers must be people who can think for themselves about their role, who can be 'reflective practitioners'.[2] And it is consistent with this that many teachers also refuse to regard children as passive receivers. During their training, they will often have been encouraged to think, not of transmitting values to pupils, but of encouraging children and young people to make their own choices. But at the same time, they will probably have been told that there are some values that must be enforced: they must not, for instance, allow racist remarks or bullying to go unchallenged. This is a tension that has not been resolved. Despite widespread recognition within teacher training and in schools of society's plurality, no adequate preparation exists to assist teachers who have to differentiate between non-negotiable values and those which must remain a matter of choice.

THE ISSUES IN SCHOOLS – ONE POLITICIAN'S VIEW

As an illustration of the way in which attempts to say something useful in this area can easily raise more questions than they resolve, I want to refer here to a speech made in 1994 by the then Secretary of State for Education for England and Wales, John Patten.[3]

Politically speaking, of course, a speech from that date may seem, by the time you read this, to come from a bygone era. Perhaps because his personal agenda happened to tie in with the attempt of the Conservative government to appeal to voters through its 'Back to Basics' campaign, Patten was unusual among recent Education Secretaries in the high profile he gave to issues about values in schools. He recognized that there are important issues about values in education that will not go away with a cabinet reshuffle or a change of government (whether from a personal and political perspective his was an adequate response to those issues is, of course, a different matter). That is why I can make use of his speech here: not to criticize a particular politician or a particular party, but to show how much easier it is to talk in platitudes than to think through the complexities of the underlying issues.

Patten began by stressing that education and values are inevitably intertwined; no school can be a value-free zone. But how does it work in practice? Patten went on to say that: 'Every school must have its own ethos, underpinned by a set of shared values.' This raises the issue of the relation between what is, or could be distinctive about a particular school, perhaps serving a specific community, and what is to be common across all the schools in one society. The statement, as it stands, fits with the idea that each school should take a clear position on its aims. But is it telling us that each school should have its own *distinctive* ethos, underpinned by its own *distinctive* values? If so, then what of the values shared by society as a whole? In other words, does 'shared values' mean values shared across the school, or shared with the rest of society?

Conservative politicians tend to take the second view, but in doing so are they paying enough attention to the diversity that certainly does exist in our society? (This issue of diversity is one that I will keep returning to.) You might interpret the idea, instead, to mean that each school will have its own set of values, which will set it apart from other schools. But then where are those values to come from, if they are not drawn from what is common in the wider society? Certainly, if teachers (not to mention governors and parents) in a school are going to agree on a shared set of values, they will have to raise some awkward questions, the kinds of questions which I hope this book may help them to answer. One of the most fundamental of those questions is, What *are* values? Here is part of Patten's attempt to answer this: 'Values are timeless: they are the very basis of our lives ... Values are an expression of a deeper truth beyond, and less ephemeral than, our material lives. They provide ideals to live up to.' The reference to 'a deeper truth beyond', reflecting Patten's own religious convictions, raises one point of controversy here. If others see values as rooted in human life, which *is* material, they are not obviously wrong. I shall be looking critically on more than one occasion in this book at the relation between values and religion.

But doesn't this quotation take rather a selective and weighted view of what values are? Certainly, some values represent high ideals, which perhaps only saints will live up to. But when people talk about values as a basis for life, don't they often have something rather more mundane in mind? Very often, these values, like our conceptions of property rights, form the basis of our all-too-material lives, and are far from timeless. If anything, we might expect greater agreement on values which are rooted, for want of a better phrase, in our late twentieth-century liberal capitalism than on values which express higher aspirations. (We could hardly, for instance, expect agreement on the value of faith in God when many people would not even agree on the existence of a God.) Perhaps it is precisely because schools *are* rooted in a particular kind of life (and are not in fact expressions of something called 'education' in the abstract – a point which I will return to in the next chapter), that it is still possible to achieve consensus on certain important values. But then we have to ask whether this agreement amounts to anything more than an agreement to use a certain set of labels – of *words* for values. The critical test is whether agreed labels translate into agreed practice. Patten, for instance, listed a number of values, including:

- regard for proper authority
- unselfishness and the need for self-restraint

- loyalty and fidelity
- the readiness to stand up for what one believes in
- respect for rational argument
- independence of thought
- readiness to resolve conflict without resort to violence

Presented simply as a list of labels, it would be difficult to object to any of these. But a review of these and other ideas as they came up in Patten's speech will show how many questions still need to be raised.

Regard for proper authority. Do we all agree on what kind or degree of authority is *proper*? Would all the cultural traditions which may be represented in one school agree on, say, the proper *limits* of the authority of teachers or of parents? Does anyone – religious leader, politician, teacher – have the authority to tell other people what to believe? I would not expect all readers, or indeed all members of one school, to agree on the answer to that question. (Many teachers may not in fact feel that they have any kind of *moral* authority *vis-à-vis* their pupils, which is one of the reasons why they may feel qualms about the role of moral educator.)

Unselfishness and the need for self-restraint. This might seem uncontroversial at first sight. But if there is such a thing as an absolute value (a notion I'll come back to in Chapter 3), this will *not* uncontroversially be one of them. People have been oppressed over generations because they showed self-restraint, and what some might interpret as selfishness on the part of workers demanding higher wages, those self-same workers might describe as standing up for their rights (and what if they have dependants to support?). And what of schools? Suppose the boys in a school seem to show rather less self-restraint, perhaps more selfishness, than the girls: should we encourage the girls to be *more* self-assertive? (Making this supposition may itself seem stereotyped; my point is concerned, however, with what a school might need to do to combat stereotypes rather than reinforcing them.)

Loyalty and fidelity. Surely here we have to ask 'to what or to whom?' Remember E. M. Forster's hope that if he had to choose between betraying his friends and betraying his country, he would have the courage to betray his country. Don't we have to add to loyalty and fidelity, the willingness to ask whether the object of one's loyalty is worth it? (Think of the millions in Eastern Europe and Asia who remained loyal to the Communist Party for years before finally being critical enough to reject it.) Or if you feel that expressing such sentiments only encourages the disintegration of society, how would you make the necessary distinctions?

The readiness to stand up for what one believes in. Here again, much the same point applies: we can't avoid the question of the *value* of what someone believes in. And what do we say of respect for 'proper authority', when standing up for what they believe in leads the likes of Gandhi and Martin Luther King to disobey that authority?[4] Of course, we could say that in such cases the authority in question is not *proper*; but in any particular situation that judgement has to be made, and education presumably has a responsibility to prepare people to judge what is proper authority and how much respect us due to it; likewise when they should take a stand for what they believe in and when they should be willing to compromise (see Chapter 5).

Echoing a common theme of liberal (with a small 'l') educationalists, Patten next insists that 'we must enable our young people ... to make an informed choice of their own values as they mature'. In the same speech, as we've seen, he sets out his own list of core values. Later he endorses further specific values, like the desirability of a mother and a father in the family. Now it's not uncommon, even if it is inconsistent, for someone both to believe that certain specified values should be transmitted from generation to generation, and to maintain that people should make their own choices of values. Politicians may be able to get away without answering in detail the question of which values are up for choice and which, if any, are not; it's more difficult for teachers. Most schools won't take the view that whether to make racist remarks or not is something on which individuals can make their own choice. But it's far from easy to spell out just how to draw the line between what is a matter of choice and what isn't.

Patten went on to say that teaching values 'also means fostering the development of a strong moral conscience, to cope with new situations where the familiar rules do not give an entirely clear answer'. Some people talk as if this notion of conscience provides all the answers: moral education is just about developing people's conscience, and once people 'have' a properly developed conscience, they'll know what to do, and (more importantly) they'll actually do it. If only it were so simple. Isn't it the case that a strong moral conscience has often led people to cling to the familiar rules, with disastrous results? Is conscience merely some sort of gut feeling?

Perhaps implicit in Patten's remark is the idea of conscience as people's ability to work things out, morally, for themselves. But then it would appear that two different ideas of conscience are being conflated here; to sort out what to do when the familiar rules don't apply, what you actually need is not a *strong* conscience but an *intelligent* one.[5] And what of the situations where it's not just the lack of an entirely clear answer that's the problem, but conflict between one familiar rule and another? (For example, a pupil – maybe through her own fault, maybe not – has got herself into a situation where to tell the truth will mean betraying a friend's trust; however, if she remains loyal to her friend, she'll be forced to lie.) Is talking about conscience any help here?

This is just one example of the difficulties people can get into through relying on a familiar *word* which won't actually do the job they want it to do. I'm inclined to think we'd do better to drop this word 'conscience' altogether; at the very least, it is important to realize that any attempt to answer the question of how teachers can help to develop their pupils' conscience will depend on whether you see conscience as a matter of will-power, or as an ability to handle ideas intelligently.

According to Patten, pupils 'will learn that the existence of different views on particular issues does not reduce all values to pure relativism. On the contrary, they will find that there is much common ground ...'. As it happens, I agree with this, though it will be worth coming back to this notion of relativism later (see Chapter 3). But does this view of Patten's apply only, or especially, in the context of religious education (which is where it occurs in his speech)? Or is it something that can and should be learned in any part of the curriculum? Patten is not alone in linking moral education and religious education;[6] so it should come as no surprise that in a speech on values in education he also referred to collective worship: 'Daily collective worship ... affirms the importance of the spiritual.' This fits with the general stress in his speech on the school ethos; and it may be that some degree of ritualized activity is necessary to maintaining any particular ethos. But does the link with collective *worship* assume that the spiritual is tied to theistic religions? If the spiritual has to do with transcendence of the mundane and material, might it be found in art, or some kinds of philosophy, or a secular moral consciousness? (I'll return to the subject of spirituality in Chapter 8.)

Patten next moved on to a discussion of family values, initially in the context of sex education: 'Among the values that sex education should reflect are those of the family.' What do we mean by 'family values'? Do we mean certain benefits that arguably come to children through being brought up in families? If it was discovered that children brought up in families tend, say, to be less neurotic or less violent, then this would be *one* reason for advocating the support of family structures (though there may also be reasons on the other side). It's possible that social scientists may produce convincing evidence on such matters; in which case, citing such proof as a reason for supporting the family would have nothing to do with moralizing. (I shall have more to say on the idea of 'moralizing' in Chapters 6 and 7.) Or do we mean by 'family values' the qualities, such as affection and trust, that might hold a family together? If so, then it's those qualities that we should be trying to foster. (Have we any reason to think that qualities like this depend on the number of parents or their gender?)

A passage under the heading of 'Education for Citizenship' suggests a different view of family values: 'Family values represent, in microcosm, the values that underpin the wider society. These are founded upon an acceptance that we have obligations towards others, and in turn enjoy entitlements. Education for citizenship deals with those reciprocal rights and duties.' Does this mean that families are, or should be, held together by reciprocal rights and duties, that children should only enjoy a entitlement to care if they fulfil their obligations to their parents? Or is it rather that the values which underpin a modern, populous, market-economy pluralist state are actually quite different from the values which underpin a family?[7]

In Patten's view, the knowledge and understanding involved in citizenship should

> be linked to the development of a positive approach towards education and a 'can-do' approach to life. These include respect for rational argument, for the legitimate interests of others, and for the views and customs of different groups. They should promote a sense of fair play;

independence of thought; an enterprising approach to meeting challenges, coupled with persistence in working at solutions; and, of course, a readiness to resolve conflict without resort to violence.

Several values are packed into this paragraph. *Respect for rational argument* is perhaps one of the most central values in education generally. And it is worth noting here that if we are to have such respect, we must allow this to extend (unless there is some rational argument to the contrary) to claims about values themselves. If we say that something is wrong, we should be prepared to give our reasons and to argue the case. Perhaps too we should be prepared to give up thinking that something is wrong if we can't see any reason why it is.

Again, of course, there is a lot more to be worked out when these values come into play with each other. Does *respect for ... the views of different groups* mean not arguing with them? Or if you think someone else's views cannot be supported by rational argument, isn't it more respectful (though not necessarily more tactful) to try, by rational argument, to show them that they're wrong? (Of course, it's always possible they might show you that *you* are wrong.) Presumably, the use of rational argument may be part of an *enterprising approach to meeting challenges*, including challenges from proper authorities. If authorities (including teachers and heads) are to show respect for rational argument, presumably they must always be prepared to listen to what claims to be rational argument, and if they think it doesn't succeed in being rational, to explain patiently why this is so. Do they cease to be *proper* authorities if they fail to do this? On the other hand, authorities know that sometimes decisions have to be made, and *persistence in working at solutions* doesn't mean that the argument can go on endlessly. At such times, they may have to act on the basis of what they take to be good reasons, even though they know that others don't agree. But it is quite another matter to appeal to some supposed basis (such as, 'this just is the way things are done') for which they couldn't give a rational argument themselves.

As for *readiness to resolve conflict without resort to violence*, this may not by itself sound like a specifically educational value, but I think it can be argued (rationally) that anyone concerned with educational values must be committed to this value too. As with the previous values, to take this one seriously will have further ramifications through a school. On the face of it, it commits schools to endorsing a ban on corporal punishment; and, perhaps more interestingly, it gives a reason for including some form of peace education in the school curriculum (for what is peace education intended to do if not to make it less likely that people will resort to violence as a way of resolving conflict?). I shall have more to say on the value of non-violence in Chapter 9.

CONCLUSION

What this discussion has shown, I think, is that the difficulty often faced by teachers lies not in outlining the values which a school stands for, but in recognizing precisely what this endorsement will mean in practice, particularly if some of the values do not sit comfortably together. Since the discussion so far has raised many more questions than it has answered, to help teachers approach this issue of the questions of values, we need now to proceed more systematically. To this end, and to understand how issues of values will fit into the broader context, we need to reflect on aims in education generally. This is the task for the next chapter.

NOTES

1. For a discussion of the usefulness of the language of competences in education, see Bridges (1996).
2. This phrase was made popular in a number of professions by Schon (1983).
3. Extracts from the speech are taken, in the order of their appearance, from a circulated text headed 'Secretary of State's Address to the Oxford Conference in Education: 5 January 1994'.
4. For an accessible introduction to the moral issues raised by civil disobedience, see Singer (1973).
5. Singer, pp. 92–104, distinguishes two main senses of 'conscience' in the context of conscientious objection.
6. See pp. 89, 92 below on why the two should not be too closely linked.
7. Further consideration of this point could lead on to large issues in social theory and political philosophy: in particular, an ongoing debate between what has come to be known as 'communitarianism' and its rivals, labelled as 'individualism' or 'liberalism'. See also the Afterword.

CHAPTER 2

Education and aims

WHAT IS EDUCATION ABOUT?

If we start from a lofty enough vantage point, we might answer that education is about keeping civilization going. Perhaps it is worth reminding ourselves of this before coming down to earth. The English philosopher Thomas Hobbes, in the politically unstable times of the seventeenth century, bewailed the conditions that people would endure if – so he argued – there were not a strong central government:

> In such condition, there is no place for Industry; because the fruit thereof is uncertain: and consequently no Culture of the Earth; no Navigation, nor use of the commodities that may be imported by Sea; no commodious Building; no Instruments of moving, and removing such things as require much force; no Knowledge of the face of the Earth; no account of Time; no Arts; no Letters; no Society; and which is worst of all, continuall feare, and danger of violent death; And the life of man, solitary, poore, nasty, brutish and short.[1]

Today, there are still prophets of doom who will suggest that, as regards the continual fear and danger of violent death, our present condition is not much better. And it is always possible to point to parts of the world, shaken by civil wars or terrorism, where the description will seem to fit. Nor, after the experience of three centuries since Hobbes's day, can we have much confidence in strong government as a solution.

But for the majority of people reading this, life is probably not so bad. There is an understandable tendency for public comment to focus on criminality and violence, and to suggest that schools should be doing something about this. Hence the calls for renewed efforts in moral education when particularly horrifying cases fill the media. But the broader picture is one in which we do have Technology and Science (clearly referred to by Hobbes, though not by those names), Arts and Letters and Society. We do have a degree of civilization. (Of course, as with many broad-brush statements, to call a society 'civilized' is only partly a factual description; it is also an evaluation, albeit one which most readers of this are likely to share; but we should be reminded from time to time of Gandhi's comment when asked what he thought of English civilization, that it would be a fine thing.) For most people reading this, and even for most of the people going through schools in affluent countries today, the chances are (and statistics *are* relevant here) that life is not going to be solitary, poor, nasty, brutish and short.

In terms of material conditions, that has a lot to do, of course, with medicine, science and technology; and material conditions aside, arts and letters, science and technology provide many of life's pleasures and meanings. And these human activities, these social traditions of enquiry and practice, would not last from one generation to the next without education. We will not get far in thinking about values in education if we don't recognize how much of what is important in life depends absolutely on education – at least in its broadest sense (exactly how much depends on schools is a more detailed question). It's a commonplace that world development is partly a matter of educational development (which is not to prejudge the question of how far that development should everywhere follow a Western model). And try to imagine what your own society would be like after one or two generations if no knowledge or understanding was passed on from one generation to another. It's highly debatable how far the avoidance of Hobbes's so-called state of nature actually depends on any particular moral or political system, let alone on strong government; it's hardly debatable at all that it depends on education.

So, it's part of a civilized society to have Arts and Letters and Science and Technology; and not just to have them, but to care about what is good in these enterprises, and to recognize what can go wrong in them. In the modern world, education has brought these values within reach of more of the population than ever before. Increasingly, people are becoming aware both of how much is wrong in the world and that the knowledge by which it could be improved is available, if only it could be harnessed. Education, when it is working well, enables people to appreciate what is of value, helps them decide what is going to matter in their own lives, and lets them acquire the skills and knowledge to do something about it. It's in this sense above all that teachers have always and unavoidably been teachers of values. Indeed, this kind of teaching of values would exist in schools irrespective of the presence of anything that could be called *moral* education.

So far, so good. But all this may seem to be just high-flown rhetoric. How do we make anything more usable out of it? By some more careful thinking, I suggest, about aims in education.

AIMS AND VALUES

Thinking about aims is a way of getting a clearer picture of what it is we are trying to do, and about what would count as doing it well. Our aims are closely related to our values: we aim at things that we value, that we think are in some way worth achieving. (But not all of our values can underpin aims; there may be some things we think are good which we are powerless to bring about.)

John Dewey, the American pragmatist philosopher and educationalist, said 'education as such has no aims. Only persons, parents, and teachers, have aims, not an abstract idea like education.'[2] There are two important points I want to take out of this. First, the fact that we have a certain notion of education does not, by itself, tell us anything about the aims we ought to pursue. Secondly, given it is people who have aims, it may very well be that different people approach education with different aims.

To illustrate the first point, think of what the words 'education' and 'indoctrination' convey to you. As a speaker and reader of English, you recognize these words, and the chances are that they convey two rather different ideas to you. For instance, 'indoctrination' may suggest an attempt to brainwash an individual into believing something regardless of evidence or reasoned argument; while 'education' might suggest that someone's opportunities for thinking and reasoning are being opened up and extended rather than narrowed down. If the words convey to you something like these two meanings, then you can use these words to express two different kinds of aim: the educator (in your vocabulary) will be aiming at something quite different from the indoctrinator.[3]

Now, there would be nothing idiosyncratic about such an interpretation – these words, with *something* like these meanings, are common currency. But the fact that we have these words tells us nothing by itself about what we *ought* to be aiming at. If someone thinks that teachers *should* aim to inculcate certain beliefs (perhaps religious or moral ones) in people in such a way that the people concerned will never be able to question these beliefs, then the fact that you wouldn't call this 'education' does not necessarily mean that there is anything wrong with the aim. People are free to say that if education is about opening up people's minds, making them critical and enquiring and so on, then education is not what they think schools ought to be aiming at. Of course, we often use the word 'education' to refer to a social institution, namely the enterprise which teachers in schools are professionally engaged in. But in that case it's an open question as to whether education (in this institutional sense) should be about *educating* people (in the sense of opening minds) rather than training them for jobs, or moulding their behaviour, or even just keeping them off the streets.[4] I shall in fact be using the term 'education' mostly in the institutional sense, to denote formal education or schooling; but I shall also trade on the common ambiguity of the word, so that when I argue in Chapters 11 and 12 that values education should, precisely, be *education*, I shall mean that it should not be indoctrination or (mere) habit-forming or training, but should be concerned, above all, with knowledge, understanding and rational thought.

Thus, teachers and schools cannot establish what they *should* be aiming at just by appealing to the meaning of words. There's a real area for debate here, and the debate will turn on values. This brings us to the second point raised by the quotation from Dewey: that different people may have different aims for education. Even where many people may share the same underlying values (and that is not something we can just assume), the fact that they are involved in education in different ways may give them (quite properly) different perspectives and hence different priorities. In their day-to-day work, teachers will often find that they are concentrating on relatively short-term objectives which could be articulated in terms of the learning outcomes they hope their pupils will achieve. To a certain extent, those same learning outcomes may be part of what at least some pupils are aiming at for themselves; but equally, pupils may have many other aims of their own which are not necessarily compatible with those of the school (it's relevant here that schooling, from their point of view, is compulsory). Parents of pupils may have aims for their own children (that they get a certain kind of job, for instance) where it might not be right for a teacher to have specific aims of this kind for individual children (that this pupil should succeed in this particular way, for example). At the same time, as members of the staff of a school, teachers are likely to be involved with others in formulating the aims by which the school as a whole presents its conception of itself to pupils, parents and a wider public.

Among other concerns, a school's statement of aims may express some of the values which the school wishes to put into practice: one will often, for instance, find a reference to the school 'respecting the individual'. Notice what an aim of that sort does and does not do. It *does* set up a certain guideline or principle which members of the school can try to follow; what it *does not* do is tell anyone what the purpose of the whole exercise is. Such an aim may help the school both to respect broader ethical concerns in the way it operates and to do its work effectively; but an aim of this kind does not tell us what the work of the school is. If the school didn't exist, we wouldn't create it just for the purpose of trying to ensure that people within the school respected each other. If schools in general didn't exist, this kind of aim – an internal aim, if you like – wouldn't give anyone a reason for inventing them.

WHAT CAN WE DO WITH SCHOOLS?

So there is a different kind of question to be asked, namely, 'what are schools for?' This question is, in a sense, one for a whole society, though it is still one on which anyone, whether teacher, parent, politician or pupil, may have a view. It is a question which takes for granted a certain context, namely that schools exist, and as such it is not an abstract question about the aims of education *per se*. In fact, the reader approaching this question is likely to be asking it in a still more specific context: what will be the role of teachers and schools as the twentieth century closes and a new century begins? (Here, and at some other points in the book, I shall refer to the context in late twentieth-century Britain; but readers elsewhere can take these references simply as illustrations of more general points.)

Wherever there is an education system regulated by the state, teachers work within a context in which some aims have been either explicitly set or implicitly assumed by legislation: in the case of England and Wales, the Education Reform Act 1988 included a statement of aims which I'll have occasion to quote in Chapter 8. But the actual aims assumed in the legislation seem to have been largely derived from a context of tradition and existing institutions. The legislation was concerned above all with instituting a National Curriculum, and the range of subjects of that Curriculum offered nothing new (nor, apparently, was derived from the statement of aims); it appealed instead to what, in practice, has become a canon of subjects which is recognized across most of the world: the dominant language of the society in question; mathematics; sciences (generally dominated by an established core of physical and biological sciences); historical and geographical studies with a content often highly relative to the particular society; literature, music and arts to various degrees, and again with a content that is at least in part culturally relative; useful second languages; various practical, technical and vocational skills.

The National Curriculum of England and Wales, in the form in which it was introduced in 1988, is not untypical of this canon in its list of foundation subjects: English, mathematics, science, technology, a modern language, history, geography, art, music, physical education. Such is the influence of the established canon that it is likely to structure the aspirations towards mass schooling even of those countries which have not yet been able to achieve it.

Now, in mentioning this canon of subjects I do not mean to suggest that it can't be challenged. Far from it. I mean only that if I am to say something of immediate practical relevance, I can't start with a clean slate. Yet even the traditional canon of subjects is surely not as firmly entrenched in the thinking of most of us as is the institutional form in which we tend to expect that canon to be delivered: schooling. Legislation can be repealed, our ideas about the curriculum of schools *could* be radically altered, but the fact of the existence of schools and teachers would be, in modern societies, much harder to change. The existence of schools can be challenged, of course: the 1970s saw a brief flourishing of de-schooling literature, which suggested that universal compulsory schooling was not the answer either for the modern societies which already took it for granted or for the developing societies which were following the model.[5] The intellectual case for that position can still be made, and perhaps the fact that in the 1990s there seems to be little talk of de-schooling society only demonstrates the power of the school that writers such as Ivan Illich were seeking to expose. But whatever the arguments, the chances are that we are stuck with schools in something like their present form (within which the disputes about comprehensive or selective intake, large or small size, even state-run or independent are only so many details). And it is this that provides the context for our questions about aims (more so, even, than any set of assumptions about the curriculum). (Notice that the context I'm speaking of is one in which for the vast majority of children attendance at school is, *in effect*, compulsory even though there may be provision in law for alternatives such as education at home.)

It's perhaps surprising then that we don't more often ask the question: Given that we have a system of universal and compulsory schooling, how best can we use this system? What should we try to do with it? What does it enable us to achieve that we couldn't achieve without it? Is what we can achieve through this system so important that it would justify creating the system now if we didn't already have it? The way I have set up the question might suggest that I shall be concentrating on the ways in which the institution of education may be of value to a society as a whole, to the neglect of any consideration of what it can do for the individual. But it can be very misleading to think in terms which set up an opposition between what is good for society and what is good for an individual. If we had to make a choice, say between developing in people the capacities which will enable them (individually) to lead fulfilling lives and giving them the skills and attitudes which will equip them as cogs in an impersonal machine, then there would be a real divide between aiming at the good of the individual and aiming at the good of society. But it is not necessarily like that. If, for instance, your view of a good society is one in which all individuals can lead unrestricted and fulfilling lives, then no contradiction would exist between aiming at the good of the individual and aiming at the good of society. In fact, even without being idealistic, it's clear that many aims do cut across the individual/social division. Giving people skills which will enable them to get productive jobs, for instance, will in many cases be of benefit both to the individuals concerned and to others within society.

Without, then, worrying too much for the moment about what is good for society and what is good for the individual, it may be more fruitful to look at some of the different kinds of aims that can be suggested for education. If we think again of what I have called the traditional canon for the curriculum, we can see that this has not only faced challenges recently from other concerns competing for a place in the curriculum, but has in fact always faced challenges to its dominance.

MORAL AND POLITICAL CONCERNS

Perhaps the longest-standing of these concerns outside of the traditional canon of subjects appear in the moral and political area. Society has often looked to schooling to make people morally better, but approaches to this concern vary greatly. In some societies it has been widely assumed, at least until recently, that the moral aims of schooling are to be achieved largely through religion. Perhaps for this reason religious education was a compulsory subject in English schools long before the advent of the National Curriculum. But as we know, in other countries, such as the USA, religious education, or at any rate instruction in any particular religion, is excluded from the curriculum of state schools, so that moral aims perforce have to be pursued in some other way. Some countries do include courses in ethics or morals explicitly in their curriculum. To the extent that morality is treated as a matter of public rather than private concern, such courses are likely to overlap with the concern to promote good citizenship. This highlights another of the very common concerns which societies expect their school systems to address: that education should enable people to be good citizens, and perhaps, in democracies, politically active citizens.

Some of the ethical and political aims of schooling reflect perennial concerns: the moral and social functions of education were recognized in the Greece of Plato and Aristotle and the China of Confucius, as well as in the practice of many societies in which there was little formal reflection on education. But in addition to these concerns, and often on the basis of the same underlying values, there are specific issues which appear urgent at a particular time: for example, that education should foster a multicultural non-racist society; that it should advance the cause of equal opportunities between the sexes; and that it should promote citizenship in a wider than nationalistic context.

Then there are those concerns which arise because of technological developments: for example, the widespread promotion of skills and understanding in information technology. And while the preparation of people for some vocational role has never been far from the forefront of thinking about formal education, the particular content of careers education is obviously affected by technological as well as by social changes.

Then again (and this is really an overlapping category rather than a distinct one), there are claims which arise from perceived dangers which an educational response may do something to mitigate. One such is 'education for natural disaster reduction', which involves preparing people to cope with earthquakes, floods, etc. in the hope that this may reduce the scale of the *human* disaster.[6] In a similar way, HIV/AIDS education has been promoted in some countries as a way of reducing the spread of AIDS by influencing the choices which human beings make in their personal lives. And then there were the calls for peace education, which were probably at their strongest at the height of the Cold War (though there is much more than this to peace education,[7] some of the impetus behind its development must have been a response to the perceived threat of nuclear war).

How are we to assess all the varied calls for this and that issue to be addressed in education? Can we say, for instance, that given certain real threats, then it follows that we should do whatever we can in schools to reduce the dangers? Actually, of course, the amount of controversy generated around peace education and HIV/AIDS education shows that the argument can't be that simple. In each of these cases, people on both sides were appealing to their sense of values. Yet if we look deep enough, we may well find that there is some common ground.

Most people would agree that formal education should in some way improve people's lives, whether individually or in societal or even global terms. Even the view that the mass of the population should be educated so as to serve more effectively the interests of a privileged class would be an attempt to justify education by its contribution to *some* people's quality of life. Most importantly, perhaps, there is room for different interpretations of what constitutes a better life: that people acquire intellectual interests which make their lives richer; that they develop skills which enable them to achieve worthwhile aims of their own; that they are less at risk from the antisocial behaviour which *other* people might engage in if they were not taught how to behave; that they keep the wheels of the economy turning, so increasing the general wealth; that they live in harmony with nature; that they live in obedience to divine law. All of these and many more, represent different opinions about the benefits of education. Here again, our values necessarily come into our assessments of what makes one kind of life better than another.

We cannot look here at all the possible permutations of values which could come into such assessments. Instead, I shall pick out just one difference that seems to underlie many actual disputes over the aims that should be pursued in schools: namely, the difference between, on the one hand, values that have traditionally been specifically associated with the idea of *education*, and on the other, values that might be seen as basic to any kind of worthwhile life. Education has often been seen as especially concerned with knowledge and understanding, rationality, and the more elaborated and refined kind of appreciation, both of the natural world and of human creations, that becomes possible only through education. But schooling may also promote what in a sense seem more basic values: health, a sense of security, adequate nutrition and shelter, freedom from injury and, in the end, sheer survival (possessing the skills necessary to support oneself will be, at least, instrumental in enabling individuals to secure these basic values). The difference between 'educational' values and 'basic' values, as it enters into actual debates, is likely to be one of emphasis. It is not that some people care only about one set of values, others about the other kind; but that, where schooling is in question, people will differ on the balance to be struck between one kind of value and the other. In that way, the question about the aims to be pursued in schooling could be seen as a question of *priorities*, between those who seek to promote the 'higher' or more specifically educational values, and those whose aim is to promote the more basic values.[8]

But to see it this way is actually misleading. These are not two independent sets of values; rather, they are in a symbiotic relationship with each other. The basic values are fundamental to almost anything else that is of value in human life, including educational values. If, for instance, people perish, whether through disease, natural disaster, the despoliation of the environment, or war, their opportunity to realize any higher values is simply deleted; and when societies are thrown into chaos by events, whether natural or humanly contrived, there is little chance of enjoying the satisfactions of the life of the mind that education can make possible. But the relationship also holds good the other way round: without knowledge and rationality, and technologically informed skills, we have little chance of doing much to mitigate the assaults which the world, both natural and human, can make on our most basic values.

If the question were only a theoretical one of priorities, it could be endlessly debated. But the interrelationship between these values is not only theoretical, it is mediated, in the most practical way, through the actions of persons in their own lives. This is true at more than one level. It is clearly true in the case of those whose education leads them into specialized fields. It would not, in the modern world, be realistic to try to equip every individual to meet every one of his or her needs independently; we are all of us dependent to varying degrees on specialists for much of the basis of our quality of life, and schooling has a large role to play in promoting an environment in which the production of specialists can flourish.

But the relationship between the promotion of educational values and the promotion of more basic values is not only mediated through the actions of specialists but also through the skills and capacities which any individuals may exercise in their daily lives; and through the actions of all persons in their capacity as moral and political agents. Since the exercise of these capacities will involve the working out in practice of values which have been partly formed through education, we shall need to look not only at the way in which values underlie any conception of aims in education but also at the way in which values may enter explicitly into the *content* of certain aims. In what ways should the promotion of values be part of the aims of education? And which values should these be? As I said at the end of Chapter 1, we need more thinking about values in general before those questions can be answered. But first, can we suggest any guidelines which might help to resolve differences about educational aims in general? I think we can at least list some questions which it would be worth asking about any suggested aims.

SOME QUESTIONS ABOUT EDUCATIONAL AIMS

1. *Is the aim for something of positive value?*
2. *Is it something that can feasibly be realized or at least promoted through formal education?*

Together, these two questions perhaps capture the minimal requirements for any aim of formal education. Some things which we would generally regard as uncontroversially positive (such as an optimal combination of rainfall and temperature from the point of view both of the production of food and of people's pleasure in the weather), it is doubtful whether education can do much, at least directly, to influence. There are other things schools are very likely to be able to achieve (such as subjecting the majority of young people to years of boredom) which are not likely to be seen as valuable.

3. *Is what is aimed at something that can be seen as both good for individuals and good for society, or at least as not merely benefiting the few at the expense of many others, or the majority at severe cost to a few?*

A fault of the first kind, arguably, might be a concentration on the academic achievement of high-flyers; a fault of the second kind, which might arise unwittingly, could be the formulation of aims in terms which assume normal oral communication, thus disadvantaging those whose speech or hearing is impaired.

4. *Are the aims of broad relevance rather than narrowly specific?*

Since it is unrealistic to expect education to accomplish everything we might want it to do, we should give priority to goals which can be realized in conjunction with other goals which are also worth achieving. Those aspects of the curriculum, whether in content or in method, which can serve more than one purpose will have a preferential claim over aspects which can serve only one particular purpose. This suggests that some broad overarching concern, such as promoting the capacity for rational and critical thinking, will have a stronger claim, *other things being equal* (but see question 7), than specific aims like, say, education for natural disaster reduction or HIV/AIDS education, because the overarching aims can contribute, even though not directly, to the same goals as the more specific educational endeavours, and to others as well.

5. *Is what is aimed at something that teachers and schools are particularly well placed to promote? Or is it perhaps something which would come about anyway, independently of formal education?*

In the education profession we perhaps too easily slip into thinking that if something is worth doing, it is worth doing – or in some way preparing for – within formal education. There are many other sources of learning and experience (a point the de-schoolers were right to emphasize), and many desirable things may happen even though teachers do nothing about it. There is, however, at least a case for saying that schools should concentrate on things which schools are necessary for.

6. *Is what is aimed at something that it is important for everyone to have (achieve, be exposed to, etc.)?*

This is not to rule out the existence of options within any individual's career in formal education, but it's worth remembering that one of the things a system of universal compulsory education can do is to ensure that everyone is exposed to similar experiences (and there may be nothing else in modern society that can do this – even television is not watched by *all* children). Are there things that everyone *should* be exposed to? (And if not, should there be universal compulsory schooling?)

7. *Is what is aimed at something which has a justified place in education because of its sheer importance, regardless of the other considerations above?*

It's not inconceivable that we might consider a particular aim to be *so* important that we should devote all possible means, educational and otherwise, to realizing it. The avoidance of global environmental disaster might fall into this category as could the avoidance of nuclear war. If formal education really were to be subordinate to one exclusive aim, it might be radically different from what we are used to. But in fact, few people probably do want to see education geared to just one aim, however important it might be. In other words, we recognize in education as elsewhere a plurality of values.

8. *Can what is aimed at be pursued without violating any moral values in the process?*

If a particular aim, however valuable, could only be achieved by subjecting all pupils in school to half an hour of torture each day, most people would rule out that aim. More likely is the case in which a certain aim – perhaps people's refusal to engage in a particular kind of behaviour – could only be reliably achieved through methods which some people, but not all, would count as indoctrinatory, so that equally some, but not all, would rule out that aim.

If we ask how far education (in the formal institutional sense) should be concerned with aims that fall under the headings of moral education and/or the transmission of values, these questions may be helpful. The first two questions direct us to ask what it would be desirable for schools to do in the area of values, and what would be feasible; but before we can say much more even on those questions, we need to clarify what we are talking about when we speak of values in general, and of moral values in particular. That is the task I'll start on in the next chapter.

NOTES

1. Hobbes *Leviathan* Part 1, Chapter 13. See Hobbes (1968) p. 186. First published 1651.
2. Dewey (1916) Chapter 8. John Dewey's classic *Democracy and Education* is still well worth reading. Dewey is often recognized simply as an advocate of child-centred education. In fact, his educational theory is part of a well worked-out theory of the relations between individuals and society, and of the nature of knowledge and thought. See especially Chapters 1–4, 8 and 9.
3. The most thorough and recent analysis of the concept of education is to be found in Walsh (1993) pp. 3–35, from which readers can also follow up the classic analytical treatment of the concept in Peters (1966) and other philosophers of education influenced by him.
4. See Barrow (1981) Chapter 2 for a clearer than usual treatment of education as just one among many possible aims of schooling.
5. I contributed to this literature myself: Haydon (1977).
6. Haydon (1996a).
7. I shall refer to peace education again in Chapter 9. The 'much more' has to do partly with understanding the many ways in which people can come into conflict, personally as well as nationally and internationally, and partly with practical methods of non-violent conflict resolution.
8. For different accounts of the variety of kinds of value entering into education, see Walsh (1993) Chapters 1, 2 and Bottery (1990).

Further reading

Wringe (1988): An introductory text, reviewing a variety of positions about aims in education concerned (i) with the development of qualities and capacities in the individual for the individual's own good; (ii) with what is good from the point of view of society; (iii) with the pursuit of aims seen as intrinsic to education and valuable in their own right.

White (1982): A philosophical argument which first reviews some accounts of aims which, in White's view, are unsatisfactory, then develops the author's own view (at that time), which puts heavy weight on individual autonomy. White also looks at the practical implications of his account.

O'Hear and White (1991): Written, ten years later, by the same
philosopher of education in conjunction with the headteacher of an
inner London comprehensive school. Published by a left-of-centre
think-tank, it was intended as a contribution to political debate rather
than an academic text. It develops a view based on the qualities which
are desirable in democratic citizens, rather than on knowledge or skills
for their own sake.

Part II
Values

My intention in this part is not to give a definitive account of values; I am more concerned to emphasize their variety. Not only are there moral and non-moral values, there are different interpretations of moral values.

While the notions of a plural society and a multicultural society do not appear in the title of this book, they are part of the context assumed throughout – a context which surely has to be assumed by any book on values in education now. That is why, after making some distinctions between moral and non-moral values in Chapter 3, I turn in Chapter 4 to conflict of values, and in Chapter 5 to the values of compromise and tolerance that come into play because other values conflict.

Values and moral values

A VARIETY OF VALUES

If we ask the question, 'What are values?' it is much easier to draw up a list of examples than it is to give a general account of what kind of thing a value – any value – is. In looking at John Patten's speech in Chapter 1, we encountered at least, I would say, the following values:

- regard for proper authority
- unselfishness
- self-restraint
- loyalty
- fidelity
- readiness to stand up for what one believes in
- respect for rational argument
- sense of fair play
- independence of thought
- persistence in working at solutions
- readiness to resolve conflict without resort to violence

Given the context of the speech, it would not be surprising if most of these struck us clearly as 'moral values', though it may be that some of them – possibly respect for rational argument and independence of thought – would not naturally occur on many people's list of such values. We could easily add to the list more words for values which may not be moral ones, e.g.:

- security (a sense of security)
- comfort
- cheerfulness
- convenience
- intelligence
- efficiency

- cost-effectiveness
- neatness

I'll come back to the question of what makes a value a moral one. First, one thing to notice about all these examples, whether moral or not, is that they are abstract ideas rather than concrete objects. This doesn't mean that it's not possible for people to value concrete objects; it clearly is. You might value your house or your car or your watch (I don't mean in the sense of 'putting a specific monetary value on it' but in the sense, roughly, of 'caring about it'). All sorts of things can be important to us, can matter to us, and in that sense we can value them. But it seems (as a fact about the English language) that we tend to use the word 'values' to describe the more abstract ideas.

These abstract ideas tend to embody qualities which can characterize objects or institutions, or indeed whole societies, or can characterize individual persons. Take 'tolerance': we can speak of a tolerant society or of a tolerant person. In fact, all or most of the examples we took from Patten are personal qualities: they are ways that people can be (or fail to be) in their thinking and action. As it happens, we have in English an old word which we can use as roughly equivalent to 'a morally good way a person can be in their thinking and action'. The word is 'virtue'. Though it's rather fallen out of use in everyday talk, it will be useful here to say that, for instance, readiness to stand up for what one believes in is a virtue. (Of course, you will only agree with this if you do think this is a good quality for a person to have; if you think that something else on Patten's list, perhaps 'fidelity', is not a good quality – or maybe if you think that, while positive rather than negative, it is not very important – then you will not see it as a virtue.)

But our values, including moral values, do not have to be expressed by speaking about virtues. If Patten, for instance, instead of speaking of unselfishness, had said that people ought not to pursue their own wants at the expense of other people, then he would have been expressing much the same value, but putting it as a rule of behaviour. Often we can refer to what seems to be the same value either in terms of a rule (e.g. 'don't tell lies') or in terms of a personal quality (truthfulness). Reference to rules allows us to be more specific about the kinds of behaviour we want to praise or criticize ('Do what your teachers tell you' is more specific than the idea of respect for proper authority); reference to personal qualities says more about the motivation behind a person's behaviour, as we shall see in Chapter 6. So in some contexts it will make a difference whether one thinks in terms of personal qualities or in terms of rules, but since people sometimes express their moral values by referring to moral rules, I want to use the term 'value' in a broad enough way to include talk of rules as well as qualities.

PEOPLE HAVE VALUES

I hope by this point it is clear enough what I mean when I speak of values. At this stage, we do not need to raise metaphysical-sounding questions about the real existence of values. *People* value things, and prominent among these are the qualities of people (themselves and others), and the ways that individuals can be and act. Since we are concerned in this book with issues that people think about and discuss when they are formulating education policies, it actually makes good sense to concentrate, not on the question 'What *are* values?' but on the role of values in people's thinking and behaviour. For whatever else may be true of values, it is true that persons value things (using 'things' in the widest possible sense, to include personal qualities, states of affairs, anything that people can be aware of or have a notion of), and in that sense at least that persons have values, or acknowledge values.

But, you might wonder isn't there something more than this to values, more than just the fact that people value things? What about Patten's idea that 'Values are timeless: ... an expression of a deeper truth beyond, and less ephemeral than, our material lives'? Certainly, many people would endorse this thought, so it is worth spending a while to try to examine what is involved in it.

Perhaps it is the case that no value is timeless. We can recognize that one generation might value what another doesn't. Take as an example something which possibly doesn't involve *moral* values at all: our ideas about natural beauty in landscape. We are told that prior to the romantic movement in poetry and painting, Europeans saw rugged landscapes of bare rocks and mountains as hostile (to human purposes) rather than beautiful.[1] Assuming that we can accept some such broad generalization, we could just say that our ideas of beauty changed: people began to put a certain positive value on things they had not previously valued in that way. If we give no more than this kind of account, then timeless values are unnecessary. But many people would give a different account, insisting that the beauty of rugged natural landscape is a timeless value, but that it is only in recent centuries that people have begun to recognize this; previously they were blind to it.

If some people feel this way about aesthetic values, more will probably feel compelled to say it about values which they see as moral. If we believe that slavery is wrong, it doesn't sound very plausible to suggest that it only became wrong when people (some people, most people?) began to think it was wrong. We are more likely to say that its being wrong is a matter of values, which are themselves timeless (perhaps the values of freedom or of dignity, or the value of personhood), even though it may have been only in recent historical times that most people have either recognized these values or accepted the full implications of them. (To call a value timeless is, I suppose, not to say that it has always been there – or we would have to say that the value of human dignity existed before there were any human beings – but rather that it is somehow independent of time altogether.)

If we concentrate in an educational context, and for certain purposes, on *people holding values*, that doesn't preclude speaking of values as embodying some kind of independent existence or reality. That's why earlier I also used the idea of people 'acknowledging' values, which suggests that the value is already there to be recognized. If we think of human dignity, say, as a timeless value, we are acknowledging not only that some people do in fact value human dignity, though that will be true, but also that they are right to do so (and that people who don't are in some way mistaken or blind to this value). Already here some difficult questions are emerging about the sense in which values could have a real existence or an objective truth about them.

I am not going to spend much time discussing these questions, as it would be impossible to resolve them to everyone's satisfaction (or even to my own), and even to survey the arguments which have occupied moral philosophers for centuries would turn this into a quite different kind of book. The book is premised, rather, on the assumption that something worthwhile can be said and done about values in education without a stand having to be taken on questions of the objectivity or subjectivity of values and the like. Some people think that there are objective values, and others insist that all values are subjective, while many people perhaps are confused about the whole issue – and *this* is the situation that teachers have to work in.

Thus, while I don't attempt to settle questions about the timelessness or reality of values, I do take seriously the fact that many people (I suspect most of us some of the time) do *treat* many of their values as being more than just the preferences they merely happen to have or which society enforces. I am also aware of the fact that people can get seriously muddled by some of the terminology in this area: objectivity, subjectivism, relativism, 'absolute' or 'universal' values, and so on. So I have added a cautionary note about such terms at the end of this chapter.

Before turning to the question of what distinguishes a person's moral values from any other values they may hold, there is a possible ambiguity we should clear up about what counts as a person *having* certain values. Do a person's values lie in what they profess to value, or in what they actually put weight on in their behaviour or (if we are talking about personal qualities) in what they are actually *like*? Probably the answer is all of these. You might say that people's real values are shown in what they do, since when they talk about their values people may be insincere or self-serving. Yet what people say about their values – their professed beliefs about values – can't be neglected; on the contrary, it is where much of the conflict between people over values originates. In any case, if somebody fails to be, say, as kind as they would like to be, it doesn't mean they don't genuinely value kindness. After all, as John Patten said, our values can provide us with ideals; someone who fails to live up to their own ideals may still genuinely hold those ideals.

WHICH VALUES ARE MORAL ONES?

Accepting that people's values are revealed both in what they say and in what they do, our next question – since people's concern about values in education most often seems to be a moral concern – is to ask what it is about some values which makes them moral ones.

Notice first that we're not asking about the distinction between moral and immoral (or morally right and morally wrong); we're talking rather about the distinction between moral values and other sorts of values, be they aesthetic or purely personal, or whatever. Suppose, for instance, that you think (a) that no twentieth-century European music is as good as some earlier European music, and (b) that it is wrong for people who are not married to each other to sleep together. Then (a) expresses an aspect of the aesthetic values you subscribe to and (b) expresses an aspect of your moral values (probably; though as we shall see in the next paragraph it will depend on the reason you have for your view). Suppose someone else thinks (a) that some rock music is (musically) as good as any classical music and (b) that there is nothing wrong (in itself) with unmarried people sleeping together. Then you may think that the other person's musical judgement is depraved or uninformed and that their moral views are corrupt; and if the person acts on their views you may think their behaviour immoral. But it remains true that the distinctions between (a) as aesthetic and (b) as moral hold in their case as much as in yours: that there is nothing wrong with unmarried people sleeping together expresses (or may follow from) an aspect of *that person's* moral values (the relevant aspect in this case may be that they do not think this is a moral matter at all).

This also shows, I think, that we can't distinguish someone's moral values from the other values they hold merely by the content of the values – by what they say or what they're about. Admittedly, if asked to name some moral values, we might mention notions like honesty or truthfulness, or alternatively, if our thoughts turn to rules, we might mention 'don't steal' or 'don't tell lies'. But even these *might* not be moral values, at least on one quite commonly held view of what makes something moral (of which we'll see a lot more in Part 3). 'Honesty is the best policy' is a piece of advice appealing to the person's own self-interest; some would say that this means it is not a matter of morality at all (similarly the near-equivalent 'don't deceive people because you might be found out'). 'Don't sleep around' might well be a moral view, but it could also, in the days of HIV and AIDS, be a piece of health advice. Similarly, 'Don't eat meat' could be a moral view (from an ethical vegetarian) or, again, merely straightforward health advice. And even a criticism of rock music, while it is most probably an expression of aesthetic values, could be a moral judgement on the content of some of the lyrics (indeed, the plots of Mozart's operas leave a lot to be desired by some people's moral standards, too). So what makes someone's views moral ones may not be, so to speak, their surface content, but what kinds of reason the person has for them. That, of course, leads us to ask what makes reason a moral reason? We'll come back to that later.

There are other features, too, which may help to distinguish people's moral values from the other values they hold. (Incidentally, whether someone actually uses the label 'moral' of some of their own values is only one feature, and probably a rather minor one. Some people have reasons of various kinds, as we'll see in Chapter 6, for not liking the *word* moral': they may not want to think of themselves as making moral judgements. But I would be surprised if they didn't turn out to have some moral values, whatever they might choose to call them.) Which of your values, then, will count as moral ones? Let me at least mention some features which may distinguish some of your values from others; and let me suggest very

[handwritten: Indistinct differentiation between values & Moral Values.]

roughly, that the more of these features your values exhibit, the more clearly those values will be moral values.

- Some of your values have to do with the way people behave; not all of them do. What kinds of music you appreciate, for instance, will have a lot to do with your aesthetic values, but these will not necessarily say anything about how people are to behave. It won't necessarily follow, for instance, that your preference for one kind of music over another means that you think that everyone producing or listening to music *ought* to produce or listen to music only of that kind, or that they are doing something wrong if they don't.

- Following on from that, some of your values (unlike aesthetic ones, perhaps) may be ones you're inclined to express by using words such as 'ought' and 'ought not', 'right' and 'wrong'. Of course, this only begins to narrow down the field a bit; using these words doesn't necessarily mean you're expressing anything moral ('you ought not to do that calculation that way; you've got it wrong').

- Some of your values may be ones you consider to be particularly important, ones that in the end you would have to stand by, even if you were to give up on or compromise on all sorts of other things. (But see Chapter 5 on compromise.)

- Some of your values you may think make claims on you, as it were, 'from outside', independently of how you happen to feel or what is convenient for you at a certain time. You might realize on a particular occasion, for instance, that it will smooth over a difficulty if you tell a lie; but the idea that you ought not to tell a lie may still be there, and you may feel that you can't just decide to ignore it.

- Some of your values you may think apply not just to you but to everyone (that is, they are 'universal'). Perhaps this will be the case just because you do feel that these values make some sort of claim 'from outside' (and so they can't be making that claim just on you). That one kind of music is better than another, you might think is a matter of preference – if not just your personal preference, then a cultural preference. After all, we're well aware that there are different musical traditions, and some of us acknowledge our ignorance about most of them. But some values – say, the wrongness of torture – you may think everyone *ought* to recognize, even if not everyone does.

- Some of your values may be ones which you don't think are just a matter of what you happen to prefer or choose. Suppose you do feel, as a general rule, that you ought not to tell lies (I won't get into the question now of whether there can or can't be exceptions). Still, you might say to yourself that this value is one you choose to acknowledge. When trying to think in general terms, people will often say that ultimately moral values are all a matter of choice or personal preference. Yet most people, at least, will not think that all of their preferences are on the same level.

To follow up a number of these points, and to introduce one or two further ones, think about something you feel strongly opposed to – for example, racism. Can you really put your position on this issue down to just your personal preference: that you just happen to prefer an environment free of racism, as you might prefer a environment with plenty of trees in it (not for any ecological reasons, but just because you find it more pleasant)?

If you really thought that moral values were about nothing but personal preference, you could not argue with anyone about their values, and it would be difficult to see how you could disapprove of their actions (I suppose, if you prefer coffee, you don't disapprove of someone else having and exercising their preference for tea). Now, you may say that you don't disapprove of other people's values – perhaps you want to say that everyone is entitled to his or her own values, that they are all equally valid, or something of that sort. Many people now do think like this about various matters – sexual preferences, for instance – which, in an earlier generation, people thought of as in no way a matter of choice. But my example of racism was intended to suggest that, perhaps, there are some things which you cannot sincerely treat in that way. If you don't feel this way about racism, try something else – child abuse, maybe. I would be surprised if you couldn't find something, perhaps many things, that you feel are wrong. And it is difficult, when contemplating something which seems to you quite clearly wrong, to think that this is just a preference you happen to have. (This doesn't mean you have to go around condemning people – that's a different point, which we'll take up in Chapters 6 and 7.)

What does this show us? What it doesn't do is show us that moral values *are* objective – to demonstrate that would take a lot more argument, if it can be shown at all. (It would also need some more careful sorting out of ways in which it would even make sense to think of values as objective – on which I shall say a bit more below.) But it is still important that people – probably most people, at least some of the time – tend to talk about certain values as if they are objective. This reflects the significance which certain values may have for the person who holds them, and I am suggesting that it is largely this fact which determines whether they are among that person's *moral* values.

At this point it would be convenient if we could say that there is just one kind of significance which values must have for a person if they are to count as moral values. But in fact I think the situation is more complicated, because different people do have different conceptions of what moral values are (even if most people's conceptions are only implicit, never spelt out even to themselves), and so we can say that there are different kinds of significance which moral values can have for people. A person, for instance, who thinks in terms of simple and general rules of behaviour, which admit of no exceptions, has a different conception of morality from one whose approach, explicitly or implicitly, is in terms of a plurality of values which have to be realized as fully as possible in the concrete situation (a contrast which will be relevant in Chapter 5 and again in Chapters 6 and 7). A person who sees the values they recognize as being both objectively and universally valid attaches a different significance to those values from someone who sees their values as the conventions of a society of which they happen to be a member. The difference is not necessarily that one person attaches *greater* importance to their values than the other;

the difference is qualitative rather than quantitative. The person who sees their values as the values of their culture, rather than being universally valid, may still be very attached to those values, and may care greatly about them. Conversely, the person who sees their moral values as being universally valid may nevertheless in practice not care deeply about them (for all those people who pay lip-service to the idea of universal human rights, there must be relatively few who are actively trying to do something about ensuring that they are everywhere respected).

Probably the most striking difference, and one that is very important educationally, is that for some people moral ideas are intimately tied up with religious ones, and for others they are not. The most obvious difference this makes is that people who have no religious belief cannot attach any religious significance to their moral values. They *may* still see certain values as having some special kind of importance, but they are likely to have more difficulty than religious believers in saying much about this whereas, for religious believers, almost invariably their moral values will have religious significance. There is still room, even given some religious connection, for different kinds of significance – the idea that moral demands simply are commands of God is only one kind of account, and (to many Christians at any rate) would not be the most plausible. Yet in one way or another, it remains true that in the thought and experience of a believer it is possible for an offence against moral value to be at the same time an offence against religion, whereas for the non-believer this, obviously, is not possible. (There will be more in Chapters 4 and 8 about the ways in which moral values can have religious significance.)

I suggested above that one kind of difference between moral and non-moral values would rest in the kinds of reason that can be given for them. But it seems that we have to recognize at least two different kinds of reason that can back up moral values. For religious believers, the fact (if there are such facts) that something is against the divine order of things (what is experienced or believed to be the divine order) may be sufficient to make it morally wrong. For non-believers, it may be that the only kind of reason that can make something morally wrong is that it is in some way bad for other people (or animals), hurts other people (or animals) or shows disrespect for people. Both these kinds of reason appeal to something outside of the individual's own interests and preferences. But their differences are important too, and underlie a lot of disagreement about values in a plural society, where for many liberal and secular thinkers the *only* question of moral relevance about anything is 'does it do any harm?', whereas for some religious thinkers that question will be largely missing the point.

Some of the secular thinkers may want to confine the notion of moral values to ones that they can justify in their own particular way. But I don't think they have good reason for that. What kinds of values count as moral values is a question that might be answered, in various contexts, by an appeal to any of the features I've already mentioned. As a matter of empirical fact, it will be the case for many people (though probably a minority in the UK) that the values they see as most important, as bearing on their conduct towards others, as making claims on them independently of their own preferences, and so on, will be experienced as having a religious significance. Furthermore, the reasons they would give, if pressed, for the importance of these values, might also be couched in religious terms. At the same time, they may use the word 'moral' of these values. Where the use of the word 'moral' is established by long usage, there is no more justification for secular thinkers to try to wrest it away from religious believers than there is for religious believers to try to deny the word to those who use it within a secular framework. This does not, of course, prevent these different users in some cases disagreeing, from their different perspectives, about what is right and what is wrong.

OBJECTIVITY, RELATIVISM, ETC. – A CAUTIONARY NOTE ON TERMINOLOGY

Specialized terminology is often indispensable for specialists when they are talking to each other, and where there can be a precise definition of the terms. But while there *are* people who specialize in talking and writing about moral matters – including moral philosophers, moral theologians, psychologists studying moral development, and others – they don't share a specialized, agreed vocabulary. Instead, there are terms which have either been borrowed from everyday language in the first place or have made their way back into it, terms which anybody may use when they get into talking about moral values, but which have no agreed technical definition. I mean terms like 'absolute', 'relative', 'subjective', 'objective' and 'universal'. I feel it would be useful to say a bit more about such terms here – but only to show how easily they can be misleading, and as a guide to your own thinking if you still feel the need for these terms.

Of the examples I've mentioned, objective/subjective and absolute/relative provide a useful pairing, giving us two dimensions with two opposing positions on each; but sometimes people use 'objective' as more or less equivalent to 'absolute' and 'subjective' as more or less equivalent to 'relative', while they may use 'universal' as more or less equivalent to 'absolute', too – in which case five terms are only helping us to mark one distinction, which seems a waste of resources.

'Objective' and 'subjective'
'Objective' may be used of claims or beliefs which can be true (or false) independently of the thoughts, feelings or viewpoint of the person who makes the claim or has the belief. The simplest and least controversial examples we can give of an objective truth will describe states of affairs in the physical world: for example, the structure of the solar system. We can use the term 'objective' here because we assume that there is an actual state of affairs, a part of reality, which is independent of what anyone thinks. Notice that the idea that something is objectively true (using the term in this way) is *not* the same as the idea that we are *certain* of its truth. Things we are certain of may turn out to be false (many people used to be certain that the sun revolved around the earth). The point about objectivity (as I'm using the term now) is that the truth or falsity of something doesn't depend on what we think or feel about it – and that means,

among other things, that it doesn't depend on whether we feel certain or uncertain about it, or even on whether we agree about it. That there was a time when people disagreed about the movements of the earth and the sun doesn't show that this is a purely subjective question.

So what is 'subjective'? My preference for sugarless coffee is surely subjective – it is a matter of taste. But already we need to be careful. It is a fact that I prefer coffee without sugar. That it's a fact about me – about an individual person – doesn't by itself make it any less a fact. Like other facts, I can tell it to you, and you can learn it. What is *not* a fact is that coffee without sugar tastes better, full stop.

So what about values, and moral values in particular? There are lots of facts about what people value, just as there are facts about people's tastes. And the fact is that, on some matters, different people think different things: for example, some people think capital punishment is right in certain circumstances and some that it is always wrong. But just as in the example I gave earlier of the time when people disagreed about whether the earth revolved around the sun, the fact that people disagree doesn't by itself mean that the whole matter is subjective. If someone says that capital punishment is wrong, they usually mean that its being wrong is *not* dependent on what they, or anyone else, thinks. (If they really think it is wrong in this way, they will be willing to say 'it will still be wrong, even if everyone – including me – misguidedly comes to think it is right'.) There is no inconsistency in someone recognizing that people have different views about the rightness or wrongness of capital punishment, and still maintaining that there is an objective truth of the matter.

But suppose someone says that while there might be an objective truth of the matter, we have no *objective procedure* by which we can establish this. Here we are shifting towards a different sense of 'objective'[2]: when someone says that there is no objective truth in moral matters, they might mean *not* that there is no truth of the matter at all but (merely) that there is no truth *that can be established in the way that the claims of science are established*. But if that is what someone means when denying objectivity to moral values, their claim may not be very controversial. I said that the simplest examples we can give of objective matters of fact are of states of affairs in the physical world. Unfortunately, such examples don't help very much in thinking about values, because values, whatever they are, are not states of affairs in the physical world. If values have a real existence, they don't manifest it in the way that trees and rocks do, or even in the way that electrons and electromagnetic forces do (and if there is an objective truth of the matter about values, we don't at any rate have the same kinds of procedures – sense perception, hypotheses and the experimental testing of hypotheses – for establishing it).[3]

But there is quite another and perhaps more promising way in which we could establish an objective truth about moral values without having to say that they exist in the world. If this sounds paradoxical, think of mathematics. At least at the level taught in school, there are plenty of objective truths in maths: '$7 + 5 = 12$' is correct, and is about as objective as one can get; there really isn't room for dispute over it. But to say that is not to say anything in particular about *how* there can be objective truths in maths, and it certainly doesn't commit us to believing that numbers, or sums, or answers, really exist in the world in a way that is quite independent of the fact that there are people doing maths. If intelligent beings had never evolved on earth, would it still be true that $7 + 5 = 12$? What to make of that question, what sort of reality mathematical truths have and whether they are timeless, is all a matter of interpretation, and forms one of the more esoteric branches of philosophy. But we don't have to be able to understand the philosophy of mathematics in order to treat maths as a field in which there are objective truths. In effect, we can here run the first two senses of 'objective' together. We do have objective procedures for establishing answers in mathematics – not the same procedures as those of empirical sciences, but if anything more clear-cut – and that may be enough to entitle us to speak of objective truth here.

In the same sort of way, the question 'if human beings had never existed, would it still be true that human dignity matters?' is one that it is difficult to make sense of. (Perhaps it would be easier if we were to conceive of a God, equipped with a God's-eye and a timeless perspective.) But we do exist, and we do have moral ideas and systems, and *if* within those systems we have procedures, ways of thinking, by which we can arrive at answers about certain values, then that might be enough to entitle us to speak of objectivity. It would make a difference here whether we thought that we had ways of thinking which would, if they were properly followed, lead everyone to the same answers. In the case of truths about the physical world, as we've seen, we can make sense of the idea that while everyone agrees, everyone *could* be wrong. In the case of mathematics, however, it's not clear that we can make sense of this. What, again, of moral values? If *everyone* had reasons for thinking that, say, torture is wrong, could everyone be wrong about this?

Perhaps it would still depend on what *kind* of reasons people had for thinking this. This brings us to yet a third (related) sense of 'objectivity': the idea of persons being objective in the way they look at and think about something – that is, adopting an unbiased standpoint detached from their own particular preferences and inclinations. It's very plausible that objectivity in this sense would form part of any way of thinking (assuming one even exists) that might lead people to agree on moral values. I shall myself use something like this idea in Chapter 7 when I defend morality against some of its critics.[4]

'Relative' and 'absolute'

As with 'objective' and 'subjective', it is probably best to clarify the terms 'relative' and 'absolute' in contrast to each other. But first, I want to put on one side the fact that people sometimes use the word 'relative' to make a contrast, not with 'absolute' but with 'universal' in one of its meanings. It is a matter of fact that different people in different parts of the world, at different times and in different cultures, have held and do hold different moral beliefs (on infanticide, for instance; or even on head-hunting[5]). Sometimes when people say that values are relative they intend no more than to report this fact of actual variation. The contrast to that would be to say that some values are universal, meaning that everyone shares them.

Whether there are any values which are universal *in this sense* is a question of fact, which could be settled by reports from anthropologists, sociologists and so on. However, it's unlikely that there are any values which literally everyone holds (since 'everyone', if we mean it literally, would have to include, for instance, psychopaths). But there may be some values which exist in every human culture. And it is consistent with this that there may also be considerable variation.

What I said above on objectivity should show that the fact there is variation in the values people hold doesn't by itself mean that there is no objective truth of the matter (faced with the fact that some people think it is right and meritorious to cut off the heads of people from the next village, we still have the possibility of saying that they are wrong). But the word 'relative' has a more distinctive role when we use it to say that there are some truths which are objective *but also* relative to a context. That July is one of the summer months is true, but this truth is relative to geography (it's true in the northern hemisphere but not in the southern). When a weather forecaster, standing in front of a map of England which shows a temperature of 35° Celsius says, 'it will be hot today', this is not a subjective report but it *is* relative. It's relative to what the inhabitants of England have come to expect, and it's also, in a wider sense, relative to the range of ambient temperatures that human beings are adapted to (inside an oven 35° would be fairly cool). Judgements of hot and cold are always relative to something, with the exception of the physicists' 'absolute zero'.

Such a phrase does illustrate the best use for the term 'absolute' – to indicate that something is not relative to anything else at all. Unfortunately, where values are concerned the same value might be relative (and therefore not absolute) in respect to some things but not others. The least misleading use for the idea of values being relative is to say that they are relative to cultures. This is very different from saying that 'anything goes'; rather it is saying, quite objectively, that there are some things that go and some that don't but that what these things are is relative to culture or tradition. If, for example, you were to say that it is wrong (and you meant that it *is* wrong, not just that it's considered wrong) for a Muslim girl to marry someone her parents don't approve of, but not wrong for a non-Muslim girl, you'd be expressing a relativist view of this kind.

The most thoroughgoing account of values as absolutes is, I think, that of the philosopher Kant (whom we'll encounter again from time to time). He held that there are moral imperatives which are binding on any being capable of following them – that is, on any rational being not just on human beings. It would be, for instance, wrong for any being which is capable of communicating truth or falsehood to tell a lie (so if you meet aliens from a flying saucer, you know that it would be wrong for them to lie to you). Now many people probably consider that there are moral values which apply to all human beings by virtue of something to do with human nature; Kant could have labelled these people as relativists. For his own part, Kant was the most uncompromising kind of absolutist, holding that there are moral truths which are not relative even to anything to do specifically with human nature or the human condition.

In Kant's account it was also the case that the application of a moral imperative could not be relative to particular circumstances – in other words, if it's wrong to tell a lie, it's wrong full stop, without exceptions. Yet it does seem possible to distinguish here two notions of absolute values, which correspond to different respects in which values could be relative. We might want to say that truthfulness is always and everywhere an important value – in that way it would be absolute, not dependent on culture – but at the same time, we may want to stress that its importance could in a particular case be outweighed by other values (such as saving life).[6] Thus, the rule 'never tell a lie' would *not* be a rule with no exceptions. Unfortunately, when people speak of moral absolutes, it is often unclear whether they mean that there are values which are not relative to culture, or that there are rules which can never admit of an exception. The second position – that rules such as 'don't tell lies' or 'keep your promises' or even 'don't deliberately take the life of an innocent person' could *never*, under any circumstances, have a justified (though perhaps tragic) exception – is one which few people probably hold.

'Universal'

We have already looked at one definition of the term universal values – namely, the rather implausible belief that there are values which are actually held or recognized by everybody. But another sense of 'universal' is to say that a value *applies* to everyone (which makes it almost equivalent to 'absolute' in the sense of 'not relative to culture'). Thus, the right not to be tortured is not universal in the first sense, since there are apparently people in the world who don't recognize or respect it; but if you say that it is universal in the second sense, you mean that it applies to everyone, that *everyone* (regardless of race, religion, culture, etc.) has the right not to be tortured.

What I have said about these terms will hardly have cleared them up, but it may at least have shown why they can cause trouble (and why my arguments in this book will rarely rely on them, although I shall find it useful in places to refer to the different senses of objectivity). I would suggest that before embarking on any discussion of moral values, you establish the extent of people's understanding of these words. If there is clarity, and agreement about meaning, well and good: these terms will then serve as useful tools for the discussion. But if, as is more likely, the meanings are unclear, or the words mean different things to different people, then spend some time trying to tighten up the definitions. If time is precious, however, then it is probably better to avoid these terms altogether.

NOTES

1. See Schama (1995).
2. I don't mean to suggest that there aren't intelligible connections between the different senses I'm picking out; but to trace the connections would be too complex a process for this context.
3. I say little here about the question of whether moral values have some kind of real existence in the world, and if so, what kind. This is because, so far as I am aware, the notions of moral 'realism' and 'non-

realism', in that terminology, are largely confined to philosophical debate. (This technical notion of 'moral realism' is, of course, different from the sense of a realist as someone who takes pride in not expecting very much by way of moral behaviour from actual human beings in real-life situations.) I am doubtful whether we can make sense of the notion of values having a real existence independently of human thought unless we are seeing values as in some way attributes of a (really existing) God – and even then the interpretation may be difficult. I have a little more to say in Chapter 8 about whether a denial of the real existence of moral values need make any difference to our sense of morality.

4. There is a thorough, fascinating, but not easy, treatment of the questions of objectivity and subjectivity, not just concerning values but in knowledge and experience generally, in Nagel (1986).

5. 'A European peasant, beheading a woman from a neighbouring village whom he happened to encounter on his way home from the fields, would be locked up as a criminal lunatic; whereas in a Naga village a youth returning with a human head captured under similar circumstances earns the insignia of a successful headhunter.' von Furer-Haimendorf (1967) p. 1; see also pp. 97–101.

6. I have in mind here an example of Kant's, which I'll refer to in Chapter 5.

Further reading

On values in general see also Almond and Wilson (1988); and in an educational context Walsh (1993), Chapter 8, 'Basing Values on Love of the World' and Garforth (1985), Chapter 3.

On the issues raised in the last section see Williams (1976) (subjectivism and relativism); Mackie (1977), chapter 1 and Hare (1981), chapter 12 (objectivity); Wilson (1987) (absolutism).

CHAPTER 4

Conflict and plurality in values

What do values have to do with conflict? One answer is that they may help to reduce conflict; another that they may cause conflict. We shall look at both connections here, and in doing so I have more to say about value pluralism.

VALUES AS A CONFLICT-AVOIDANCE DEVICE

In Chapter 2 I mentioned Hobbes's claim that human beings, left to their own individual devices, would lead a life that was 'nasty, brutish and short'. In Hobbes's view, the human condition being as it is, the potential for conflict is always there and has to be restrained.

What are the sources of this potential conflict?[1] Some of them lie in the nature of the world we live in: what we want does not automatically come our way; we have to make efforts to acquire what may be in short supply, and in demand by others. This by itself would not necessarily lead to conflict, if it came naturally to human beings to resolve amicably and co-operatively any difficulties which the world lays upon them. But in fact it seems that human beings are essentially concerned with their own individual interests, and often take a short-term view.[2] Besides, while the pursuit of individual self-interest is enough to produce conflict, human beings also sometimes display an active malevolence towards others. And, further, there are limitations in human capacities: in knowledge and intelligence, understanding and imagination.

If this is the human condition, something is needed to prevent human life being always and everywhere 'nasty, brutish and short'. Morality provides part of what is needed. Not that an established moral system would be sufficient in itself to prevent conflict: for Hobbes, only a human authority, endowed with enough coercive power to keep people in check through the making and enforcement of laws, would suffice. But there are many forms of self-restraint that can hardly be enforced by law: moral prohibitions, and not only legal ones, can deter people from doing what, if no such prohibitions existed, they would do at others' expense. I'll refer to this as the Hobbesian picture of morality.

This, then, is the sense in which moral values can be seen as one factor in reducing the level of conflict among human beings. If everyone were to pursue his or her own advantage or immediate desires amorally, there might be far more overt conflict between people than we actually experience. Morality in the Hobbesian picture is that set of values which is necessary in order to contain the potential conflict: it will consist of basic prohibitions on killing, assault, theft, lying, promise-breaking and the like; or it may comprise an all-purpose set of virtues.[3] This picture is still quite powerfully operative in our culture. It is there, for instance, when public figures, condemning, say, an increase in vandalism and theft among young people, call on parents and schools to reinforce moral values as the way to reduce antisocial behaviour. (The conflict here is between individuals and society, or between different groups of individuals, as when rival gangs clash in street fights, and the harm to the wider society is, from their point of view, a by-product.) The more firmly moral values are instilled in people, the less will be the conflict. It is a simple picture, and one that seems to give a clear-cut role to education – or at least to schools.

VALUES AS A CAUSE OF CONFLICT

Unfortunately, this picture is far too simple. Education in modern societies has to take the existence of a plurality of values into account, and so it cannot neglect the fact that there can be conflict *between* values. Indeed, values will sometimes be the very factor which leads people into conflict. So, if we put a positive value on avoiding conflict between people, we have very practical reasons for seeing whether education can prepare people to live in a society in which there are different values in play. The first step will be to understand more about how people's values can lead to conflict.

On first sight this may seem paradoxical if we take the Hobbesian picture for granted. How can moral values, which have to do with restraining one's own wants and putting weight on the interests of others, actually bring people into conflict? Yet it is a fact in plural societies that some conflicts arise because of differences in the moral values to which people adhere. In clarifying this point, I need first to say something about the sense of 'conflict' which I have in mind; then I shall go on to give some examples and look at what it is about moral values in particular that can lead to conflict.

There is a sense in which we can speak of conflict between values themselves. It is often said, for instance, that conflict exists at a social level between freedom and equality, meaning that equality cannot be realized within society without (too much) restriction on people's freedom (I am using this as an example without necessarily endorsing it[4]). There can be a conflict at an individual level between honesty and kindness, as when we deliberate about whether to tell someone an unpleasant truth. It seems a familiar part of experience that values can conflict in this way,[5] though it is worth noting that it already complicates the simple Hobbesian picture: if morality is viewed as a kind of device for reducing conflict between persons, its 'design' would appear to be deficient if it cannot work without producing its own internal conflicts. Conflict of values in this sense, though, which may be experienced by a single person, does not necessarily lead to interpersonal conflict. Here I am going to concentrate on conflicts between persons which arise because different people adhere to different moral values.

That such cases do frequently occur is characteristic of a plural society. We can, if we like, say that there is an inevitable kind of conflict here (as when we speak of conflicting opinions or conflicting points of view). Since there are many reasons for welcoming the existence of plural societies, conflict in this sense may not necessarily be undesirable. Indeed, with the benefit of hindsight over the longer term, we may come to recognize that conflict of moral positions can be a positive advantage to a society. Changes which would now almost universally be acknowledged as constituting moral progress – the abolition of slavery, the enfranchisement of women – would not have come about if everyone in society had remained content with the status quo; such changes generally have begun with a minority whose views conflict with those of the majority, or with those whose entrenched positions favour the old order. But while, with hindsight, there might be general agreement that a particular conflict over values had been resolved in the right direction, at the time it is part of the essence of the conflict that the persons in disagreement cannot stand back and take a common view on what would be a satisfactory resolution. In such cases people will sometimes resort to violence – as we have seen in the cases of abortion in the USA and the treatment of animals in Britain.

What is it about values, and moral values in particular, that is liable to lead to conflict? We can establish at least part of the answer to this by looking back at some of the features that distinguish moral values from other kinds, which I picked out in Chapter 3. For instance, that moral values are perceived by people as important: if that were not so, conflict about them would be less likely, for people are less likely to fight about what they themselves see as trivial. (Some people, as I have suggested, do not spontaneously think of what they *call* 'moral' values as important; such people may be liberals of a certain kind, and their tendency to disclaim the importance of 'moral' values, which to other people seem vital, may partly explain the difficulty that some liberals have in seeing why anyone should fight over moral values. But, to repeat, liberals who take this view are likely after all to have some values – perhaps not the ones that immediately occur to them as examples, but values such as tolerance or respect for diversity – which do function for them as moral values.)

Moral values are perceived by people as not just a matter of individual preference. If they were, conflict over them would again be less likely. This said, however, some matters of individual preference may be very important, even central, to the lives of the persons concerned. This may be true, for instance, of a career or lifestyle or lifelong ambition. But there is a sense in which what is important in my life may still be something which I don't think is particularly important in itself. ('It may be of the greatest importance to Henry that his stamp collection be completed with a certain stamp, but even Henry may see that it is not, simply, important.'[6]) Someone whose life would seem meaningless without risk and adventure might still recognize that this is a personal preference, and would not necessarily think that it should be shared by everyone (he might, indeed, acknowledge that it is better that it is not shared by everyone). But a man who thinks it important that unborn children should not be killed doesn't (just) think this is important *for him*. People are more likely to get into conflict over matters they think are *important*, full stop, than over things that are just important for them (at least, if they don't see other people as restricting their pursuit of what is important for them).

The sense that moral values have some kind of objectivity means that one person can consider another to be wrong. 'Wrong' can have a double sense here. It can mean morally wrong, or immoral: in this sense, when one person thinks that another is acting wrongly, there is not necessarily any *conflict* of moral values. It is commonly acknowledged that people sometimes act against their own moral values, doing what they themselves believe to be wrong. Here, there may be an internal conflict, perhaps between self-interest and moral obligation, but there need be no conflict of values between this person and another who criticizes their conduct; they may both share the same standards. But 'wrong' can also have the sense of 'incorrect': the person criticizing may think that the other's values are wrong. And the two kinds of judgement can also be combined: the critic may think not merely that the other's values are incorrect, but that the other is culpable for having the wrong values. Perhaps it is this kind of judgement more than any other (particularly when linked with religious belief, a link we shall come back to) which has led people to believe they are justified in persecuting others over their moral differences.

I said too that moral values, unlike some values, are to do with how people behave. Moral values are values that people, at least to some extent, live by, or think they ought to; and (because these values are seen as making some sort of claim independently of preference) people tend to expect others to live by them too. This means that differences over moral values are unlike mere differences of opinion, which may have no practical consequences even when expressed in conversation. Differences in moral values are to some degree differences in ways of living; and differences in ways of living are a more potent source of conflict than differences of opinion as such. For example, someone who can tolerate the expression of an opinion with which they disagree may find it more difficult to tolerate the fact that other people are actually living in ways they disapprove of.

But what is probably more important is that much of morality concerns a person's conduct towards others. The conduct which a critic believes to be wrong may be conduct which (in the critic's eyes) has victims. (Some liberal-minded people find it difficult to see any conduct as wrong if it has no victim.) No one suggests that someone who believes there is nothing wrong with murder should be allowed simply to live out this alternative policy. But perhaps it is too often forgotten by liberal-minded people that the person who believes that abortion is murder can hardly view policies which are favourable towards abortion as innocent expressions of an alternative lifestyle; and much the same goes for the person who condemns vivisection. (This will be relevant in Chapters 5 and 9 when we look at the scope for compromise over different kinds of moral issues.)

MORAL VALUES, CULTURE AND RELIGION

If the features of moral values which I have mentioned are ones which are liable to lead to conflict over differences in values, it hardly follows that such conflict could be avoided by doing away with these features. For such features seem to be central to much of our experience of morality; and there is probably enough truth in the Hobbesian model to suggest that a world lacking in morality would be unlikely to be a world with less overall conflict (a question I will follow up in Chapters 6 and 7). But one thing we must now notice about the Hobbesian model is that it purports to pick out features of the human condition, tending to lead to conflict, which are universal; and hence the kind of morality looked to as a remedy would also be universal. If the simple Hobbesian picture were correct, we should expect to find moral values the same everywhere. I shall not here try to resolve the debate, referred to briefly in Chapter 3, on how much in actual human values is in fact universally shared; but it is certainly true that there are cultural differences. Possibly the most plausible way of looking at these differences is to note that while there may be universal features of the human condition that are likely to lead to problems in the absence of a recognized moral code, there may be more than one possible code that will serve to mitigate these problems. Thus, it is certainly something about the nature of human sexuality which leads to every culture (even the most liberal) having some set of moral conventions about what sexual conduct is or is not acceptable; but there is more than one possible set of conventions which can prove more or less workable (where what is 'workable' is largely a matter of what enables the culture to continue).[7]

It should not be surprising, then, that different cultures have different conventions; or rather, different conventions have evolved in different human populations, and it is the differences which in part define different cultures. This is not in itself any kind of problem: even the possibility of problems only arises when cultures come into contact with each other, and particularly when members of different cultures are living in proximity (which is not intended as an argument for trying to keep societies culturally homogeneous, even if that were possible). As the possession of a particular set of moral values is one of the aspects which constitutes a human culture, so it is one of the factors which constitutes the cultural identity of individuals. Sharing a common set of values is part of what gives members of one culture a sense of belonging; and recognizing differences between their values and those of others is part of what can give a sense of other cultures being alien. In a plural society, this fact is perhaps one of the most potent ways in which differences in values turn into conflict between persons. People's moral values can be of central importance to them, not just because these are the values that they as individuals hold, but because these values partly define them as the kind of persons they are. When people find that some of their values are opposed by others in their society, they may feel that both themselves and their culture are threatened – especially if they are already in a minority in their society.

What has just been said applies particularly when the values in question are integral to a person's religion. It would be greatly oversimplifying, of course, to suggest that actual conflicts in the world which we may identify as religious are entirely about religion. Whatever example we take, we are also likely to find a variety of political, historical and often economic factors (Northern Ireland is a case in point). But sometimes a degree of simplification can be an aid to understanding, and I want here to make just such an initial simplification by focusing on the religious aspect of certain conflicts, in order to ask how far a religious conflict is a conflict over values.

I think it would be widely agreed that to have a religion is not just a matter of holding certain beliefs about the existence of God or other metaphysical matters; it is also a matter of being committed to particular values (where the commitment, naturally, does allow of degrees). It's rather artificial to speak of beliefs and values as if they were separable, but it does allow us to recognize that it is not just because of differences in beliefs that people are likely to come into conflict. Some people believe that there is intelligent life on other planets, others that there is not; we do not find rival groups fighting over these beliefs.

If it is largely because of their differences over values that adherents of various religions come into conflict, then the points already made – about why values can bring people into conflict – will partly explain religious conflict too. However, this is somewhat crude; it would be better to say, without suggesting that beliefs and values can be separated, that the beliefs already carry evaluative import. Or we could turn this round and say that the values are given their particular significance by the beliefs. Either way, my point is that the religious context of values can make a difference, not only to the content of people's values but to their significance.

It may be natural to assume that conflict over values arises because of differences in the *content* of people's values – such as the difference between the orthodox Roman Catholic position on artificial contraception and a standard liberal position – but what may be even more likely to generate conflict is not that people's values tell them to do different things, but that the values have different sorts of significance for different people. I pointed out some of these differences in Chapter 3, but we need now to examine how they can lead people into conflict. For the most part, differences between various non-religious interpretations of values do not tend towards conflict; though there is an argument, long made by some theorists of liberalism,[8] that conflict is more likely to ensue when people see their values as having objective and universal force, rather than as being simply the values of their own culture, since they must then see others as wrong and are thereby going to find it difficult to tolerate them. But this danger of intolerance, though it can apply independently of any religious interpretation being attached to values, may itself be heightened where values are perceived as having religious significance. So it is to the potential for conflict in the perceived religious significance of values that I now turn.

To repeat, the differences over values between religious believers and non-believers are not necessarily differences in the content of the values. A Christian and an atheist, for instance, may to a large extent be in favour of and against, the same things. And it is also, of course, possible for both of them either to follow the values they acknowledge consistently or sometimes to go against them. But going against one's own values cannot, for the atheist, be disobedience to God, or violation of a divinely ordained order, or *sin*. And this in turn affects the perceived importance of the values. It is not that the moral values of the atheist cannot be, to the atheist, of supreme importance, for they may well be paramount within his or her scale of values; it's rather that the very nature of supreme importance is different for the religious believer: right and wrong – at least on matters on which the religion pronounces – will have a cosmic significance which they cannot have for the non-believer.

This difference in significance wouldn't by itself yield the potential for conflict, but it can when coupled with two other factors which are particularly associated with a religious point of view (though they are not exclusive to it). One is the degree of confidence with which one's moral convictions are held. The secular moralist, aware of how much people can differ in their values, may always retain some room for the thought that others might be right after all. But the believer who has a quite unshakeable religious faith may by the same token have the strongest possible conviction of the correctness of certain moral positions. The second factor is having the strength of motivation to act on the values one acknowledges. In part, this interacts with the first factor: the stronger the conviction, the stronger may be the motivation to act. And there is also another way in which the significance of moral values for the religious believer can make a motivational difference, in that there are motives, whether love of God or fear of God, which are only available to the believer; and to the extent that the believer's relation to God is the most important facet of the believer's life, so it may furnish the strongest possible motivation.

In pointing to differences between religious and non-religious interpretations of values, I should not neglect the differences between various religious interpretations. Within the theistic religions, perhaps the most significant difference is between the outlooks of those who regard moral values, in the end, as a matter of individual conscience (though it would be misleading to call them in this context a matter of individual choice[9]) and those for whom moral values are essentially a matter of authority. To approach a moral dilemma as one on which we must ultimately make up our own mind, or to approach it as one on which we can look to scripture or a spiritual leader, represent two very different understandings of moral values. Of the major world religions it is Islam, in its more fundamentalist tendencies, which has gone furthest in stressing the need for the believer to submit his will to God's. Within Christianity, however, even in its Protestant manifestation, there is all the variation, from the most fundamentalist attempt to rely on the words of the Bible to the most liberal stress on the decision of individual conscience in the actual circumstances at hand;[10] but by and large there has been a cross-fertilization between Christianity and modern moral and political liberalism which would hardly be possible to the same extent within Islam. As regards the non-theistic religions, of course they cannot conceive of moral action as being in conformity with the will of God, but it can still be true that for Hinduism or Buddhism under their non-theistic interpretations, a moral life will be one that is in conformity with the true nature of the world; and that significance is not, on the face of it, available to a secular and materialist world-view.[11]

But while there are differences between religions, it is possible that in modern plural societies their importance is outweighed by the differences between religious and non-religiously based values. This may be seen, for instance, in the choice that British Muslims not infrequently make, when an Islamic school is unavailable, to send their children to a Roman Catholic rather than a secular school; in the fact that non-Christian religious communities in Britain by no means necessarily support the disestablishment of the Church of England;[12] and in the extent to which in the Salman Rushdie affair it has been Christians more than secular liberals who have been most sympathetic to Muslim complaints (though not to the *fatwa* on Rushdie).[13]

It would be a mistake, of course, to think that all the differences in values between, say, Muslims of Asian origin and secular liberals within Britain correspond to the religious or non-religious basis of the values. There are values which demand an explanation in terms of broader cultural patterns, rather than by reference to scriptural authority – for example, some aspects of the role of women in South Asian societies, and of the status of children in different communities. There are cultural outlooks in which obedience is a major virtue, and others where, outside of special cases, it may be looked on even with some suspicion – and this again does not seem to be primarily a religious difference. In parts of the Western world, teenagers are almost expected to rebel against parental authority at some point; autonomy of the individual is a central value in some cultures, but remains subordinate in others. And there is a long-standing, but possibly overdrawn, anthropological distinction between cultures where moral thinking revolves around the idea of shame and those where it revolves around the idea of guilt.[14]

Even where a dispute arises explicitly in the context of religion, the values brought into play may be of broader cultural relevance. The Rushdie affair is a good illustration of this. In general, the only way that liberals can make sense of offences against religion is to see them as causing offence to persons. They can then bring them under the general liberal principle that the law should only interfere in people's conduct in order to prevent harm being caused to others.[15] There are problems in interpreting offence as harm (as shown also in the debates over obscenity and pornography), but at least this perspective appears to bring offences against religion under the same conceptual scheme as other cases the liberal is used to dealing with. But this appearance is perhaps superficial, since it may be difficult for the liberal to understand the nature of the perceived offence without sharing conceptions of honour and shame, central to Islamic culture, which have become relatively unimportant in Western society.[16]

I began this chapter by referring to the Hobbesian picture, whereby moral values are essentially those which, if put into practice, will prevent the conflict that otherwise would arise among human beings pursuing their interests amorally. We can see now that this picture omits a large part of the total range of moral values; and that the values it omits are not merely at the periphery – for many people they can be fundamental to their moral outlook, indeed to their life.

NOTES

1. My answer here is not purely Hobbesian. Accounts which have some features in common include: Hume (1888), Book III, Part II, Section 1; Hart (1961), Chapter 9; Warnock (1971), Chapter 2.
2. I say 'it seems', because it is certainly disputable. Hobbes took himself to be an objective observer of human nature; a Marxist would point out that the human life Hobbes observed, and the perspective from which he observed it, were those of a particular socio-economic context (early English capitalism). Marx, as we shall see in Chapter 6, thought that this context could be transcended: the motivations and behaviour appropriate to that socio-economic context were not a fixed part of human nature.
3. See Warnock (1971), Chapter 6.
4. For a discussion of whether equality and freedom in a political context must conflict, see Norman (1987), Chapter 7.
5. See Hampshire (1983), Chapter 7; Taylor (1982); Williams (1981).
6. Williams (1985), p. 182.
7. See Hampshire (1983), Chapter 6. To say that all cultures have some conventions about acceptable sexual conduct is not to say that such conventions are central to morality; indeed, I shall suggest in Chapter 6 that there is no 'sexual morality' as such.
8. A classic argument appears in Berlin (1969). There will be more on liberalism in Chapters 5 and 11.
9. This is a case where 'conscience' must refer to an individual's capacity for judgement, rather than to strength of will – see the comments on 'conscience' in Chapter 1. On why the exercise of an individual's capacity for judgement need not amount to individual 'choice' of values, see my comments on the ethics of Kant in Chapter 7.
10. See Fletcher (1966).
11. Some ethical positions within an ecological perspective may be an exception – see Chapter 8, p. 94.
12. See Modood (1992), Chapter 11.
13. In my own experience of teaching on a large PGCE (Postgraduate Certificate in Education) course, where issues were taught and discussed in overwhelmingly secular terms, the Christians, Muslims and Jews among the students sometimes collectively expressed their approval on the rare occasions when any religious perspective was voiced.
14. See Tombs (1995) for an interesting discussion of the possible relevance of shame in education in the British context.
15. The classic expression of this liberal principle appears in Mill (1859).
16. On the notion of honour see Berger (1983); and Chapter 12 below, pp. 141–2.

CHAPTER 5

Two difficult values – compromise and tolerance

In Chapter 4 I discussed the way that conflict can arise from the differences between people's values. In a plural society, education may have a potential for mitigating such a conflict, not by trying to demolish or weaken the potentially conflicting values, but by promoting still other values which help people to co-exist with their different values. Two values which come to mind are tolerance and the willingness to compromise.

HOW WE (NEARLY) ALL COMPROMISE ON VALUES

Attitudes towards compromise are ambivalent – not only within one society but often within one person's thinking. When we look in the next chapter at why some people are suspicious of the very idea of morality, we shall find it is partly because morality may be seen as rigid and uncompromising. Yet this can also be regarded as an essential feature and strength of morality. While we can in some circumstances see a willingness to compromise as a positive value, we may also sometimes see a willingness to compromise on what one stands for as a sign of weakness; indeed, we will sometimes admire an uncompromising stand on moral principle.[1] We need, then, to look further at compromise in relation to values.

What I want to suggest here is that compromising over values should not cause us any special qualms, because there is a sense in which as individuals we very frequently, and quite properly, compromise between different values. I shall start with these individual cases.

If all situations in which values come into play were ones in which just one value clearly applied, life would be much simpler, and the question of compromise might not arise. In fact, cases where just one value applies are the exception. The first point to note is that it is easier to construct examples if we think in terms of rules, for it is these that can be most directly construed in an absolutist way ('absolute' in the sense of 'allowing no exceptions'). The rule 'never tell a lie, under any circumstances' at least makes sense in itself. By setting up this principle as an absolute, Kant was able to reach a notorious conclusion in a particular (imagined) example.

Suppose a person seeks refuge in your house from a pursuer intent on killing him. The would-be murderer comes to your door and asks 'Is he here?' In Kant's view, you must not deny that he is in your house, for you must not tell a lie (though refusing to answer might be an option).[2] (As I will make clear in Chapter 7, I don't by any means want to dismiss Kant's view of morality, but I think that we can hold on to what is central to his view without going along with this kind of absolutism.)

Many people react against Kant's conclusion, finding it absurdly rigoristic. Surely in such a case, it would be justified to tell a lie, if this was the only way in which a murder could be avoided? Now what is going on when someone reacts in this way? I would say that, whether one sees it explicitly in these terms or not, one is recognizing the validity of a compromise. Kant's conclusion is uncompromising: he is not prepared to compromise the absolute imperative of not lying for the sake of any valuable end. Most people will think that other values must be allowed to come into play here, chiefly the value of the life of the victim (and also perhaps the value of preventing the would-be murderer from committing a heinous crime and sin). And they will argue that these other values take precedence in this case, as they outweigh the importance of not telling a lie. But this does not mean that the principle of not telling a lie ceases to have any force at all.

In one respect, this example is not a good one for my argument, since to many people it will not seem to constitute a serious dilemma, precisely because it seems obvious that one ought to tell a lie in these circumstances. So let's take an example which most people would recognize as a dilemma.[3] Frances, a qualified research chemist, cannot get a job. She has two small children dependent on her. At last she is offered a well-paid job, with convenient hours, in a laboratory where research is being done on chemical weapons. On the one hand, she is opposed to chemical (or any other kind of) warfare, and dislikes the idea of contributing to it in any way. On the other hand, she is living in very difficult circumstances and she knows she will be able to give her children a better life if she takes the job. The director of the laboratory tells her that if she does not take the job it will go to another researcher whom she knew at university, and who she knows would have no compunction about working on chemical weapons; he can be expected to pursue this research with all possible efficiency. If she took the job, perhaps she would do it less effectively and, since she would rather the weapons were not produced at all, that would be better than letting her acquaintance do it.

There is a dilemma here, of course, because more than one value comes into play. If it were clear that one consideration outweighs any of the others, the dilemma would be resolved. But often this is not clear. What people then tend to do is to try to balance the different considerations against each other, and take whatever course seems to allow due weight to them all (so far as possible). In other words, people effect a compromise between different values as best they can in the circumstances. In some cases, there will be one course of action available which in itself constitutes a compromise: if, for instance, you have to decide between devoting a long time to some activity or a short time, there may be some intermediate period you can opt for. Even in something like a choice of career, where you might start by considering two quite disparate alternatives, you might think of a possibility which combines some of the best features of each.

There are other cases, however – and the most serious dilemmas will often be of this type – in which, so far as the outcome is concerned, there is nothing which constitutes a compromise in itself. There is no intermediate position between having and not having an abortion. But even in the case of abortion, the total context of relevant considerations and possible outcomes may be one in which compromise is not irrelevant. First, even an either/or decision is not necessarily made by the straightforward application of a single principle; many factors may be weighed up in arriving at it, and the alternative decided on may be chosen because it seems to satisfy rather more of the considerations than the other. And secondly, the dilemma may not present itself to the person concerned in such a sharply defined way. Even if having an abortion seems like one unitary course of action, not having an abortion could in a sense be many different things – depending on whether the child is kept or given up for fostering/adoption, and so on; and the woman who is not applying a single principle could well conclude that not to have an abortion would be the right thing *provided, but only provided*, she can be sure of various other factors.[4]

Sometimes it is suggested that the person who is willing to compromise is the one who tries to decide by weighing up which course of action will have the best consequences overall; while the person who will not compromise is the one who thinks that certain things are right or wrong in themselves, regardless of consequences. This characterization seems to fit Kant's example, but it is misleading. The person who genuinely thinks that they should always do what will have the best consequences in the circumstances is not a compromiser at all; the person is, in the jargon, a strict consequentialist, or in slightly more familiar but less precise language, a strict utilitarian.[5] Such people are probably quite rare, and this no doubt has something to do with the fact that a strict consequentialism is among the most *uncompromising* moralities there can be, for it holds to just one principle: that one should do whatever is required to achieve the best consequences. If these consequences involve, say, breaking a promise or telling a lie or even someone's death, these factors will not have any independent weight of their own; they can be taken into account, but only as some among the totality of consequences. The strict consequentialist does not compromise between the promotion of the best consequences overall and anything else.

In contrast, many of us are partial consequentialists, and by the same token are constantly compromising. We do think it important to take the consequences of our actions into account, but there are other considerations to which we tend to give independent weight: we would rather avoid telling a lie or breaking a promise if we can, and this is not just because we think that telling lies and breaking promises tend to lead to bad consequences. And at least sometimes, we may give most weight to one of these other values: we may decide, for instance, that we had better tell the truth, even though we think the consequences would be better if we told a lie. Most of us do, I think, give weight to a number of values in this way, and so it is inevitable that we often have to make the best compromise we can between them. The person who would ascribe to any single value the kind of overriding weight that Kant gave to the principle of not telling a lie (though even here I am simplifying Kant's position) is probably about as rare as the strict consequentialist. It is worth noting, too, that even if we try to avoid all reference to consequences, we won't evade the possibility of facing conflicts of values. For principles which do not themselves refer to consequences can come into conflict; you may find yourself in a situation in which you can avoid telling a lie, or avoid breaking a promise, but not both.[6]

These points about compromise do not depend on whether we talk about principles, or virtues, or simply values. If, instead of talking about a principle of not telling lies and a principle of not breaking promises, we put it in terms of the virtue of honesty and the virtue of fidelity, or if we talk simply of the value of telling the truth and the value of keeping one's word, in all cases the substantial point remains. But it does seem to be true, as I said above, that the language of moral *rules* lends itself more easily to the impression that there is no compromise to be had. If we think, on the other hand, in terms of honesty and fidelity, these are qualities which we try to exemplify and we are less likely to feel that if we allow an exception in one case, we have betrayed the value in question altogether. We can care about these values without making exceptionless rules out of them. If instead of saying to myself 'I must never tell a lie' and 'I must never break a promise', I say, 'it is important, other things being equal, to tell the truth' and 'it is important, other things being equal, to keep my promises', then I am more likely to think that a course of action is the best in a particular circumstance even though it does not fully realize the value in question.

To some people it may seem that to move away from thinking in terms of absolutes is already to have compromised too far; though, as I have suggested, it is easier to say in theory that one would never compromise than to achieve this in practice. What we have here is an instance of how the way in which we see our own values, and the kind of significance they have for us, will affect our attitude towards compromise. I want to argue next that if compromise is possible between two values held by the same person, then equally it is possible between values held by different persons.

COMPROMISING WITH EACH OTHER

Suppose first that a set of persons are members of a collective entity: they identify themselves as members of the group, and at least sometimes they think of themselves collectively as making decisions which are the decisions of the group. Many sorts of groups or institutions can be collective entities in this sense: it could be the staff of a school or members of a parent–teachers' association or residents of a local community. Suppose that the members of the collective entity have to make a decision which they see as raising moral issues. And suppose (as a simplification of greater complexity in real life) that each member puts forward just one moral consideration which he or she sees as the one on which the decision should be based. Moreover, each member puts forward a different consideration, and the considerations pull in different directions. Since they are able to meet face to face, they can attempt to reach a consensus; but it is clear that a consensus will not be reached by fastening on just one consideration and ignoring all the rest. What they can do is attempt to arrive at a decision which gives some weight to all of the considerations and tries to find a balance between them all.

Depending on the circumstances, it may or may not be possible to achieve this; but what I am interested in asking is whether there is anything irrational or reprehensible about the attempt to arrive at a consensus in this way. So far as I can see, there is not. It seems that what is happening here is in principle just the same as what happens when one person, having to resolve a moral problem, weighs up a number of values which come into play and arrives at some compromise between them. In the case of the group, the compromise is between values which happen to be held by different persons; but that does not seem to me to make compromise any less reasonable. It may even be more reasonable, since in the collective case there is the added incentive to avoid, not a personal dilemma, but interpersonal conflict.

I was assuming in that example that the members of the collective entity do identify themselves as members of it. In effect, they see themselves as constituting a collective person (a notion readily recognized in legal contexts). At least to this extent, I am supposing that they share a common interest in reaching a decision; and perhaps I am also implicitly supposing that there is no fundamental antagonism between them as individuals which could outweigh their interest in arriving at a common decision. If we change these assumptions, the position becomes more problematic. If a decision has to be made on behalf of a whole society (which is the standard case, for instance, with legislation), we cannot so readily apply the idea of a decision being arrived at through compromise. While the large number of people in question, and hence the impossibility of their all meeting face to face, is a significant factor, I suspect that the most important difference lies in the fact that members of a large society are likely to have a much weaker sense, if any at all, of themselves as members of a collective entity. So the importance attached to seeing one's own values 'win' will be correspondingly greater. Nevertheless, we know that on the broader political scale compromise can be effective. While the procedure of voting on a Bill in Parliament, say, is not itself a method of reaching a compromise (since in a given vote the decision is an either/or one), it often happens that many compromises have been made in the drafting or committee stage before a final decision has to be reached.

It still seems, then, that in moving from the individual level to the level of decision-making within a large community many of the factors which may make compromise between values possible, desirable and often unavoidable remain unchanged. In some respects, the move to the larger scale often gives more scope for compromise. There is no halfway house between having and not having an abortion, but there are all sorts of intermediate possibilities for a society between complete prohibition of abortion and complete freedom to choose on the part of individuals, and

any one of the intermediate possibilities might be a cor
number of the values which come into play.

It may seem to some readers that I have been ti
heavily in favour of compromise. It's sometimes sug
already assume a liberal point of view is comprom
while this liberal point of view may be open to secu'
many Christians, it might not be an option, for insta...
whom Islamic values will be non-negotiable.[7] Here again we ...
careful in interpreting what is at issue. In a sense, it is clearly true tnat
Islamic values are not negotiable because they are not open to compromise. If the Qur'an informs Muslims that God has commanded that
something not be done, there is no room for negotiation about the truth of
that belief (many Christians would take a similar view about the authority
of the Bible). So the value deriving from that belief is not negotiable. But
this does not mean that even fundamentalist Muslims cannot, alongside
other groups within a plural society, negotiate and if necessary compromise over what the guiding principles of that society are to be. For any
fundamentalist believer living in a plural society has reason to accept, if
only on pragmatic grounds, that the society as a whole cannot be governed
by the principles of his or her own religion. For such a person, some
compromise is inevitable in living in a plural society.

Every Muslim father who would prefer to send his daughter to a single-
sex Islamic school but who for lack of availability has to send her to a
mixed and predominantly secular school, is involved in a compromise.
Even for a father in this position the values in play will not be all on one
side. If he thought that his daughter ought not to be educated at all, and
allowed her to acquire an education only because he feared the penalties
which the law would inflict if she did not go to school, this would represent, from his point of view, a pure case of coercion by the state; it would
not be compromise. But such a case is unlikely. We can assume rather that
the father does want his daughter to have an education, that he does want
her potential (or aspects of it) to be developed. There are, in other words,
values in play which weigh in favour of her going to school, but there are
other values which weigh against her going to the only sort of school which
may in fact be available. And if proposals for abolishing compulsory
schooling[8] were ever to become a live political issue, the father I am imag-
ining would be unlikely to vote for them, for he both values education and
realizes that many children, including perhaps his own, might be worse off
if there were no free and (effectively) compulsory schooling. So he is not
unwilling to compromise if compromise he must.

Of course, none of this means that the compromise presently available is
the best possible, either for him or for the society as a whole. In fact,
policy on schooling – determining the scope of free and compulsory provision, deciding whether single-sex schools must be available, and whether
schools attached to particular religions must be available within the state
system,[9] and so on – is eminently an example of the sort of large-scale
policy issue on which negotiation and compromise do make sense as ways
of coming to an agreed policy. The current status quo owes much to historical developments which minority groups within our society have often

xpected to accommodate with little opportunity of influencing the
gements. When a minority begins to feel that the existing arrange-
ts are not acceptable to it (a perception made, of course, through the
nses of its own values), a process of change in which their own voice is
fully heard, even if it can only lead to compromise, is still likely to be better
for all concerned than out-and-out conflict. Even though there may be no
institutional arrangements by which a formal process of negotiation
between different groups can lead to change in the governing values of a
whole society (a parliamentary democratic system can at best be a very
imperfect approximation of such an arrangement), the process by which
values (or perceptions of values) do over time change within a plural
society represents a kind of informal negotiation (though one that may be
weighted too much in favour of the dominant majority), as various groups
put forward their claims and others gradually come to have more understanding of them. To engage in such a process does not mean that the
minority group is ceasing fully to hold its own values; the fundamental
values remain the same, though it is recognized that the outcome, within a
plural society, will not fully conform to those values.[10]

TOLERANCE

The idea that education, especially in a plural multicultural society, should
promote tolerance (among other aims), is one that I shall endorse in
Chapter 11. But as with so many of the values with which education has to
concern itself, there are questions about tolerance which we need to think
through if we are to take a coherent educational stand. As with compromise,
these questions will mean thinking about issues of politics and the
state. From a liberal standpoint, tolerance is a virtue in its own right,[11] but
this is not so from all points of view. But a plural society seems to need a
high level of toleration from all its members, and that means that it has to
expect toleration of differences in conduct and moral belief, not just from
liberals within its midst but also from those who do not see it as a virtue in
its own right.

Toleration is often defined, at any rate in academic discussions, as a
matter of refraining from interfering with the conduct of others although
one morally disapproves of it. Thus, the very possibility of toleration is
held to come into play only where someone – whether individual or government – disapproves of a particular practice, and has the means to restrict
it. On this understanding, it would be wrong to say of someone who sees
nothing wrong with a homosexual way of life that he or she tolerates it;
and it would be equally wrong to say this of someone who disapproves but
has no power to do anything about it. I think, though, that in everyday
speech we use the notion of tolerance or intolerance with more latitude.
We can say that a society in which homosexuality can be openly practised
is more tolerant than one in which it is concealed; and while the difference
may be partly a function of the people who disapprove of homosexuality
choosing not actively to oppose it, it may also be partly a function of
people ceasing to disapprove of it. And if someone frequently expresses
their disapproval of homosexuality among friends who already agree with

them, but takes no steps to do anything about it, I think that ordinary usage might describe that person as somewhat intolerant of homosexuality.

These, however, are semantic points, which need not cause problems in themselves so long as they are understood (and they will need to be understood by teachers who discuss tolerance and toleration in the classroom). There is a more substantial problem about toleration which has been well expressed by David Raphael (notice that he draws on some of the same points about what is involved in holding a moral position which I used in Chapter 3):

> to disapprove of something is to judge it to be wrong. Such a judgement does not express a purely subjective preference. It claims universality; it claims to be the view of any rational agent. The content of the judgement, that something is wrong, implies that the something may properly be prevented. But if your disapproval is rationally grounded, why should you go against it all? Why should you tolerate?[12]

In other words, why should you not try to stop people from going against the values which you believe to be right? Why not prevent them from acting in ways which you disapprove of? And if that leads to conflict, why should that not be justifiable, especially as the avoidance of conflict is not necessarily the highest value for people who are defending the moral values they are committed to? Why *should* people in this position be tolerant?

The liberal tends to respond to this challenge by presenting an argument of principle. Toleration will be displayed as a virtue in its own right, a higher-order value which takes precedence (at least sometimes) over the particular values which support disapproval of particular things. At a political level, toleration involves the state displaying a certain impartiality between different views and ways of life, even though there may be grounds for approving of some of these and not of others. But it is by no means easy to justify this toleration at a level of principle (it is neither easy to grasp the justification nor, if it is grasped, to get it across to sceptics). The problem has been well put by Thomas Nagel, who says that the motive for higher-order impartiality is so obscure

> that critics of the liberal position on toleration often doubt that its professions of impartiality are made in good faith. Part of the problem is that liberals ask of everyone a certain restraint in calling for the use of state power to further specific, controversial moral or religious conceptions – but the results of that restraint appear with suspicious frequency to favour precisely the controversial moral conceptions that liberals usually hold. For example, those who argue against the restriction of pornography or homosexuality or contraception on the ground that the state should not attempt to enforce contested personal standards of morality often don't think there is anything wrong with pornography, homosexuality or contraception. They would be against such restrictions

even if they believed it *was* the state's business to enforce personal morality, or if they believed that the state could legitimately be asked to prohibit anything simply on the ground that it was wrong. More generally, defenders of strong toleration tend to place a high value on individual freedom, and limitations on state interference based on a higher-order impartiality among values tends [*sic*] to promote the individual freedom to which they are partial. This leads to the suspicion that the escalation to a higher level of impartiality is a sham and that all the pleas for toleration and restraint really disguise a campaign to put the state behind a secular, individualistic, and libertine morality – against religion and in favour of sex, roughly.[13]

Though Nagel himself goes on to try to offer a justification of this 'higher-order impartiality among values', I am not hopeful of the chances of making such a justification, at a principled level, that will be convincing to all, whatever their starting position. It is doubtful, for instance, whether it could be made convincing to someone whose position is through and through an Islamic one (without causing that person to lapse from Islam). It may be better, then, to go for a more pragmatic kind of argument for toleration. Many members of religious groups in particular do not see the state which exercises liberal toleration as an ideal. Rather their ideal would be a state governed in accordance with the principles of their own religion. The enforcement of the principles of their religion by law would not be against *their* values but precisely in accordance with them. There would be nothing fanatical, for instance, in a Muslim taking this view; it would simply be consistent with Islamic principles. But at the same time, a Muslim living in Britain knows that converting the country into an Islamic state is not in the foreseeable future a realistic option. In the present context, Muslims must demand toleration from others (it is after all only fairly recently in Britain that full toleration was extended to Roman Catholics, let alone to other religions); and they could not convince others of their right to toleration from them without a willingness to extend it to them in turn.

In this respect toleration is rather like compromise: people who do not see it as a value in its own right may still see value in it within the actual circumstances, including the social and political circumstances, of their lives. Various arguments may exist for the same values; enabling people to appreciate that point may be one task which education is well placed to do. But I shall say more about how far education should attempt to promote tolerance and a willingness to compromise in Chapter 11.

NOTES

1. See Day (1989).
2. Kant's original discussion is in Kant (1927), first published 1797.
3. The example comes, slightly adapted, from Bernard Williams in Smart and Williams (1973), pp. 97–98.
4. I return to the abortion issue in connection with the perspectives of justice and care in Chapter 6.

5. A consequentialist holds that the rightness or wrongness of actions depends only on their consequences; a utilitarian is a particular kind of consequentialist, who holds that the value of different consequences should be assessed in terms of the pleasure, happiness or well-being of persons and of sentient beings generally. Strictly speaking, there can be consequentialists who are not utilitarians, because they assess consequences by some standard that has nothing to do with pleasure or happiness. It's the consequentialist aspect I'm concerned with here.
6. Ross's notion of prima facie duties (Ross 1930, 1939) is relevant here. Ross's conception is referred to in connection with compromise by Day (1989), p. 479. On Ross's notion, see also Dancy (1992).
7. See Halstead (1992).
8. See the comments on the deschoolers in Chapter 2.
9. See Chapter 10 for more on this issue.
10. Chapter 9 includes an extended discussion of how far there is scope for compromise over one particular controversial moral issue – the treatment of animals.
11. We have in English the words 'tolerance' and 'toleration'. There may be no distinction between them which is systematically observed, but the tendency is for 'tolerance' to refer to the personal attitude, 'toleration' to an actual and deliberate forbearance from interfering. The forbearance may be exercised by an institution or by the state, and it may involve positive action such as change in legislation.
12. Raphael (1988), p. 139; quoted in Mendus (1989), p. 161.
13. Nagel (1991), p. 156. Reprinted by permission.

Further reading
On compromise see Benjamin (1990); on toleration see Mendus (1989).

Part III
Morality

While the idea of morality was always present in Part II, the discussion of values and moral values did not concentrate on the notion of 'morality' as such. As compared with the whole field of values, morality seems narrower, more systematic and less open to choice – as if, while people might choose their values, they have to be initiated into morality. But if morality is a pre-existing system and moral education is initiation into it, in some people's eyes this will go against the grain both of pluralism and of education. The issues raised by the notion of morality need attention in their own right.

In Chapter 6 I consider the objections that some people have to the very idea of morality; in Chapter 7, what can be said in its favour; and in Chapter 8, whether we can make sense of it independently of a religious framework.

CHAPTER 6

What's wrong with morality?

In Part 2 we saw something of the complexity and variety of values – non-moral and moral values, different understandings of moral values, religious and non-religious interpretations. To some people the variety, while it may set a challenge, is not unwelcome, and the ideas of compromise and tolerance may set us on the right road to handling the complexities. But there may be other readers who so far feel I have avoided the heart of the matter. Aren't there, they will say, some values which education should simply set out to teach? If asked which values, these readers might turn back to the Hobbesian picture of morality which I sketched in Chapter 4. I suggested that, ignoring all the surrounding complexities and variety, the Hobbesian picture tries to set up a minimal morality which, if it does not play a major role in enriching our life or giving it meaning, should at least enable people to co-exist without conflict. A minimal morality of this kind could be very important for education. If education cannot do everything in the area of values that might be desirable, a minimal social morality might well be what it should concentrate on.[1]

But if we suggest that it is the business of education to promote even a minimal morality, there may be other readers – perhaps the same ones who will be attracted to the ideas of compromise and tolerance – who will be uneasy. Some teachers, and others who are about to go into teaching, are reluctant to see themselves as teachers of morality. What is it that under-lies the worry here? It may have a lot to do with the connotations of the *word* 'morality'. We need to explore what the notion of morality means to people; and we need also to ask the substantive question of whether moral-ity is a good thing after all. Could we be better off without morality?

Many teachers are liberal-minded people – that will often be part of the reason why they have gone into teaching. By calling people 'liberal-minded' I mean to say something about their values: that they think it is good for people to have freedoms and opportunities to live their own lives and to think for themselves. Liberal-minded people are likely to be unhappy about the idea that they might be imposing certain ways of think-ing, certain values, on other people. But when they think about the teaching context, these liberal-minded people may well agree that there are certain rules which it will be essential for a school to maintain – rules of order and non-violence without which a school could hardly function. Maintaining these rules may not be seen as imposing anything; and not everyone will see it as a matter of morality. For some teachers will say that it is only for pragmatic purposes that these rules have to be upheld inside the school; how people behave in the rest of their lives, what *values* they hold, is not (in this view) the teacher's business. And a liberal-minded teacher of this kind may in particular recoil from the idea of imposing *morality*. In this reaction I think there is more than just the liberal-minded person's dislike of imposing anything; there is a sense also that morality in itself is a kind of imposition.

I'll defer to the next chapter the question of whether there is any way in which teachers can teach morality without imposing on their pupils. For this chapter, I want to ask whether there is anything in this idea that morality as such is an imposition.

MORALITY AND SEX – A SIDE ISSUE

First, but only to get it out of the way, there is no doubt that morality has become associated in some people's minds with a rather narrow set of concerns – specifically, who sleeps with whom. This tendency to think that morality is about sex may, as many people have suggested, be a particularly English phenomenon, whose cultural roots could be traced back to Victorian times. It has, if anything, been reinforced recently by media attention to the private lives of politicians (though any argument as to why politicians should be expected to observe different standards in their private lives from those of media personalities is rarely spelt out).

Now, there are many people, particularly many young people, who don't have much time for 'morality' if this is all it is supposed to be. As I suggested in Chapter 3, though these people may not have much use for the *word*, this does not mean that they don't have moral values. That people should have the freedom to choose their lifestyle, provided they do so without harm or disrespect to others, may well be among their moral values; and in recognizing what would count as harm or disrespect to others their values will tell them that emotional as well as physical hurt is bad, that fidelity to promises is good and betrayal bad. But they will see no reason why consensual sexual relations between adults should necessarily violate any of the positive values here.

This is surely a reasonable view. It means not just that morality is not especially about sex, but that there is no special 'sexual morality'. Sexual relations may well lead to hurt and betrayal (a fact which young people may not always realize, so there is certainly a role here for a kind of consciousness-raising as part of sex education); but the standards by which these things are judged wrong will not be special to sexual relations. Some people, too, would see the attempt at even a well-meaning 'sexual morality' – where it is not concerned with the consequences to third parties – as paternalistic. Heterosexual relationships also, of course, can have enormous consequences for 'third parties' by bringing them into existence; relationships which have this potential certainly can't be seen as morally neutral. So when I describe 'morality and sex' as a side issue I don't mean that sex is a morally unimportant matter; I mean that to link morality especially with sex is misleading, because the moral values which come into play where sex is concerned are not unique to it. Those who say that sex education should be conducted within a moral framework are right, but perhaps not in the way they think; it is not that sex education should be any less concerned with the biological and social aspects of sex, but that it is best this should take place within a school where values education as a whole is taken seriously.

Now, whether you agree or not with the idea that there is no special sexual morality, it is likely to be one to which many young adults adhere; and many of them will be going into teaching. Thus, anyone who expects teachers to be moral paragons, yet cherishes this narrow conception of morality is being unrealistic. There will be people in teaching, just as there are people outside teaching, who in their private lives are involved in all kinds of sexual relationships. This does not mean that the public can have no legitimate moral concern at all about how teachers behave when they are not in school; but it does mean that this concern should not be misdirected. It may well be true (I'll raise the question again in Chapter 13) that it is better for pupils if they have teachers who are morally admirable people, or at least no worse than average. If this is right, then we should expect teachers to have a sense of moral values themselves and be prepared to live by them. But we should not demand that they conform to certain traditional rules of lifestyle when those rules may not be justified by the teachers' own moral values. The fact, for instance, that a teacher is living with someone else in a relationship not sanctioned by marriage is not, in itself, any reason why that person can't be a good teacher.

So let's, for this argument, put sex on one side and turn to a broader notion of morality. This will allow us to say (again in accordance with tradition, but not such an artificially narrowed tradition) that keeping promises, not hurting people, not telling lies, and so on, are questions of morality. Why then do some people still regard morality as some sort of imposition?

MORALITY AS SOCIAL CONTROL – CAN WE DO WITHOUT IT?

When we speak of morality in this way, as if it had an upper-case 'M', we are not just speaking of the sum total of an individual's moral values. We are speaking of something wider than one individual – something more like a *system* of demands to which individuals are subject. Some of the features of this system coincide with features of an individual's moral values which I mentioned in Chapter 5. Morality is seen as making demands on people independently of their preferences or inclinations, and perhaps also demands of a generalized kind regardless of the circumstances of particular individuals. But *where* do these demands come from, if not from individual preferences? For some religious believers it will come naturally to think of these demands as issuing from God; and that may indeed be a way of making sense of them. We'll come back to this possibility in

Chapter 8. But what is the person without any religious belief to make of this system of demands?

One likely answer is that the demands are those of society. This fits with the idea that morality is a system over which individuals have no control, but which attempts to control them. In this view, morality is just another form of social control, less formalized than law and not backed up by an institutionalized system of punishment, but still a way in which entrenched opinions and traditional ways of doing things exercise tyranny over individual lives. Morality exercises that tyranny partly through making people feel uncomfortable, perhaps guilty, about actions which might otherwise seem to them natural or harmless. It sets up rigid categories and tells people 'you must not do this' (because it comes under a certain category which attracts disapproval), and thereby doesn't allow people to make their own decisions, even though they may know their own circumstances best.[2] This conception of morality may explain why some liberal-minded teachers do not want to see themselves as promoters of morality: they do not want to be regarded as agents of social control (even if the sociology of education tells them that they cannot avoid this).

In the next chapter I will suggest that we don't have to see morality as a system that is imposed on people. But having seen why some people may take quite a negative view of morality, it will be worth asking whether we could do without it. Would we even be better off without morality?

One who thought so was Karl Marx. In fact Marx provides a good illustration of the way in which someone can have moral values but not subscribe to the *system* which is recognized as morality in a particular society at a particular time. There was certainly what, in the terms of Chapter 3, we can call a moral impulse behind Marx's criticisms of nineteenth-century capitalism. In his view, it stunted and confined human capacities, and Marx seems to have valued the free development and flourishing of human capacities almost above everything else. Yet *morality* to Marx was a form of alienation (so was religion, in much the same way). This meant that even though morality was something which had been created by human beings as part of their social form of life, it had come to be seen as having an independent existence, putting objective constraints on people. It functioned ideologically: it induced false consciousness in those who believed in the external reality of this human construct, and it served the interests above all of the ruling class in society (this is particularly clear in the case of moral rules about property, which did far more for those who had property than for those who hadn't).[3]

That it served some interests rather than others is the key to Marx's belief that human beings would be better off without morality – that is, in conditions in which morality was no longer needed. Morality presupposes economic and social arrangements in which people's interests are in conflict with each other. (We encountered in Chapter 4 this notion that morality is about conflict, and how to contain it.) Once that conflict of interests was overcome, and communist society fully established, people's interests would be in harmony. They could develop and exercise their human capacities without restricting the same development and exercise on the part of others. This does not mean that people would be operating in isolated compartments; quite the reverse. They would be co-operating with others rather than competing; promoting others' interests rather than undermining them. The most rigid moralist would find nothing to complain of in their behaviour. The difference would be in their motivation. When people in this fully developed human society didn't assault others, didn't tell lies, didn't break promises, it wouldn't be because they felt themselves constrained by some external system of rules, but because they wouldn't want to do these things, they would have no reason to, and no interests which would be served by doing so.

Marx never went very far in attempting to work out what personal and social relations would be like in a fully communist society – in his own terms, it would have been pointless to try to predict what choices people would make when they were genuinely free to make them. In any case, I am not concerned here either to defend or to criticize his ideas. I am only extracting one point, which is by no means special to Marx: the idea that morality, as a system of constraints, would be unnecessary if people's motivation was right – or if social conditions were right, because if you take seriously, as Marx did, that human beings are social animals, people's motivation will depend on social conditions.

MORALITY AND BAD MOTIVES

There is an idea here that morality involves a particular kind of motivation – a sense of being bound by constraints not of your own making, with the prospect of suffering guilt if you go against these constraints. What is by no means special to Marx is the thought that if that kind of motivation were unnecessary, morality itself would be unnecessary. The idea is there in the Christian tradition, for instance in St Augustine's 'love God and do what you will' – for if you love God, you will not *want* to do the things which morality tells you not to do.[4] The idea is present too in the emphasis which some moral theorists have put on virtues, from Aristotle to various contemporary moral philosophers.

At the beginning of Chapter 3, referring to John Patten's speech, I noted that the values he mentioned mostly took the form of personal qualities, and that we can use the word 'virtues' for those qualities we think it is morally important for people to have, or we feel are morally admirable. Now there is more than one interpretation of the sort of quality we're talking about here. Take an example from Patten's list: unselfishness. What are we saying about a person when we say he or she is unselfish? One answer might be that the person does not behave in ways that further their own interests at the expense of others. But this by itself could hardly be enough, because it only tells us about the actual effects of the person's behaviour, and nothing about why they behave as they do; so it is not really attributing a personal quality at all. To call a person unselfish is not just to say that, as a matter of fact, their actions do not benefit them at the expense of others. That might be purely accidental as far as the person is concerned, and nothing to do with what they are aiming at; it could even be that they are so incompetent at pursuing their own desires that they end up benefiting other people when really they only wanted to do the best for themself.

So in calling the person unselfish, we will be saying something about their motivation. But there are still two different kinds of motivation. First, suppose that what the person is really most concerned about is their own interests, but that they also had it drummed into them throughout childhood that one ought not to be selfish. So they do their best to follow this rule, and most of the time succeed. The person deliberately sacrifices their own desires to those of others, not because they really care about others, but because they want to do what is morally right. So the person helps others but does so rather reluctantly. Alternatively, it may be that this is a person who really does have the interests of others at heart. They do not *want* to pursue their own interests at the expense of others.

So there are different motivations here. We could raise the question of which motivation genuinely constitutes unselfishness, but there would be little point in this. Our language is flexible enough to allow us to refer to either as unselfishness; the important point is to be as clear as we can about what qualities it is that we value. Think of other words that we have for virtues. Courage, for instance. The courageous person stands up to dangers – it could be physical danger, as in facing a bully in the playground, or it could be the courage to stand up for one's convictions; it could even be the courage to stand up to the taunts of others when refusing to fight the bully. But we can again ask what motivates the person to stand up to such dangers. Is it that they are only too aware of the reality of the dangers, fear of which would normally motivate people to avoid them; except that they would then be ashamed, and so make an effort of will to face them? Or do they see the dangers positively, as challenges which they actually want to face? What of truthfulness? The truthful person doesn't tell lies (and may even go out of their way to tell as much truth as possible). Is this because, while the person often sees that it would be more convenient or profitable to tell a lie, their moral compunction restrains them? Or is it that it would never occur to them to tell a lie – they seem to be just 'naturally' truthful?

You could perhaps add to the examples yourself. The point is that whenever we talk of a quality as a moral virtue, there are likely to be at least two possible accounts of what it involves. In one account, the person's underlying motivations – self-interest, fear, perhaps a degree of callousness or maliciousness – will be of a kind which need to be restrained by an awareness of the requirements of morality. The motivation to do what morality demands will have to overcome other, non-moral, motivations. In the other account, a person will not have the virtue unless their underlying motivations are in order, and therefore do not need to be restrained or overcome. In this account, a person will not be a kind person if there is any callousness or maliciousness in them, however successfully they overcome that and always, in practice, are helpful: the person will be kind only if the good of other people – or rather, the good of the particular people they encounter – is itself one of their underlying values.

Faced with examples like these, many people will think that it is better, more admirable, for people to have underlying motivations which will make for peace and harmony, rather than to have contrary motivations which have to be restrained by a sense of morality. And if we interpret the idea of virtues accordingly, then we can say that, if people have the right virtues, morality – in the sense I've been using the word here – will be unnecessary.

This conception of virtues, as having a lot to do with one's underlying motivations, and very little to do with deliberately restraining oneself according to moral rules, goes back at least to Aristotle (though it would be misleading to suggest that there is no sense of moral rules or principles in Aristotle). Among contemporary moral philosophers, approving references to Aristotle are quite common, and criticisms of the system of morality by no means rare. Bernard Williams, Professor of Moral Philosophy at Oxford University, has argued that we would be better off without what he calls 'morality, the peculiar institution'.[5] Influenced in part by Williams, one of the leading British philosophers of education, John White, has taken a similar line in the context of education, arguing that we would do better to abandon 'moral education' as such in favour of education in altruism, which he sees as preferable in a number of ways. Morality, he suggests, brings with it rigidity, a tendency to fanaticism, an unwillingness to compromise, and the pervasive tendency to blame oneself and others for moral defects. Our ethical life, says White, 'does not *have* to be as unlovely as this'.[6] So rather than teaching morality, we should be trying in various ways to develop altruistic motivation in pupils. (You can see now why I couldn't go straight from discussing the aims of education in general to asking what place moral education should have among those aims. The whole notion of moral education has been brought into question. We need to be clearer about the place of morality itself among our values before we can expect any answers about the place of morality in education.)

IS CARING BETTER THAN JUSTICE?

A further twist to this story of the defects of morality has emerged in recent years from a different quarter – psychological research into moral development. This field was dominated for many years by the work of the American researcher Lawrence Kohlberg. He claimed to have found that as people grew up they would go through a sequence of stages in their moral thinking, and that, while some individuals in any culture would progress further through these stages than others, the *order* of the stages was the same in any culture. Now, the fact that a certain way of thinking comes later in a person's life does not mean it is better; given some standpoint from which to make the assessment, it is always possible that people's later ways of thinking will be worse than their earlier manifestations. (Indeed, the idea that formal education tends to work so as to corrupt people's earlier moral innocence has been with us at least since the educational writings of Rousseau.) Kohlberg, well aware of this point, tried to present philosophical arguments to show that the later stages in the sequence of moral development were indeed morally better than the earlier ones.[7] But the main point for the present argument is the nature of the later stages. Kohlberg's stages of development progressively move further from the individual's immersion in his own immediate circumstances (you'll see below why I use the masculine pronoun here), to the individual making consciously abstract judgements about situations, and appealing to universal principles of justice. The final form of moral thinking – Kohlberg's 'Stage Six', which he claims only a minority of the population reach – is one of consciously endorsing universal[8] principles, and judging the rights and wrongs of particular situations in the light of those principles.

Kohlberg's associate Carol Gilligan noticed that his claims about the sequences of stages did not fit very well with the results of her own research on women's moral thinking. Kohlberg had apparently not been inhibited in making his generalizations by the fact that his subjects had been predominantly male. But apart from the sex of the subjects there was also another important difference between Kohlberg's research and one early research project of Gilligan's. Kohlberg conducted his research by presenting subjects with hypothetical dilemmas – given the bare outline of a situation, with a minimum of detail, subjects would be asked whether it would be right for a person to do such-and-such. Gilligan, however, studied the moral thinking of women facing a genuine dilemma in their own lives – whether to have an abortion (she contacted the women through an abortion clinic).[9] Now it may not seem at all surprising that women in this position will not think in quite the same way as people, male or female, asked about a hypothetical case; but what we need to follow up here is Gilligan's positive characterization of the ways in which the women did think.

Gilligan in fact argued that there are two significantly different orientations in moral thinking, and that one is more associated with males, the other with females. What are these orientations? So far as labels go, one has been commonly called the justice or the rights perspective, also sometimes the perspective of separateness, as opposed to connectedness; the second, in addition to the idea of connectedness, has been named the perspective of responsibility or, perhaps most often, that of care. Look first at the responses of two adults to the question, 'What does morality mean to you?'

1. Morality is basically having a reason for or a way of knowing what's right, what one ought to do; and when you are put into a situation where you have to choose from among alternatives, being able to recognise when there is an issue of 'ought' at stake and when there is not; and then ... having some reason for choosing among alternatives.

2. Morality is a type of consciousness, I guess, a sensitivity to humanity, that you can affect someone else's life. You can affect your own life, and you have the responsibility not to endanger other people's lives or to hurt other people. So morality is complex. Morality is realising that there is a play between self and others and that you are going to have to take responsibility for both of them. It's sort of a consciousness of your influence over what's going on.[10]

It is not difficult to fit the first of these with the notion of morality as a system; whereas the 'sensitivity to humanity' which the second respondent talks about does not sound like an acknowledgement of morality, in *that* sense, at all. But for bringing out the difference in the orientations, the best illustration I have come across (perhaps because it does involve the simplification of a hypothetical dilemma which is not even presented as one about human beings) is the story of the porcupine and the moles, which has also been used in research to elicit adolescents' responses. Be prepared to put the book down for a minute or two after you read the next paragraph.

A group of industrious, prudent moles have spent the summer digging a burrow where they will spend the winter. A lazy, improvident porcupine who has not prepared a winter shelter approaches the moles and pleads to share their burrow. The moles take pity on the porcupine and agree to let him in. Unfortunately, the moles did not anticipate the problem the porcupine's sharp quills would pose in close quarters. Once the porcupine has moved in, the moles are constantly being stabbed. The question is, what should the moles do?

Well, before I continue the quotation, what do you think they should do? The report continues:

On the one hand, subjects answering according to the rights perspective point out that the moles own the shelter and are therefore entitled to throw the porcupine out. When asked what the moles should do if the porcupine refuses to leave, some of these respondents favour shooting the porcupine. On the other hand, subjects answering according to the care perspective suggest solutions like covering the porcupine with a blanket. These respondents devise compromises that defuse conflict and secure everyone's interest.[11]

The reference to defusing conflict is worth following up, since we have already looked at the potential for conflict growing out of people's adherence to different values. On the face of it, the justice orientation seems more likely to lead to overt conflict, or is, at least, less likely to defuse it. Notice that some respondents suggested the porcupine should be shot if he refused to leave. Given that moles do not normally carry guns, it may be that some subjects (one suspects boys) were using a certain licence in order to give a consciously macho response here. Even so, it makes a difference that the justice orientation, but not the care orientation, allows scope for this. In this dilemma a justice approach starts by setting off the claims of the moles and the porcupine against each other; a *conflict* of claims is seen as the chief feature from the beginning, and the assumption is implicit that the solution must be all or nothing, one way or the other. Since this will inevitably mean that one side loses, within this orientation what counts as a solution to the problem is not necessarily a *resolution* of the conflict. The alternative orientation sees the conflict between individuals as *constituting the problem*, so that a solution is not reached until the conflict has been resolved.

Now it might look as if the differences shown up here are differences in the content of people's values: some saying, in effect, 'the most important thing is to uphold justice and respect people's rights'; others that 'the most important thing is to maintain relationships, defuse conflict and secure everyone's interests if possible'. But if these are differences in content, they are not like the relatively specific difference between yes and no answers to the question, 'is abortion wrong?' The different perspectives do not so much give different answers to the same question as display an interest in asking different questions. Faced with a given problem, some people tend to approach it by working at the level of general principles, asking whose rights are at issue, and what justice demands. For these people, any reasoning about a moral issue starts from principles expressed in a very general form and which are seen as universal – in this case it might be the principle that people have a right to control access to resources which they have created for their own use, or it might also be a right to shelter – and then draws from the general principles a conclusion for the specific case. Others tend to approach the specific problem without working from the general level first: they will ask what is at stake in the relations between the persons involved; who might be hurt and how can hurt best be avoided?

Consider the abortion issue again. If we think in terms of rights, we ask whether the foetus has a right to live and whether the mother has a right to choose whether to have the baby or not. If this is the question, then we have to answer in favour either of the foetus or the mother, or else we are simply faced with an impasse. And for many people, especially if they are thinking at the level of state politics and legislation, this *is* the question. But for many women, if they are pregnant and there are reasons of some kind for not having the child, the issue of rights will not be the question. Their question is not about the rights of foetuses in general or about the rights of women to choose. A particular woman's (or teenage girl's) question is about what to do in this situation, in this particular relationship, or lack of relationship, with the father, with her parents, with others who might or might not be involved in caring for the child. In fact, the woman's dilemma only arises because a general answer in terms of rights isn't sufficient either way. If a woman really thought that a foetus had an absolute right to life,[12] that would immediately settle the question against an abortion; but it's not surprising that a Catholic mother in Gilligan's study, even though she had always thought of abortion as murder, found that this thought, rather than removing the dilemma, merely added another aspect to the whole problem. And if a woman thought that she had an absolute right to choose – to choose either way, for any reason whatever, or for none – then she could toss a coin. But, of course, the problem is only there because the woman has other values which come into play. Having the child or not having the child is going to make a lot of difference, not only to the existence or non-existence of an individual human being – to whom the mother may already feel some sort of relationship – but to the mother herself and to the other people who are part of her life.

So taking one perspective or the other does not predetermine a particular answer to a dilemma. The rights orientation will tend to set off the rights of the mother against the rights of the foetus, but different persons using this orientation may come down on one side or the other. The care orientation focuses more on an ongoing complex web of relationships, unique to each situation. So it's even more clear that to take this focus does not predetermine what the answer will be.

While the recent attention to these differences arose from research on women's moral thinking, it would be an oversimplification to suggest that men think in terms of the rights or justice orientation, women in terms of the care orientation. Rather there appears to be a predominant focus to the thinking of each individual, which may be either of justice or of care. For most males the predominant focus is that of justice, as it is also for a considerable number of females (in other words the justice orientation seems to be predominant, irrespective of gender, in the North American culture where the research has mostly been done); but for many females (and relatively few males) the predominant focus is that of care. At the same time, most individuals seem to be able (perhaps with a little prompting) to appreciate the alternative orientation to their own predominant one.[13]

In my own experience of talking to teachers about these orientations, I find that most, male as well as female, tend to find the care orientation more congenial.[14] It seems to embody more concern for the individual person (which surely is one of the values which motivates many teachers), whereas the perspective of justice or rights appears, in contrast, abstract and impersonal. Of course, that someone finds one orientation more attractive when the two are described (and the description may itself not be neutral) does not imply that the same person will tend to use that orientation in their own thinking. I cite the apparent attractiveness of the caring orientation here only because it forms yet another angle of attack on the idea of the system of morality.[15] (In Chapter 12 I shall ask whether teachers should be trying to promote the use of one orientation rather than the other.)

So far we have encountered several lines of attack on morality which all seem to portray it as a rather unattractive, even alienating, idea. The kind of motivation it can involve – doing something, not out of love or fellow-feeling for other persons, but out of a sense of obligation, perhaps backed up by feelings of guilt if one fails; the sense that it is abstract and impersonal; the impression that it is imposed from the outside – all of these can add to the unattractiveness of the idea of morality. In addition, many people are uneasy about passing moral judgement on others. This uneasiness may be expressed in the pejorative terms 'moralizing' or 'being judgemental', suggesting a censoriousness which is unattractive in itself, and may too often be linked to hypocrisy.[16]

It's not surprising, then, that it may be difficult for teachers to inspire pupils with a lively sense of morality, or that many people going into teaching, particularly if they have themselves been brought up in a liberal atmosphere, feel that, even if they knew how to do it, they would not want to impose morality.

If the arguments of this chapter held sway, we would have to agree with John White that we should be trying to move 'beyond moral education'; taking Bernard Williams's conclusions seriously, we ought to be trying through education to prepare people for a world without morality, attempting instead (the 'instead' is important) to cultivate in pupils altruism and caring. But it may be premature to reach that conclusion. Having examined what there is to be said against the system of morality, it is now time to see what there is to be said for it.

NOTES

1. On the idea of a minimal morality in an educational context, see White (1982), pp. 78–88; White (1990), pp. 43–5.
2. There is nothing very radical about this view; there was something of it, for instance, in the writings of the Victorian liberal and utilitarian John Stuart Mill; see especially Mill (1859).
3. See Lukes (1985).
4. It's worth remembering in this context that Christ is often cited as one who was more concerned with motives than with strict adherence to the letter of the conventional morality of his day.
5. Williams (1985), Chapter 10.
6. White (1990), p. 53.
7. Kohlberg (1981).
8. In the sense of 'universal' meaning 'applying to everyone' – see Chapter 3.
9. Gilligan's report of this and other studies, and her interpretation of the results, is in Gilligan (1982).
10. Lyons (1988), p. 21. Reprinted by permission.
11. Meyers (1987) p. 141. Reprinted by permission. Copyright 1987, Rowman and Littlefield.
12. In the sense of 'absolute' meaning 'without exceptions' – see Chapter 3.
13. See Gilligan et al. (1988). It's worth noting that any realistic dilemma is likely to give some scope for thinking within either of the perspectives; think, for instance, of the dilemma of the research chemist in Chapter 5.
14. I have found the same with nurses, again with no obvious gender difference. Incidentally, probably the commonest response to the story of the moles and the porcupine among the teachers and nurses I've asked has been that the moles should dig a bigger hole.
15. Dancy (1992) helps one to see how Ross's notion of prima facie duties may be illuminating in making sense of the justice/care distinction, and thereby links this topic with that of attitudes towards compromise (though Dancy himself doesn't use the language of compromise).
16. For more on 'moralizing' and on popular suspicions about morality, see Hare, 'How did morality get a bad name?' (in Hare (1992)) and Midgley (1991).

CHAPTER 7

What's right about morality?

In Chapter 6 we looked at a number of problems that arise with the idea of morality as a system: that the sort of motivation it appeals to may not be desirable; that it is abstract and impersonal; that it involves the imposition on people of something alien (the last point is one that many teachers may worry about). I suspect that while some readers will be sensitive to these points, others will wonder what the fuss is about; for them, morality is just there, and it is right, and it has to be passed on to each new generation. This diversity among the reactions of readers reflects one more aspect of the pluralism of our society: people don't just have different ideas about what is right or wrong; the very ideas of 'right' and 'wrong' mean different things to different people.

THE QUESTION FOR EDUCATION

In view of this diversity, one strategy which it would not be very helpful for me to try to take in this chapter is the one that says, 'morality is just there, and it's right, so we have to pass it on'. It's true that if there is an objectively right moral system, then it would seem sensible to pass it on; just as if certain beliefs about the existence and nature of a God are objectively right, it would seem sensible to communicate them (though in each case it's a further question whether it should be schools that do the passing on). But first it has to be established that certain identified beliefs are right, or, in the case of morality, that a certain understanding of its nature and content is objectively right. Now philosophical arguments that attempt to do this abound, and inevitably spawn disagreement about the nature and content of morality. So if I were to try to use the strategy that morality is 'right' and should be transmitted I would have to establish, to every reader's satisfaction, the rightness of one particular interpretation. The book would then become a treatise in moral philosophy, and whatever the conclusion of my argument, it would still be controversial.

We need a more pragmatic approach. There is room for disagreement about the nature and content of morality, but what is less controversial is that morality as a system does have a degree of social reality. Some people, at least, do still speak of moral obligation, or of certain things as being morally wrong. People will sometimes refrain from doing something because they think it is wrong, or conversely, will do something because they believe they ought to; and sometimes people will express moral approval or disapproval of what others are doing. To some degree, thinking in this way elicits social approval, though the picture is ambiguous here: making moral judgements about others also quite commonly arouses *disapproval*. In any case, since some people do grow up using words like 'right' and 'wrong' in something like a traditional sense, it must be the case that this way of using language, this way of thinking, is being passed on from the older generation to at least some of the young.

But none of this can be taken for granted – not even the language in which morality is characteristically expressed. Morality, as such, is after all a phenomenon only of language-using creatures. That is not to say that it doesn't have biological roots. Among non-human animal species, one individual will sometimes act in a way that benefits other individuals of the species at its own expense (evolutionary theorists, begging a lot of questions, have labelled such behaviour 'altruism'). And it would be taking the refusal of anthropomorphism too far to deny that some animals can *feel* (something like) what we would label as 'care' or 'concern' for others – at the very least, we can accept that female animals in many species may feel this for their offspring.[1] Much of our language of morality might appear intangible if we couldn't sometimes link it to *feelings* and motivations which may well be biologically programmed into us and which (by the same token, if you accept evolutionary theory) we share with other species. But what other species certainly do not have is the *language* of morality. They cannot say things like 'that is wrong' or 'I have a moral obligation to do this'. And since they cannot say these things, they also cannot think them; there is no non-linguistic feeling or experience which could be *equivalent* to these thoughts, even if certain feelings may characteristically underlie them. No creature, for instance, could experience a sense of moral obligation without having a concept of obligation, and this involves knowing that word or a close equivalent to it.

The language of morality is something which has developed within human communities, and like other parts of language it is spoken by each generation only because it is passed on by the older generation. But language does not, of course, remain static; whole areas of it may undergo a change in significance, or may fall out of use altogether. It's not impossible that this could happen with morality. It's already likely that some children grow up with little sense of morality; where there is a degree of scepticism, and a diversity of conceptions of morality, a plural society can't just assume that it will survive willy-nilly. In these conditions, formal education, rather than everyday conversation and family upbringing, could be the major agency by which morality survives. But, as we have seen, not everyone thinks it good that morality should survive. And if we would be better off without morality, then we should not be using education to promote it. Rather than moral education, if that means education in morality, we should be educating people to live without morality.

So there is an important decision facing formal education: to try, deliberately, to promote morality, or not? In Chapter 6 I indicated some of the problems with morality; I want to suggest here that there is still something to be said for it. In so doing, I shall address the problems outlined at the beginning of this chapter: the criticisms about motivation, about abstractness and impersonality, and about the imposition of something alien. And I shall add a further question (to be followed up in Chapter 8): can we make good enough sense of morality to see how it can be promoted in present conditions?

MORAL MOTIVATION AGAIN

Take first the question of motivation. One kind of motivation is shown by helping someone who is in distress because their welfare matters to you; another kind by helping out of a sense of moral duty. Most people reading this will probably feel that the first kind of motivation is preferable; but it does not follow from that that there is never any place for the second.

The philosopher Kant, in his writings on morality, was concerned to distinguish a sense of moral right and wrong from all the other motivations that could move people. He wrote, for instance, of 'spirits of so sympathetic a temper that ... they find an inner pleasure in spreading happiness around them and can take delight in the contentment of others as their own work'.[2] These are people to whom altruism is second nature: in spreading happiness around them they are doing what they want to do. And precisely because of that, there is nothing specifically *moral* about their motivation: they are simply following their inclinations rather than a sense of *morality* ('moral' as contrasted with 'non-moral' rather than 'immoral'). Now it is surely a good thing that there are people like this; that is not, I think, in dispute. And it may even be that if everyone was like this, all the time, there would be no need for morality (though what I say later about justice may make us hesitate before accepting that conclusion). But it is a matter of fact that a lot of people are not like this, which is why it is still important that people are capable of being moved by considerations that go against their own inclinations.

Kant, speaking of the type of person who enjoys spreading happiness, formulated the following hypothesis:

> Suppose, then, that the mind of this friend of man were overclouded by sorrows of his own which extinguished all sympathy with the fate of others, but that he still had power to help those in distress, though no longer stirred by the need of others because sufficiently occupied with his own; and suppose that, when no longer moved by any inclination, he tears himself out of this deadly insensibility and does the action without any inclination for the sake of duty alone ...[3]

So, this person is capable of helping someone in distress despite his own sorrows, because he is able to say to himself (and mean it), 'this is what I ought to do'. Think of the good Samaritan. In the biblical story (Luke 10), he was moved by compassion or pity for the man who had been mugged and beaten. But if he had been moved by a sense of moral duty, the victim would still have received his help. The importance of the moral motivation, I am arguing, is that it can operate even where fellow-feeling doesn't.

Take another case: a real, though an artificially constructed one. A number of experiments by psychologist Stanley Milgram have gained a certain fame or notoriety. In these experiments, the subjects were led to believe that they were inflicting electric shocks on other participants – people who were innocent victims, except that they were not doing very well in the supposed learning experiment. On the experimenter's instructions, they were supposed to inflict what they had been told were high-voltage shocks to the point of causing severe pain and distress.[4] Relatively few subjects refused to go along with the experiment. What sort of motivation could have led to more people refusing to be party to this infliction (as they believed) of suffering?

In reply, we might say 'altruism' or 'compassion' and certainly we can suppose that if the experimental subjects had been sufficiently altruistic or compassionate towards their victims they would not have gone along with the experimenter's instructions. But then we have to conclude that a lot of ordinary people were not sufficiently altruistic or compassionate. To put it this way may mislead, if it suggests that the issue is one of *how much* altruism or compassion people have. The point is, rather, that these qualities are unlikely to be directed towards everyone equally. These experimental subjects may have been kind and considerate spouses and parents; they may even have felt they were showing altruism towards the experimenter by not wanting to mess up his experiment. Certainly, they had mixed motives in many cases (Milgram's book about the experiments devoted a good deal of attention to the question of their motivation[5]). To go against the experimenter's instructions would have been uncomfortable and embarrassing, and would have taken some courage. Besides, most subjects will have felt a duty to go along with what the experimenter asked of them.

But if some of these people were acting out of a sense of duty towards the experimenter, doesn't that show that a sense of duty can itself be dangerous? Certainly, it can be dangerous if it amounts to obedience to authority or to tradition. But that is not the kind of motivation I am talking about or that Kant had in mind. In Kant's conception the moral motivation is informed by reason: it requires people to think for themselves about what is right and wrong, not to follow others uncritically. Guided by this motivation the experimental subjects, far from believing that they must go along with the experimenter's instructions, would have said, or at least, would have had the capacity to say, 'No. This is immoral. I will not do it.' (Some people, but not many, did respond in this way.)

Suppose that one of the experimental subjects (who were mostly male), perhaps a person of a normally benevolent and kindly disposition, was having an off day. Like the person in Kant's example, he was depressed and fed up (maybe he was taking part in the experiment because he was bored, had nothing better to do, and was getting paid for it). He had no particular fellow-feeling for the victim. If anything, he felt bloody-minded: if he himself was in such a bad state, why shouldn't someone else suffer too? It seems to me it is in just such a case that the sense that there are certain things which are morally beyond the pale, whatever one's own inclinations, could operate; and that in this situation there might be no other kind of motivation that could lead to a refusal to inflict the suffering.

The kind of motivation I am talking about it one that, I think, many readers will be able to recognize. It cropped up, as it happens, in a discussion document from the National Curriculum Council (NCC) for England and Wales in 1993, which put at the head of its list of the qualities to be developed in moral education, 'The will to behave morally as a point of principle'.[6] The document was referring, I take it, to the capacity to act, not out of one's immediate inclination or desire (even though this might be thoroughly benevolent) but as a result of recognizing that there is a way one *ought*, as a matter of principle, to act. I cannot see that there is anything instinctive about this kind of motivation; if we are capable of having it, it is because we have acquired it.

WE SHOULD CARE ABOUT JUSTICE TOO

The idea that there are things we ought to do 'as a matter of principle' brings us to the second kind of criticism of morality that I want to take up here: the idea that by seeing everything in terms of 'principle', moral thinking will, very often, miss what is distinctive to and important in the concrete circumstances. We saw in Chapter 6 that thinking in terms of general principles is characteristic of the kind of moral approach which Kohlberg argued for and which Gilligan, and others influenced by her, have criticized. We need to look further at what is at issue here.

As I said, most teachers in my experience, faced with the story of the moles and the porcupine, will suggest, perhaps, that the moles should dig a bigger hole rather than turn the porcupine out because he has no right to be there. But it could very well be that the setting of the story in an imaginary animal world makes it easier to give such a response. Suppose it's your own house, the schools and colleges have broken up for the winter holidays and your family is together for once, when a homeless person, who's been sleeping rough, knocks at the door. Would you be more inclined then to appeal to some general rights and principles?

There is no doubt that, especially if we are settled in a relatively comfortable existence, we can use an appeal to our own rights to legitimate, in our eyes, a limitation to our co-operation and identification with the interests of others. This is a criticism of the appeal to individual rights which goes back at least to Marx. But the trouble here is not the language of rights as such, but the content we put into it. We could, after all, instead of appealing to our rights to decide who has a place in our own home, put more weight on everyone's right to adequate shelter.[7]

The issue I want to raise is not who has which rights, but whether we do well to think at all in terms of rights and justice and general principles, when there are critics (some influenced by Gilligan) who think that we need only to attend to the circumstances of particular concrete situations. I would suggest that the notion of justice is an important one to hang on to, precisely because it does not let us concentrate purely on the immediate situation but leads us to make comparisons between the lot of persons in different situations.

The motivation of caring and concern in the concrete situation is directed towards the particular others who impinge on us. When the moles in the story take the porcupine in, they are not thinking of its rights; rather they are responding directly out of concern for the creature. The other side of this is that there may be porcupines out there who don't get cared for at all. We expect a teacher to have concern for the pupils being taught. But we cannot expect that this concern will just happen to be equally distributed towards all the pupils. In addition to the concern that the teacher is capable of feeling for individual pupils, it may take a sense of fairness or justice to see that none of the pupils is favoured at the expense of others, that no one gets passed over. The notion of entitlement clearly has a place here.

While caring is important, we need to remember that it is, in the first instance, caring towards particular others. A community of caring persons would be one in which everyone acted in a caring way towards particular others. But this would not, by itself, guarantee that everyone was cared for, or that everyone's needs were met. To ensure this, a more impartial view is also necessary. We need the idea of justice, even though it may not come so naturally to us (the philosopher Hume described justice as an artificial rather than a natural virtue[8]). Our ideas of justice have been constructed in the course of human society; as with the idea of moral obligation, we can only be motivated by the notion of justice through having certain concepts, being able to use a certain kind of language.

If we need justice, we also need people to care about justice. Caring about justice is not the same thing as caring about particular others; it is compatible with caring for particular others, but it is also the case that to do what is just sometimes means making particular others, whom one cares about, worse off than they would otherwise be. Rather than caring about particular others, the guiding motivation here is caring about justice itself (this direction of the caring towards an idea, rather than towards specific persons, is part of what makes justice an artificial rather than a natural virtue). And to care about justice is an instance of what I have been calling moral motivation: it can call on people to act in a particular way, not because they are so inclined, not from their natural benevolence, but simply because this is what justice requires.

Justice will sometimes be necessary to correct too great an immersion in the concrete morality of a particular community.[9] We have too much experience of xenophobia and racism to suppose that the traditions, the respected ways of doing things, of a particular community can be relied on without some more universal sense of what is owed to all persons simply as persons. To illustrate this, imagine that in Milgram's experiment the experimental subject identifies with the experimenter as one of the same community, but identifies the victim as a member of a different group towards whom the subject is habitually prejudiced.

So far I have been suggesting that even when there are bonds of fellow-feeling within a community which will support altruistic behaviour, a principled sense of morality is still important. But there are many people in the modern world who do not feel part of a concrete community. While education should do what it can to promote a sense of membership of concrete communities, we must also provide a moral education for those who may not feel this sense of belonging – which could, in a modern society, turn out to be any of our children.

Even if there is no active hostility or prejudice to be overcome, a sense of justice and the existence of generally recognized rules can be important in providing some reliability and predictability in people's lives. You may well think it desirable that another person acts out of their sense of concern for the particular others in the concrete situation; but if all you knew about how a person would act was that they would do what they thought best in the concrete situation, you could not be sure how they would act towards you when you are the concrete other in the particular situation. Whereas if you know that the other person recognizes certain generally acknowledged principles or rules, you have some basis for relying on the person acting accordingly. In public and social contexts especially, this degree of reliability can be very important.[10]

While I have been speaking in this section mainly about the idea of justice, the points I have made could be generalized to apply to the idea of morality as such, or at least an important aspect of that idea. By this, I mean the notion that there is something I ought to do which, while I may have to think hard about what it is in the particular situation, still doesn't depend on what I happen to think or feel about this situation (notice that this is in effect one of the notions of objectivity which we looked at in Chapter 3). If I have no notion that there is something which would count as getting it right, or at least that some courses of action would be better than others for reasons which don't come down just to how they affect me, then there will, in a sense, be nothing to stop me doing what I want to do in that situation. This doesn't mean that I shall necessarily be selfish. It may very well be (if I am at all a caring person) that in a concrete situation I shall act partly on my feelings for other people in the situation, and these feelings may well be altruistic. But if this is all that is motivating me, it may still be too easy for me to follow what are after all my inclinations, without sufficiently modifying them to take into account the point of view of the others (including their conception, rather than mine, of what is good for them).

What I need here is a degree of objectivity in the way I look at the situation – objectivity in the third of the senses I picked out in Chapter 3. I need a degree of detachment – which doesn't mean not caring what happens but does mean seeing things in an unbiased way. One way of achieving this is simply to pursue the idea of objectivity in the first of the senses of Chapter 3 – namely that there is a right answer, or at least an answer which is better than some, which I am trying to see my way to. This doesn't mean that I have to apply some broad abstract generalization, like 'don't tell a lie' or 'don't break a promise (whatever the circumstances)'; there is no guarantee in advance that what I ought to do in the particular situation will involve nothing but the observance of simple rules of that kind. Rather, I'm suggesting it's the very idea that there is something which would be 'the right thing to do', or at least that certain things would be 'the wrong thing to do', which makes a difference here. Even with all the difficulties that idea raises, we might be worse off if it wasn't part of our repertoire of ideas.

That still leaves us with the question, 'how do I go about establishing what would be the right thing to do?' To come to the remaining sense of objectivity which I mentioned in Chapter 3, is there a procedure, a specific way of thinking, which I could follow that would help me to do this? I've already said enough (both in taking seriously some of the objections made by critics of morality, and in what I said about compromise in Chapter 5) to suggest that the right way of thinking will not be a matter of rigidly applying simplistically formulated rules. But it would be a start, at least, to ask oneself seriously, and even systematically, how the situation appears from the point of view of each of the other people involved. In other words (and you will probably find this a quite familiar idea), I ask myself what it would be like to be in their shoes. And having tried to answer that question (which again involves not the rigid application of rules but possibly a good deal of sensitivity and imagination), I ask myself whether I can still endorse what might at first sight have seemed the right thing to do.[11]

The importance of taking a view which is, in this way, objective but not oversimplified also casts light on the common idea which I noted towards the end of Chapter 6, that there is something suspect about passing moral judgement on others. There *is*, rightly, something suspect about it if one's own judgements about others are liable to be made without a full knowledge of the circumstances of the case; and there is also something impractical in treating social problems (which may need political and economic responses) as if they could be solved by the making of moral judgements. In such cases the pejorative word 'moralizing' may be appropriate. But this does not mean that it can never be right to make judgements on the rights and wrongs of other people's conduct. If, in my own case, a consideration of how other people are affected by my actions can give me reasons for thinking that it would be wrong to do such-and-such, then in principle, if I know enough about the case, I could cite similar reasons for a provisional conclusion about what somebody else is doing. And if I am in a position to be able to talk to the person concerned, then I can explain why I think his or her conduct would be wrong, and my reasons can be open to discussion in turn. In so doing, there need be no arrogation on my part of any spurious moral authority.

Furthermore, and this is perhaps of particular relevance to teachers, in saying to someone that I think their conduct is wrong, and being prepared to give my reasons and discuss them, it is important to recognize that I am not necessarily condemning the person; I need not be saying that he or she is a bad person, and I certainly need not be, and should not be, getting annoyed or uttering insults. Indeed, since expressing a moral judgement about somebody's conduct – as opposed to keeping it to myself – is itself something I do, it is as much subject to moral appraisal as any other piece of conduct. There may be occasions when, even though I could amply defend my judgement about someone else's conduct, it would be better – morally better – to keep it to myself, perhaps because uttering it would do more harm than good. But by the same token, there may be occasions when I *ought* to tell another person that I think his or her conduct is wrong, perhaps because there is a third party whose interests would not otherwise be taken into account. All this, again, may be especially relevant to teachers. Though we won't be discussing moral education as such until Chapters 11 and 12, it seems unlikely that teachers could get children into the habit of using moral ideas in their own thinking if the teachers themselves did not employ them in their dealings with the children. It's worth remembering, of course, that we use moral ideas in praising others for doing what is right as well as for criticizing them for doing what is wrong: there would certainly be something suspect about passing moral judgement on others if the only judgements we expressed were negative ones.

MORALITY WITHOUT IMPOSITION

So far in this chapter I have suggested some reasons for thinking that human affairs will improve if people display – in addition to other sorts of motivation – the capacity to act out of a sense of general moral requirements, including those of justice. But it is still true that morality conceived in this way could be something imposed on people as a form of social control. Since teachers who want to educate rather than indoctrinate – in terms of the distinction mentioned in Chapter 2 – will not be happy about imposing something on pupils regardless of their capacity to think for themselves, we still need to reply to the criticism that morality is a form of alienation.

Our response needs to be, I think, straightforward in outline, though it requires a lot of care to fill in the details. It is that a sense of moral requirements properly understood does not have to be – or rather, cannot be – imposed from outside, but must be acknowledged through a person's own thinking. For moral philosophers this idea is, again, very much associated with Kant; but in developing it, Kant himself was drawing on an idea that was strong in the tradition of thought which he was brought up in (namely Lutheran Christianity). This is the idea that to be moral one has to be autonomous; to be following the dictates of others – whether of tradition, of the whole society, or of the God one believes in – is not to be acting as a moral being at all.

We have to be careful with the notion of autonomy here, as it can easily be misleading. When we speak of people thinking for themselves, making their own decisions, we expect them to come up with a variety of answers – from which it would seem to follow, in a moral context, that there was no objective right or wrong. But this modern association of autonomy with 'anything goes' must be put on one side if we are to understand the idea of morality as self-generated rather than imposed.[12] The comparison with mathematics, which I have already used in Chapter 3, may help. Any self-respecting teacher of maths will want pupils to work out answers to mathematical problems for themselves – as opposed to, say, copying from someone else or from answers in the back of the book. But it does not at all follow from this that any answer is as good as any other. (I am thinking here of calculations within set parameters, rather than the kind of mathematical investigation where there may indeed be more than one way of going about the task.) Thinking for oneself is not incompatible with the existence of a particular answer which, if one is doing the thinking properly, one will eventually discover.

We need to adopt similar positions with regard to morality. It is not a field of free creativity; there are rational considerations. As a matter of rationality, there are moral claims which we have to recognize. But *we* have to recognize them, rather than blindly following answers given by others.[13] If something like this is right, then the idea of imposing morality on others becomes a contradiction in terms. People will have to appreciate the force of moral thinking for themselves, and there will be a role for moral education, not in imposing anything, but rather in enabling people to see what in the end they will have to see for themselves.

All this leaves us, however, with a question which may seem much more problematic in the case of morality than in the case of mathematics: whether we can make morality intelligible to the people who have to do the thinking. I have said that morality is largely a matter of having and using, with a sense of its signficance, a certain kind of language. But if we are trying to educate people to think for themselves, we must expect that they will cast a critical eye on the language we encourage them to use; that they will ask questions like, 'What does it mean to say that something is wrong or that I morally ought to do something?' Do we have an answer?

I shall call this, which is the topic of the next chapter, the problem of making sense of morality, and will look again at the question of the relation between religion and morality, and between both of these and the idea of spirituality. The reason for raising this question again is that there will be little future for morality if we can't make sense of it outside of a religious context, yet it is the lack of that context for many people – and in a sense for a whole society[14] – that raises the problem of making sense of morality in an acute form.

But before turning to that issue I want to discuss further the idea that there could be ways of thinking which people can follow for themselves and which, if they are properly pursued, will lead to determinate answers. In my analogies with maths, I have assumed that the appropriate thought process is one that each individual can follow for themself. And we often make similar assumptions about morality, as indeed did Kant in his reference to a moral compass which the individual could use (the test of universalizability).[15] But in recent years the German social theorist Jurgen Habermas has suggested that the right kind of thinking (given, I would add, certain assumptions about the kind of issue in question) is one that can only be carried on in dialogue.

In Habermas's theory of 'communicative ethics'[16] the initial idea, very roughly, is that within a community where there are conflicting interests the way to resolve moral disputes is through dialogue. This by itself will not sound surprising, but it already moves away from the assumption that any individual by his or her own rational thought can see the right thing to do.[17] Habermas is saying that where the moral problem arises from a clash of interests, then out of dialogue, if the dialogue is unconstrained,[18] something could emerge which is in the interests of all. In that kind of situation, at least, we have a collective version of the idea that there is an objective procedure, the outcome of which will be what is right – in this case, what it means for something to be right will be that it is what would emerge from unconstrained dialogue.

I have stressed the kinds of assumption involved, because it would be difficult to fit all moral disputes, even in principle, under the idea of dialogue in which common interests can emerge.[19] For one thing, people do not necessarily see the moral stance they take on certain issues as being a matter of anyone's interests: this is true of a good deal of religiously based moral beliefs, and we shall see in Chapter 9 that it is also true of the positions which many people take on issues of abortion and the environment. For another, communicative ethics seems not to take account of parties which, as we shall also see in Chapter 9, cannot themselves be participants in a dialogue. Nevertheless, Habermas's arguments may turn out to be very fruitful; I shall mention them again in Chapter 12 in connection with the role of discussion in values education.

NOTES

1. Some of the issues about non-human altruism were famously popularized – but not necessarily clarified, so far as the use of the words 'altruistic' and 'selfish' go – by Richard Dawkins in *The Selfish Gene* (1976). Philosophers who have sorted through the issues about the biological bases for altruism and morality include Midgley (1979b) and Singer (1981).
2. Kant (1948), pp. 63–64 (first published 1785).
3. Kant (1948), p. 64. (The language is, of course, that of one particular translation from the German.)
4. No shocks were actually inflicted, and the 'victims' were actors. The set-up was explained to the real subjects of the experiment – the people who thought they were inflicting the shocks – afterwards. See Milgram (1974).
5. Milgram (1974), chapters 10–13.
6. NCC (1993), p. 5.
7. The notion of rights is one that needs to be treated with care. Like other notions mentioned in Chapters 1 and 3, it can cause confusion unless the parties to a discussion are clear about how they are using it. Human rights, children's rights, animal rights, the right to life, a woman's right to choose, the right to holidays with pay, the rights of trees and the right of criminals to be punished – all have been spoken of. To go no further than bare assertion about rights – as when one side in the controversy over abortion asserts a woman's right to choose and the other side asserts a foetus's right to life – leads only to an impasse. Then it is better either to avoid the word or be prepared to look in detail at what it means to attribute a right to someone or something, at who has which rights, and how we can know it. All this needs extended discussion, which I have decided not to attempt in this book, since it would mean too great a diversion from the main line of development of the ideas. For more on rights,

see Waldron (1984, 1993); and in an educational context, Snook and Lankshear (1979); Wringe (1981); Haydon (1993a).

8. See Hume (1888), Book III, Part II, Section 1. Hume's account of the way in which justice remedies some of the defects of human nature bears some affinity to the Hobbesian account of morality which we looked at in Chapter 4.

9. The notion of the ways of doing things of a particular community, in contrast with an abstract and universal sense of morality, is a notion sometimes referred to by the German word *sittlichkeit*, used in this sense by Hegel.

10. Kymlicka (1990, pp. 262–86) makes this point well in the course of an illuminating discussion of the ethical perspectives of caring and justice.

11. I shall come back to this idea in Chapter 12, where I shall also refer to the writings of Richard Hare for the more careful formulation which the idea needs. See Hare (1981, 1992).

12. Confusion with the modern connotations of autonomy has often contributed to misreadings of Kant. Secondary sources on Kantian ethics are not necessarily reliable (I am a secondary source). I am grateful to Lenval Callender for his forceful arguments about Kant and his modern interpreters.

13. This ties in with the idea of morality as being universal in its form and content, in that it can be recognized by the exercise of the rationality which all normal human beings are capable of, independently of their particular cultural circumstances. In Kant's account, the central moral claim is that all moral agents are to be treated as ends in themselves, never solely as means to ends; this is often in modern jargon interpreted as 'respect for persons'. See Downie and Telfer (1969).

14. See the discussion in Chapter 10 of the idea of a secular society.

15. Kant (1948), p. 69.

16. See Habermas (1990a, 1990b).

17. The idea of conscience which we encountered in Chapter 1 also incorporates the thought that in the last analysis the answer to a moral problem is something which individuals have to come to for themselves.

18. In some of his writings Habermas referred to 'an ideal speech situation' – a notion which we'll encounter again in Chapter 10 (see note 2 to that chapter).

19. Habermas has acknowledged that, in terms of the justice/care distinction, he sees morality within the justice perspective. See Habermas (1990b) pp. 171–88; and Benhabib (1992) on Kohlberg, Habermas and feminist critiques.

Further reading
On moral motivation see Mill (1962b), chapter 3, and in relation to moral education Jones, R. (1980) and Straughan (1982, 1988b). On the role of feelings in morality see Oakley (1992), and on caring Noddlings (1984).

CHAPTER 8

Making sense of morality – and spirituality too?

A PAROCHIAL PREAMBLE

If there are any aspects of human experience which are potentially universal, rather than merely local or temporary phenomena, we might think that morality and spirituality would be good candidates. But the first part of this chapter may be among the most parochial parts of the book, because it is responding to some particularly English states of affairs.

Unlike the USA, where a separation of Church and state is enshrined in the constitution, England has an established Church. Without this, the 1944 Education Act might not have made religious education a compulsory – at that time, the only compulsory – part of the school curriculum; and legislators in the 1990s might not have been trying to ensure a substantially Christian content in that part of the curriculum, not to mention predominantly Christian collective acts of worship in schools. This compulsory presence of religion has made it easy, in England, for people to think that moral education in schools can safely be left to the practitioners of religion and of religious education. That many people do in fact associate morality closely with religion is not an English phenomenon; it is the entrenchment of religion in schools that sets us apart from a country like the USA, where the question had to be faced earlier of whether, and how, moral education could be taught in schools quite independently of religion.[1] In England, systematic attempts to develop a theory and practice of moral education quite independently of religion have appeared relatively late on the scene.

It also seems a rather English phenomenon that in 1988 a concern with spirituality was written into the legislation governing the school curriculum. The Education Reform Act required every school to have a curriculum which would:

(a) promote the spiritual, moral, cultural, mental and physical development of pupils at the school and of society;
(b) prepare such pupils for the opportunities, responsibilities and experiences of adult life.

As mentioned in Chapter 2, the content of the curriculum the legislation laid down was not derived in any systematic way from that statement of aims. But the point which concerns us now is that a legal requirement was laid on schools to promote the 'spiritual, moral and cultural' development of pupils. It's likely that the word 'spiritual' was put there to ensure that there would be, within the preamble of the Act, a legitimation of the role of religious education in the curriculum. Even the drafters of the legislation probably felt that in a liberal and plural society, they could not quite demand in law the *religious* development of pupils and of society. The word 'spiritual' seemed to offer a broader scope. And indeed, the teaching profession, faced with having to make sense somehow of a legal require- ment to promote spiritual development, has not been slow to take advantage of that broader scope. After a flurry of documents from the NCC, SCAA and OFSTED, a consensus seemed to be emerging by the mid 1990s on at least two things: that spiritual development did not necessarily have to be tied to religion, and that spiritual and moral development were not the same thing, but were nevertheless difficult to disentangle.

Since it would be a pity if a discussion of morality and spirituality were itself to turn out to be purely ephemeral, I shall not spend time trying to unravel the intricacies of these particular documents. (Even if you are teaching in an English school, you may well have a new set of documents to cope with by the time you read this.) But we do need in more general terms to disentangle, if we can, the three items of religion, spirituality and morality. And the importance of doing that in the context of this book is that, as I said at the end of Chapter 7, we do need to be able to make sense of morality. For many people, religion used to provide this. If we now have to make sense of it independently of religion, we may still find that the notion of spirituality, or something like it, has some useful work to do in making sense of morality.

I think it unlikely that this particular *word* 'spirituality' is indispensable, but I would not go as far as John White, who 'would advocate an absolute embargo on the use of the terms "spirituality" or "spiritual development" in all official documents on education, all conferences on education; all in- service courses for teachers, all inaugural lectures'.[2] In the beginning was that word, and the word is with us, whether we like it or not, so we might as well see what we can do with it. Indeed, if we didn't have it, we would probably have to invent a different word to do the same job.

MORALITY AND RELIGION

I referred at the end of Chapter 7 to the conception of morality, which I associated in a quite unrigorous way with the philosopher Kant, by which morality has to be autonomously endorsed by each individual. There is no doubt that morality, in that conception, is logically distinct from religion, since we are not acting as autonomous moral agents if we follow an alleged religious authority. The word 'alleged' is important here, since there are many alleged religious authorities, and we have to assess their claims. This idea might be difficult to accept, might even seem blasphemous, if your standpoint is from within one of the established religions; but it should not be difficult to accept if you think of the many contemporary claimants to the title of religious authority. Think, for instance, of the brief notoriety of David Koresh and his sect in Waco, Texas, widely reported in 1993. If you reject his claims to religious authority, it is presumably, at least in part, because you do not think he was a standard of goodness, a moral exemplar. In other words, you have some values already which you use as standards, and by those standards you find the claims of someone like Koresh wanting. But logically the situation is the same even with the most firmly established religions. Kant, for instance, from a position firmly within Protestant Christianity, was able to write that 'even the Holy One of the gospel must first be compared with our ideal of moral perfection before we can recognise him to be such'.[3]

So it is certainly possible to drive a logical wedge between religion and morality. And so far as experience goes, morality for very many people in the modern world is experienced in entirely secular terms. This is certainly something that schools have to recognize. The biggest danger in always linking morality in schools with religion is that if people reject religion they may reject morality along with it. At the same time, it remains true that if you have a strong religious belief, you probably don't see your morality and your religion as distinct; I have already stressed in earlier chapters that moral values may have for a religious believer a significance which they can't have for a non-believer. Among these differences is that the problem of making sense of morality doesn't arise for the religious believer in the same way as it does for the non-believer.

I need to explain further what I mean by the problem of making sense of morality. There is a perspective – that of a sociologist or anthropologist, perhaps – which allows us to look at morality from the outside, and from that perspective it certainly seems that we don't need to refer to religion to make sense of morality. We can see morality essentially in the Hobbesian way, as a social device by which, by and large, people benefit, because it restrains the exercise of human impulses which might otherwise be acted out in anti-social ways. We can also try to give biological and evolutionary explanations of morality, as sociobiologists, for instance, are trying to do.[4]

I see no reason why morality within education should not be studied from the outside in these ways. If we can detach ourselves a little from that traditional canon of subjects that I spoke of in Chapter 2, it may even seem odd that whereas 'Politics' or 'Economics' or 'Psychology' can be school subjects, at least at the upper levels of secondary education, 'Morality' as a subject of study never seems to figure in the school curriculum (unless it is, misleadingly, as part of religious education). I suspect, though, that some people will object to the idea of morality being treated from the outside as a subject of study at school level, because they feel this will weaken whatever force it has from the inside. I do not think that need be so (any more than being a student of comparative religion is incompatible with being a believer within one faith); but it is true that the view from the outside is not the same as the view from the inside.

Essentially, the problem of making sense of morality is the problem of how it is to be seen from the inside. The question is roughly this: can I understand morality, not just as a system and a way of using language which I can observe (some) other people in society following, but as something which I can intelligibly see myself as part of, something which I am on the inside of and which has meaning and force for me? There is another question which is related to this one, namely, what's in it for me? Why should I take any notice of morality? What will I get out of it? This has been debated at least since Plato had Socrates pose the question, 'Why should I be just?'[5] It is a question asked from the perspective of an individual who is interested only in his or her own well-being (roughly the kind of individual Hobbes had in mind). The question can be given an answer, of sorts. It may well be that life will go better for you if you respect morality rather than ignore it when it seems inconvenient for you. It's not always easy to get away with behaving immorally.[6] But on the other hand, people do sometimes get away with it. So to reply to the question, 'Why should I be moral?' with the answer, 'because it will be in your best interests' is not very persuasive.

As an answer, it may also seem to be beside the point. It doesn't just happen, as a matter of fact, that being moral sometimes means we can't do what would be in our own best interests. The requirement is built into morality (in the conception many of us have of it, and in the Kantian conception that I referred to in Chapter 7) that we act for *reasons* that are not to do with our own interests, which sometimes means that we may have to act in the face of these interests. There are occasions when, morally, we ought to be self-sacrificing, and while it may be good for the interests of society as a whole that we have a set of ideas that makes such demands, it won't cut much ice to say to an individual who is basically self-interested, 'sacrificing your own interests is in your interests'. Sometimes, it just isn't: which is why there can still be a problem, from an individual's point of view, in making sense of morality.

A WIDER FRAMEWORK OF MEANING?

The first step towards solving this problem (but only a first step) is to recognize that we don't make sense of things only by seeing that they are in our own interests. It's a common mistake, at least in Western thought, to suppose that this is the only way of doing it; and religion has not been immune to that mistake. When religion has said to people that they will reap the rewards of heaven if they are good, and be damned to hell if they are bad, then it has been assuming that people can only make sense of morality in terms of their own self-interest; and it has been trying to show them that, despite worldly appearances, it really is all in their interest after all. But, of course, once people give up any literal interpretation of the idea of heaven and hell, that appeal no longer has weight. Much religious teaching now doesn't make any use of the idea, partly because many people no longer believe it, and partly because much religious thinking would agree with Kant that if you are really only acting for the sake of your own interests, however long term, you're not being moral at all.

If the only way religion could offer to make sense of morality for the individual was by an appeal to self-interest, secular defenders of morality would have nothing to learn from it. But in another way religion does, for its believers, help to make sense of morality, and it might be that this way has something to offer even to people who have no religious faith. Religious belief can help to make sense of morality by enabling moral demands to be experienced within a wider framework of meaning, so that, while they can still be seen as independently valid, they are not isolated from other aspects of a person's life. It seems to be true of us as human beings that we can act in a certain way, not just because doing so serves some self-interested desires, or even because it serves non-self-interested desires relating to particular others (in the way that advocates of an ethic of care often speak of), but because it makes sense as part of a life which is itself understood as part of something larger. Religion can provide a set of concepts and beliefs in which the 'something larger' can be expressed. It is worth asking whether there is some wider framework of meaning, within which morality can be located, which might be available to the non-believer.

Here it is interesting that some modern religious thinking has allowed traditional beliefs about God or the transcendent to be questioned, while retaining the traditional language; so that the language can still provide a framework of meaning even though it is not interpreted in the traditional way. For instance, one way of making sense of moral demands within a religious framework, without seeing them as arbitrary commands of God, is by *identifying* central moral values with the God which is worshipped. Some of the more radical versions of this move lead to an account which Marx would have recognized, by which God becomes (or rather, always was) a projection of human concerns. Thinkers who take this kind of line have been seeking to make sense of, or to retain a sense for, religious language and practice within a world, and an intellectual culture, in which it is increasingly difficult to maintain wholeheartedly or with integrity all the older supernatural beliefs which went with such language and practice.[7]

Talking of God becomes, in such accounts, a way of talking about deep human concerns, about what we most care about, about what we recognize as most important in the world. God becomes a projection of human values; but what is most significant for the present argument is that, for such writers, taking this view of God does not mean, in their own eyes, that they have become atheist. The language and the practice of religion which they are a part of still has meaning for them. Consider, as an accessible example, the book *God in Us*, written not by an academic theologian but by an ordained Anglican, Anthony Freeman, who at the time of writing it was still a parish priest.[8] He claims that giving up a belief in a literal, supernaturally existent personal God 'out there' does not leave a large hole in his life.[9] It is the language, the practice, the whole 'mind-set' of religion that makes the difference, and this can continue, this can still in fact have very much the same meaning, after the belief in its literal truth has been abandoned.

The relevance of this to our question about making sense of morality is that it may be possible for moral language to make sense even if we consciously take a sceptical view about the reality of moral values. Let me spell out the analogy a bit further. Some people want to go on using religious language, though they cannot accept a literal reading of many scriptural claims, and in fact see religious ideas as a projection of human concerns. In the same way, others may want to go on using moral language even though they are not at all sure that moral values have any reality independently of human concerns. Whatever the case with religion, we may all have good reason for hoping that people will go on using moral language, at least some of the time, even if we ourselves are not sure how to interpret it.

When we reflect on the way we attribute qualities of good and bad, right and wrong, to people or to conduct, we may think (as have some philosophers, at least since Hume in the eighteenth century) that we do not observe real qualities that exist independently of our perception, but rather project these qualities on to the world. Such a view does not mean that we can simply invent and apply whatever moral labels we like: our moral conceptions will certainly reflect in some way underlying human concerns that are real aspects of human nature, of the human condition in the world or of rationality as a quality which humans possess; and it may well be possible to argue that there are good reasons for holding to some particular conceptions of right and wrong and rejecting others. Thus, it may be possible to establish a sense in which certain moral claims are objectively valid. But, as I noted in Chapter 3, it is hardly controversial that claims about objective rightness and wrongness cannot be resolved in anything like the same way that we might settle claims about things, like rocks and planets, that could exist quite independently of any human thought or action. So recognizing that the language we use for moral values does not pick out something existing independently of our thought need not stop us using the language for the same purposes, or even experiencing the same effects on our feelings and motivations that this language has always carried.[10]

But there is another important feature of the analogy. Some religious believers have begun, albeit gradually, to think of the language they use as a projection of human concerns; but they have come to this after starting from more traditional or orthodox religious interpretations. The religious language and practices already make sense to them, have meaning for them; it is not so surprising, therefore, that a change in intellectual interpretation need not destroy that meaning. What is much more doubtful is whether someone who had never held a religious belief on a more traditional interpretation could find any meaning in religious language and practice if, from the beginning, it were presented in an avowedly 'projectivist' way. Since there are indeed in modern society (more so in Britain, incidentally, than in the USA) many who do grow up without encountering religious language and practice from the inside (and since it is not plausible that enforced 'religious worship' in schools can do much to change that situation), we can hardly advocate religious language, however thoroughly demythologized, as a route towards moral meaning for society at large through the state education system.

In a similar way, someone may be able to take the view that moral language is (merely) a projection of human concerns, that there is nothing other-worldly or transcendent about moral claims, and still find the same force in that language, *if* that person has already been on the inside of moral language and is accustomed to using it in thinking about his or her own conduct and that of others. But if we were to present moral ideas for the first time to someone who had never encountered them, it's doubtful whether we could convert them to these ideas if we could only, in effect, represent the ideas as a sophisticated form of social control. And here there may be an important role for educational institutions, a function to perform on a social rather than an individual level: to ensure that moral language itself is kept alive by getting people used to using that language – because others around them are accustomed to use it – even before they begin to reflect on it critically. Only if the language is available, will it be possible for someone to be motivated by the thought, 'I ought not to do this' or 'I have a moral obligation to do that'. Only if that possibility is there, is there any point in asking the next question – on what understanding of moral language is it possible for someone to be moved by it?

INDIVIDUAL (AND SPIRITUAL) UNDERSTANDINGS OF MORALITY?

This is another instance when the long-standing question, 'Why should I be moral?' is misleading. In the history of philosophy this question has often been conceived as addressed to the rational individual, as if it were a question that could be answered for an individual, in isolation from any consideration of membership of a community. Interpreted in that way, there probably is no satisfactory answer to it.

Where someone has a tangible sense of membership in a community with concrete others, and can also see the importance that morality has for real people in a real community, then sceptical questions about morality may have no real weight – and in any case a distinctively moral form of motivation may be less necessary. But this is a relatively straightforward example. What of the person who is thoroughly alienated, who has no sense of real community with anyone else, or has a sense of community with a sub-community which is itself alienated from the wider society? It is in such a case, if anywhere, that the force of morality may be needed (as I suggested in Chapter 7), but also where it is most difficult for morality to be experienced other than as an alien imposition.

Think, perhaps, of what is needed if a teenager is to reject, on moral grounds, peer group pressure to join in with some antisocial behaviour. The community they identify with is the immediate peer group; the wider community is not real to them in the same way. Yet it could perhaps become sufficiently real to move the person if they could ask themself seriously a question like, 'Could I justify what I am doing to others in terms which they couldn't reasonably reject?' They may recognize that there is no way, in practice, that they could persuade their associates to change their minds. Yet if the person sees clearly enough that what they are proposing to do is something which other people, from their point of view (perhaps as victims), would have every reason to reject, this could be enough to enable them to go against the peer group.

What is happening here is that a distinctively moral kind of motivation is operating – the desire to be able to justify what one is doing.[11] This may on the face of it sound a rather thin and secondary kind of justification: it is not like acting out of love for one's fellow creatures, and no doubt truly altruistic, caring people would not go through life constantly asking themselves whether what they were doing is justified. Yet it is a form of motivation that can operate quite strongly with human beings (it is closely related to the caring about justice which I spoke of in Chapter 7), and one which it is possible to cultivate, indeed may be well worth cultivating.[12] To ask whether one could be justified in one's actions will involve seeing whether others (assuming they were being reasonable), could approve of what one is doing, and that may very well involve putting oneself in other people's shoes, in the way that I mentioned towards the end of Chapter 7. That is why imagination as well as reasoning is involved. Even if someone doesn't care about the concrete others, they may be moved – by seeing themselves, in effect, as part of a notional community, of the community as it ought to be, even if to some degree members of their own concrete community would reject what they are doing.[13]

What has all this to do with spirituality? Just that the notion of spirituality (assuming that we can provide an interpretation which may be useful in education) will have to do with the sense of oneself within a wider framework of meaning.[14] By this I mean something not just cognitive, but involving a person's feelings as well. If we thought of someone as quite 'unspiritual', we might mean that the person is immersed wholly in the concerns of the immediate and mundane world. Spiritual development would have to do with achieving a sense – a *felt* sense, beyond mere verbal expression – of connection with, even perhaps membership of, some larger whole. For many people historically, that sense of belonging to something larger has been expressed in religious ways, but it need not be. There will be something of the spiritual, too, about identification with a wider human community, or, for some people, with a community wider than the human, involving all of life on earth, the biosphere.[15] For others, it may be a matter of seeing oneself as a part, an almost infinitesimally small part but nevertheless a part, of the universe.

Moral development, then, not necessarily in the sense of becoming more moral in one's behaviour, but in the sense of coming to have an awareness of a place in a moral scheme of things, can also be spiritual development.[16] Kant, whose conception of morality I do find in a way inspiring, though I can hardly claim to be following it, said that only two things filled him with awe – the starry heavens above and the moral law within. As we understand more and more about the 'starry heavens' through astronomy and cosmology, the cognitive understanding does not by itself make the vastness of the universe any less awesome – and that can, importantly, be true both for people who see a divine purpose behind it and for those who see it as a product of blind physical forces. A moral sense, which links one, sometimes in spite of one's own inclination and preferences, to other people and to a wider world is also a remarkable thing, whether one sees it as a divine gift or as a purely human achievement.

There is another analogy, too. The universe is there, independently of the perceptions or reactions to it of human beings, but persons may react, or fail to react, to it in very different ways. Morality as a system of values might also have some content which is the same for everyone, but people may relate to it differently. In other words, the idea that there is something very personal and individual about moral development is not inconsistent with the idea that there is one common core to morality. We might say, instead, that there is an area of spiritual development which involves each person's individual response to a common set of moral ideas. If, in the end, one sees these moral ideas as a purely human creation, that should not belittle them. Those who are inclined to see themselves as taking a modern, or indeed postmodern, view of things, may find it worth reflecting on the fact that it is possible to see moral ideas and ideals as a contingent human creation and still be moved by them. If it's possible at all, it will only be possible through education.

NOTES

1. See Kohlberg (1981), e.g. chapter 8.
2. White (1995), p. 16. Though we disagree about the use of this word, my argument towards the end of this chapter does have some affinity with White's.
3. Kant (1948), p. 73.
4. See Chapter 7, note 1 and Midgley (1979a).
5. Plato: *The Republic*, Book 1. It was Thrasymachus who pressed the question; while the rest of the dialogue concerns Socrates's attempt to answer it. See Foot (1978) pp. 125–30 for a modern discussion of the question.
6. See Hare (1981), chapter 11.
7. Among the writers associated with this kind of move are (perhaps going from the less to the more radical) Paul Tillich, John Robinson (the Church of England bishop whose *Honest to God* (1963) caused something of a stir) and Don Cupitt (see Cupitt (1980) and a succession of later works).
8. Freeman (1993).
9. He was, however, removed from office as a result of publishing the book. The case was reported and discussed in the English press in the summer of 1994.
10. This view has been explored, under the headings of 'projectivism' and 'quasi-realism' by Blackburn, first in Blackburn (1984), Part 2 (a book on the philosophy of language) and in more detail in Blackburn (1993). Blackburn associates the view with Hume (see Hume (1988), Book III, Part 1). For a critical view of projectivism, see McNaughton (1988).
11. The argument is developed by Scanlon (1982). Scanlon's position is of the variety known as 'contractualism' (or sometimes 'contractarianism'): roughly the idea that morality functions as a kind of implicit or hypothetical social contract, so that I can test my moral positions by seeing whether they are ones which reasonable people would contract into (or, in Scanlon's argument, couldn't reasonably contract out of) as a basis for existence in society.

12. Scanlon suggests that moral education is largely about cultivating the desire to be able to see one's conduct as justified, with an understanding of what kinds of consideration can count as justifications (I'm sure there are aspects of moral education which Scanlon is overlooking here).

13. At least in my own thinking, there is a link here with Kant's notion (Kant (1948), Chapter 2) that we should live as if we were members of a kingdom of ends, by which he means (if it is possible to express it both intelligibly and in one sentence) that we should act in the way that we can conceive of all members of society acting, if every member of society were to treat every other member with the respect due to persons, and never to treat another as purely a means to his or her own ends.

14. My own interest in and understanding of the idea of the spiritual owes a lot to discussions with Shirley Rowan, whose research, when published, will be recommended reading. See also Carr (1995) and Mott-Thornton (1996).

15. Something like this sense of identification with a wider whole may underlie many people's strong moral concern for other animals and for the environment, when this is more than a utilitarian concern for the welfare of future human beings – see Chapter 9.

16. I have heard Roger Straughan make something like this point.

Part IV

Some value controversies in and about schools

This book has been stressing the complexities of the issues about values which teachers need to understand and to handle. Teachers face controversial issues involving values both within their teaching and in their thinking about questions of educational provision and organization. This part illustrates these points by discussing just two sets of issues, chosen from a multiplicity of issues, all of which cannot possibly be discussed here.

1. Most teachers at one time or another, in primary schools, in secondary schools in the context of personal and social education, or in the course of their subject teaching, are likely to have to handle controversial issues which extend outside their own specialism. Anything which is a controversial issue in society could come up in schools if it is not artificially excluded. Even the list of cross-curricular themes which the NCC tried, not very successfully, to introduce into the school curriculum of England and Wales in the late 1980s shows something of the possible range: environmental education, health education, economic and industrial understanding, citizenship education, careers education. There is not space here even to survey all the controversies involving values which can come up within those themes (see Haydon 1992).

    In order to illustrate here the importance of recognizing different kinds of values, and the potential that the differences hold both for conflict and for compromise, I shall refer briefly in Chapter 9 to three issues which have in fact led to violent conflict outside of schools, and are likely to generate lively discussion when they come up within schools: abortion, the environment and the treatment of animals. These may sound like a disparate set of issues, but there are interesting connections between them; and they all raise the question of whether people can be justified in resorting to violence in support of a moral position.

2. The issues just mentioned are, of course, ones for anyone and everyone in society, not just for teachers. The same is true of the second category: issues directly about schools. But here it would be especially surprising if teachers were not from time to time, perhaps in the staffroom rather than

the classroom, engaged in discussion about some of the following: selection by ability; ways in which schools are funded and governed; parental choice; the desirability or otherwise of private schools. All of these raise issues of values. In Chapter 10, I focus on just one issue which connects quite closely with points I've already made about how values can be different in content, and differently interpreted, from within or from outside of a religious position: should all schools in a multifaith society be secular, or is it acceptable, or desirable, that there should be schools committed to a particular faith?

CHAPTER 9

Fighting for a cause: violence, persuasion and education

NON-VIOLENCE AND EDUCATION

We saw in Chapter 1 that John Patten included among the values which education should promote the readiness to resolve conflict without resort to violence. He included it almost in passing, as if it was obvious that people would agree. And indeed I think most people would agree, at least so long as they are not pressed too hard in relation to issues they feel strongly about. For in fact some people do resort to violence in cases of conflict, and it is not always for the sake of their own interests, let alone for the sake of the violence itself. If someone resorts to violence for the sake of it, as may happen in bullying, they are more likely to be creating a conflict than attempting to resolve one. But many people do resort to violence for the sake of others or for the sake of what they see as a matter of rights or principle. Think of the recent history of South Africa and of Northern Ireland; think of protest and direct action in Britain and North America over abortion, animal rights or the destruction of the environment.

Patten said nothing about how schools should promote this particular value, but there will be a number of things that schools can do: by their ethos, their rules (which will not necessarily be made and imposed from above), by teachers' example, and through techniques of conflict resolution and mediation that can be taught.[1]

But why should schools have any particular concern with this value? I would suggest that it is not an optional extra; nor is it of concern only to make the work of the school run more smoothly. Anyone has reason to value the non-violent resolution of conflict if they recognize values which have more traditionally been seen as the concern of education, such as rationality and autonomy. These are not just values which have been popular in liberal philosophy of education and which, incidentally, figure in Patten's speech ('respect for rational argument', 'independence of thought'); it is doubtful whether anybody would deny that there are some circumstances in which it is better for people to be rational than irrational, to think for themselves rather than merely follow what others tell them (since there is no guarantee, especially in a plural society, that the others will be 'proper authorites'). But the resort to violence is, in a sense, the direct negation of these values. To pursue a dispute by violence is not to settle it by reason, and does nothing to ensure that the conflict will be resolved in the way that might be most reasonable, all things considered. And to use violence against persons is generally to interfere with those persons' pursuit of their own goals, plans and hopes, and thus to interfere with their autonomy.

However, it does not follow from this argument that violence, or indeed the interference with people's autonomy, is always wrong. There may be cases in which the settlement of a conflict by rational discussion is not possible or has been tried and failed, and where the readiness to use violence at the expense of someone's autonomy may be justified in defence of others. If one believes that the resort to violence can never be justified, one has to be not merely a pacifist so far as war is concerned but also an opponent of any use of constraint by police or prison officers. In effect, one has to be an anarchist, and trust that there will be less violence without the state than with it. That is another illustration of how difficult it is to hold absolutist positions, without at least the willingness to make careful and sometimes complex distinctions.

But it clearly should be possible for schools to promote the readiness and capacity to resolve conflicts non-violently without taking a stand for an ethic of complete non-violence in all circumstances. At the same time, though, and as one instance of a general concern for independence of thought, a school needs to develop in its pupils the ability to think for themselves about whether violence is ever justified, and if so, when. That question explicitly, in general terms or in one of its particular applications, may very well come up for discussion in schools. I want to say more here, then, about the reasons that may lead people to use violence in a cause which they see as moral. This will also give me the opportunity to bring out an important distinction between different kinds of value, or between consequentialist and other kinds of argument about the value of life and of the environment.

ABORTION, ANIMALS AND THE ENVIRONMENT

At the end of the discussion of compromise in Chapter 5 I referred to the kind of informal negotiation over values which can go on between groups within a plural society. It seems a desirable principle for a democratic and plural society, not just that questions of values should be publicly discussed and negotiated but that no one's voice should be excluded from the discussion for reasons of gender, ethnic identification, religion, disabilities, or whatever.[2] But some of the most deeply held values encountered in our society concern parties (or objects) who (or which) cannot themselves join the discussion, such as unborn babies, people in a persistent vegetative state, non-human animals, and trees and other aspects of the natural environment. (But in the case of human beings born and living with disabilities, however severe, we should, if at all possible, acknowledge that they do have a voice in the discussion, and that the onus is on the rest of us to find ways of listening to it.) The discussion which goes on about, for instance, the morality of abortion or the treatment of animals does not, and cannot in any literal sense, include the very parties which the discussion is about. The conflict which can arise over these issues is not conflict with the unborn child or (by and large, in a culture in which the animals dangerous to human beings are mostly in captivity) conflict with the animals. This fact itself may increase the danger of conflict breaking out, and make compromise more difficult between those persons who hold different moral positions on the issues.

Some of the issues over which people get into conflict are issues concerning the interests or the rights of those same people. When people are in conflict over an issue like this (it might be, say, over the distribution of resources to which both sides have a claim), each side at least has the possibility of shifting ground, of making some concession on their own behalf; this opens the possibility of a compromise, which would in the most direct sense be a compromise between the parties concerned. The situation cannot be quite the same when people see themselves as defending those who cannot defend themselves – as when they are speaking for unborn children or non-human animals. The unborn or animals cannot enter into a compromise; and their self-appointed defenders may feel that they cannot compromise with the interests or rights of those who cannot compromise for themselves. (I am here, in effect, expanding on a point I made in Chapter 4, that many things perceived as moral wrongs are perceived as actions having victims.) Perhaps this partly explains why, in recent years in Western societies, people have been willing to turn to violence over issues of this sort. Violence on behalf of those who cannot defend themselves may, because it is clearly not selfish, seem more defensible than violence on one's own behalf, even if those fighting on their own behalf can claim (as many oppressed minorities fighting against their oppressors have been able to claim) that they have justice on their side.

The case of defending the natural environment raises some issues which are similar, and others which are quite different. There are, roughly speaking, two quite different kinds of concern about the environment. First, people can be concerned about the effects which action on the environment has for other people and animals. This category subdivides as well:

1. Someone may be concerned about the effects of a policy on themselves, as when people protest about a motorway going too close to their own house. Their protest may be justified, but it will not be a case of protest in defence of others.
2. Someone may protest about the effects of a policy on other people, and these may be people who are not able to speak for themselves, because they don't yet exist. Into this class comes protest about the storing of nuclear waste, on the grounds that it could create a dangerous environment for future generations.
3. Someone may protest about the effects of a policy on animals – again, it could be the effects on existing animals, or the effects on future animals who might, for instance, have a harder struggle to survive because of changes in their habitat.

All the subdivisions in this first category have something important in common – the reason for objecting to a course of action is its effect on living things, whether persons or animals, which have feelings and interests, can suffer pain, and can therefore be harmed or benefited. In terms I introduced in Chapter 5, the reasons are consequentialist, because they are concerned about consequences, and utilitarian, in that they assess the consequences in terms of the interest or welfare of sentient beings. In the sense in which I'm using the terms here, only *sentient* beings can have interests or welfare, because only beings that can experience something can suffer pain and misery (and sometimes feel pleasure and happiness too). So there can be reasons for objecting, say, to fox-hunting (sheer pain and probably terror too) which can't apply to cutting down trees (assuming that people's education in biology leaves them with no good reason for attributing feelings to plants).

It doesn't follow from this that we can morally do what we like to trees, but it is true that many reasons for not doing what we like to trees will be of a different kind. This is the second kind of concern about the environment: many people treat the destruction of the natural environment as bad in itself, quite apart from any consequences for people or animals. And that is because they see the natural environment as being of value in its own right, not just good for sentient beings which may benefit from it or depend on it. (You can probably see for yourself that reasons of both kinds may be put forward for saving rainforests.)

So, again, there are two different kinds of reason for objecting to the destruction of a beautiful landscape. One is that people in future will no longer be able to enjoy its beauty. That is another consequentialist and utilitarian reason: it says that what is bad about the destruction is that the landscape will no longer be there to bring pleasure or aesthetic satisfaction to people. The other kind of reason is that the landscape, or the beauty of the landscape, has value in itself, quite apart from whether anyone gets satisfaction from seeing it.

There is in fact a similar difference in people's thinking about the value of life, a difference which lies behind some of the controversy, and some of the misunderstanding, over issues such as abortion and euthanasia. To some people, the only value of a human life can be its value *to people*, including its value to the person whose life it is. When human beings are in a persistent (and irreversible) vegetative state their life has no meaning and no value *to them*; if they have no consciousness, no experience, then it makes no difference *to them* whether they live or die. Similarly for a foetus, at least in the early months of pregnancy, it makes no difference *to it at that time* whether it lives or dies. Of course, a normal foetus in normal circumstances will develop into a person consciously living his or her life. But if we say that it would be wrong to abort a foetus because, if it lives, it will probably have a good life, that is thinking in terms of consequences, and by the same reasoning we could say that it will be right to abort if we believe that it would probably have an unhappy life. Neither argument is saying that there is anything wrong *in itself* in destroying a foetus, independently of the consequences.

Nevertheless, many people do think that. They think that the life of any human organism, including a foetus or an adult in an irreversible state of unconsciousness, is valuable *in itself*; and for some people, human life is the most valuable thing there can be. These ideas are at least part of what is meant by the sanctity of life. We can find further meaning in that idea, and perhaps have a further reason for holding it, if we believe that any human life is the creation of God. But the notion of sanctity of life is not confined to theists.[3]

It's not my purpose here to decide issues about environmental ethics or the morality of abortion. The distinction between consequentialist reasons and the valuing of things or states of affairs in their own right is, however, an important one, and neglecting it could well lead to confusion in discussion or to some points of view not being taken seriously. The same distinction comes up in relation to animals as well. When people campaign to save the whale, it is usually the survival of a species as a whole that they are concerned about. Now a species doesn't have feelings, though the individual members of it may. People may also, of course, be concerned about the suffering of the whales that get harpooned or the young that are abandoned. But if there were a painless way of killing all the rest of a species at once, there would be no objection to that on grounds of the suffering of the individual animals; but there certainly would still be objections, because the existence of the species itself is valued.

In what follows, and returning to the issues about whether violence can be justified in defence of beings which can't defend themselves, I'll take the treatment of animals as an extended example, but confine the discussion to reasons that come down to the welfare of animals.[4] I shall not speak here of 'animal rights', because the language of 'rights', is another piece of terminology which can cause a lot of trouble.[5] For the issues to be considered here to arise, it is not necessary to claim that animals have rights, only that the fact that a form of treatment causes an animal suffering is a moral reason – not necessarily a conclusive one, but still one that counts – for not treating it in that way.

ANIMALS, VIOLENCE AND EDUCATION

One observation about the dispute over the use of animals is that, on one side at least, it is likely to be motivated almost exclusively by moral considerations (in the sense in which moral considerations are contrasted with considerations of self-interest). What else would motivate people to campaign for the ending of cruelty to animals? Even when this concern has led a minority to use violent methods, it is still plausible to see their motivation as predominantly moral, though others judge it as misguided. On the other side, which in this context includes a mixture of overlapping categories – among them animal experimenters, suppliers of fur, and arguably all those who simply eat meat without qualms – there may be a large measure of self-interest.[6] But there are also moral views on that side, from those who simply see nothing wrong with using animals in whatever way suits human purposes, to those who argue, at least in the case of medical research, that the use of animals is amply justified from a moral point of view.

The issue is also one of relevance to relations between cultural groups within a multifaith society. The Islamic method of slaughtering animals has at times been a point of controversy, especially where the issue is whether state schools should supply *halal* meat. And it has not been unknown for animal rights issues to be taken up by right-wing groups to fuel racism. As with the Salman Rushdie affair, or the role of women in traditional South Asian cultures, the issue is one on which liberal supporters of toleration and equality of respect within a multicultural society are likely to be uneasy. Liberals are also, of course, likely to be unhappy about violence without necessarily wanting to condemn it outright.

Are there, then, any reasons that should persuade campaigners for animal welfare that they ought not to resort to violence, even though they feel that the odds are stacked against the innocent victims they are fighting for? I want to suggest that the reasons for compromise and negotiation still have weight on questions of animal welfare, even though the intended beneficiaries of the campaigns cannot be party to the compromise. Precisely because animals cannot speak for themselves, how they are treated depends on the moral values of the society. It will only be through changes in the prevailing moral climate of a society, that significant changes will come about in the treatment of animals. It is, then, appropriate and inevitable that it is between the conflicting moral positions of persons that the issue is played out.

To try to arrive at a moral consensus or a basis for legislation which will improve animal welfare *is* to work for the defence of animals, even if someone has to compromise and retreat, at least temporarily, from the stronger position to achieve this. This doesn't mean, of course, that there aren't moves which an individual can make, and may feel morally obliged to make, independently of whether they are having any effect in shifting a broader social consensus. The person concerned could become a vegetarian, avoid cosmetics tested on animals, or join peaceful demonstrations, independently of how many other people are doing the same. But it does not follow that the same person would be justified in resorting to violence against other persons who disagree or who take no action. The reason for the difference is that in the case of individual non-violent action there are no strong countervailing moral values which have to be set against the defence of animals. In deciding, say, to be a vegetarian, a person may not be compromising at all between different moral values; if the person is making some sort of compromise, it is likely to be that in giving some weight to reasons such as their own convenience or lack of social embarrassment – which they might acknowledge are not really moral reasons – the person is not going as far as they might, perhaps only becoming vegetarian rather than vegan.

As an aside, and bearing on the general theme of compromise between values, it is worth adding that compromise of this sort does not seem to me to merit the opprobrium sometimes (disingenuously?) laid on it. The argument often heard, that if one does not eschew absolutely all human benefit from animals one has no business taking any steps in that direction at all, collapses in the face of the argument that if it is the welfare of victims one is concerned with (rather than one's own moral virtue), something can be a great deal better than nothing. The same would go for the argument that one has no ground for criticizing or trying to avoid violence unless one is prepared to be a complete pacifist; for the victims or potential victims of violence, less violence is almost always better than more.

Think, then, of a person who is inclined towards using violence against other persons, or endangering other persons, in order to promote the cause of animal welfare, but who does stop to think about it. At the risk of gender stereotyping, I'll assume that he is more likely to be male, and I'll call him the activist. What values should weigh with him, in addition to those which led him to protest in the first place? The values which weigh in favour of campaigning for animals are still the same; but on the other side now there is the value of non-violence against persons. For anyone to whom this value is an absolute, the case against violent action will be clear-cut. However, it may be that an absolutist stance towards non-violence is itself too uncompromising. In the present case I would have to say that the activist may rightly recognize that there are values having some weight on each side of this decision, both for and against the use of violence, so that whatever he decides will involve some compromise.

But if the activist is not appealing on either side of the case to an absolute principle, then it will be quite appropriate that he should give a lot of weight to the question of whether his proposed methods are likely to promote the cause. He must therefore look to the broader social context, asking seriously whether violent methods are actually more likely than any others to achieve what he wants to see, given that they are also certain to antagonize many of those whom he would presumably wish to win over. Since there is no good reason to think that the non-violent methods available to campaigners for animals have been exhausted, any case for violence in my view becomes very weak at this point.

How far might the available non-violent methods themselves be educational? Any such methods will, of course, be indirect from the point of view of animal welfare, since they will be seeking to influence human behaviour towards animals in the longer term, rather than seeking directly to change the conditions of animals living here and now. From a consequentialist point of view, however, indirect and long-term methods will sometimes do more good in the end than direct ones. So campaigners for animal welfare may well decide to take their message into schools. But then the question arises whether this is something that can legitimately be done in schools. I suggested in Chapter 2 that the kinds of aims people may try to pursue through schools are indeed many and varied. But in practice the pursuit of any aim needs some degree of consensus, and there would not, in the face of many competing aims, be widespread consensus on pursuing the cause of animal welfare through schooling (if there were, in some society, a much greater consensus on the ethical aspects of the treatment of animals, it might seem natural in that society that the values concerned would be among those 'transmitted' by schools). Even though schools are not bound to be committed to educational aims and values (where 'educational' has connotations of independence of thought and rationality), the pursuit of such aims is likely to be less controversial. We can ask, then, whether the promotion of animal welfare – or other controversial ends – in schools is compatible with educational values.

Someone might think it is not compatible, because the goal to which campaigners for animal welfare are committed is not itself education. But it does not follow from the fact that people are pursuing aims which can be characterized quite independently of education that they cannot use genuinely educational means towards those ends. Indeed, if they believe that evidence and reasoned argument supports their case, and that other people, if unbiased, will see this, then they have every reason to use educational means. Campaigners for animal welfare might make a judicious calculation that people who are encouraged, in an openly educational way, to think about the treatment of animals are on the whole likely to end up taking a position opposed to a great deal of current treatment of animals. They cannot be confident that this will be so in any individual case: an individual who thinks critically about these issues may end up siding with the carnivores and vivisectionists (just as some philosophers do, though other philosophers have been in the forefront of arguments for changing our treatment of animals).[7] But all that the campaigners need, to be able to use educational means in pursuit of their cause, is a degree of confidence that, by and large, educated and informed people who think about animal welfare are likely to decide in favour of the animals.

So people who have a liberal concern for educational values need to ask campaigning groups – and for that matter, sponsors – not whether they have a disinterested concern for education for its own sake but whether the methods they would use or support are themselves educational. A distinction will still have to be made between education and propaganda. Campaigners might, for instance, be coming close to pure propaganda if they did little more than present harrowing pictures of laboratory experiments. If instead they engage pupils in discussion, accept criticism, are willing to admit that there might be difficulties and grey areas in their case, what they are doing would be educational. While the distinction may be far from clear-cut in practice, I would suggest that it is important for the campaigners themselves to try to keep it in mind (if only for the reason that if they do not, they will have little cause for complaint against campaigners on the other side waging their own propaganda drive).

What of the issue of *halal* meat, which might be seen as something of a test case for the values of toleration and compromise in a multifaith society? If a new religion were to spring up which advocated child sacrifice, there would be very few outsiders who would advocate toleration of its practices; most people would feel the issue so clear-cut that it would hardly constitute a test case. Why should liberal defenders of animal welfare (I shall call them 'liberals' for short) be any more tolerant of Islamic methods of slaughtering animals? Of course, liberals may believe, or at least hope, that liberal education and reasoned argument will have their own influence in the end; but what should be their attitude in the meantime? Let me give at least some indication of how that question might be answered. Any compulsory restriction of Islamic slaughter would be perceived as an imposition of the values of the 'host culture' on a minority. In fact this would be a correct perception, even though the majority culture would be making this imposition on moral grounds, not just to demonstrate its dominance. The question is whether, in this case, the imposition would be justified (as it surely would in the case of child sacrifice).

Liberals would first have to be quite sure (and not just assume in advance) that the Islamic method of slaughter is less humane than ordinary non-Islamic practices. Then they must be aware of the broader context in which this particular question arises; if liberals could be sure that there are few other ways in which Muslims (in common with members of other minorities) are discriminated against, they might have more ground for confidence in justifying this particular imposition. If such an imposition were made, perhaps there ought to be some concessions in other areas made in compensation. Then, liberals have to consider whether the value of protecting animals outweighs the value of respecting other cultures, especially those aspects of other cultures which are tied up with religion, and whether alternative approaches are available. If Muslims in Britain have to compromise in some ways with the dominant culture (while not ruling out in principle that they might convert all British people to Islam, but never expecting it in practice), then liberals may also have to make compromises (while not ruling out in principle that they might convert all Muslims to vegetarianism).

The liberals have also to look at their own record and practices. The liberal tradition has by no means been free of the attitude that animals, with the rest of the natural environment, are so much material to be exploited for human purposes, including the satisfaction of scientific curiosity (perhaps it had better be said, though it should not be necessary, that to suggest that not all scientific use of animals is justified is by no means to take a general 'anti-science' stance). And in a predominantly secular society there are many millions who, with no justification from any particular moral or religious tradition, and with no sense that *they* have to defend a culture which is seriously under threat, continue to eat animals whose slaughter, whether 'humane' or not, is actually unnecessary, since eating meat at all is unnecessary.

If we could suppose some sort of society-wide negotiation over the treatment of animals, in which all points of view could be put forward, criticized and, if possible, defended, I suspect that the outcome would lead to an improvement in the overall lot of animals, and that the greater part of the improvement would come about through changes in the practices of the dominant, more-or-less secular, more-or-less liberal community.

NOTES

1. At the broader and more academic level, there is the potential influence that might be exercised through the study of conflict and peace. Taking both levels together, there is, in other words, peace education. Peace education is treated at some length in the unpublished report referred to in the Acknowledgements. See also Hicks (1988).
2. This principle will also be relevant in our discussion of the secular society in Chapter 10, and in relation to equal opportunities in Chapter 13.
3. Of the many published discussions of the ethics of abortion and of

euthanasia, one of the most enlightening I know, on both topics, and one of the most accessible to the layperson, is Dworkin (1993).

4. I have an interest, and a position, to declare. It seems to me that there are very strong moral objections against many of the ways in which animals are treated, and that anyone, once they recognize these reasons, ought at least to be a vegetarian. The most straightforward argument goes roughly like this (without the qualifications which would be needed to make it watertight):

   1. We ought to avoid causing suffering if we can do so at little cost to ourselves (this sounds like a pretty minimal moral principle which it would be difficult to reject if we recognize any moral principles at all).
   2. By not eating meat we can avoid (some of) the suffering which is inevitably caused by the large-scale rearing and killing of animals for food, and we can do this at little cost to ourselves, since we don't need to eat meat.
   3. Therefore we ought not to eat meat.

   See Singer (1976) for an argument of this kind, with evidence to back it up; and Clark (1977) for a very different argument, which would, however, agree with many of its conclusions.

5. See Chapter 7, note 7.
6. Baier (1985), p. 142. The final section of this chapter may well appear more partisan than most parts of the book, for reasons given in note 4 above. But I do not mean to imply that there is no argument on the other side, or that teachers in their treatment of controversial issues should be any less balanced in their handling of this issue than of others.
7. For an example of a philosopher critical of those mentioned in note 4, see Frey (1980). See also Carruthers (1992).

CHAPTER 10

Secular society, secular schools and citizenship

Should all schools in a modern society be secular? Or, if that would be too illiberal, should all state-supported schools be secular? The issue arises because many parents within religious traditions feel, not just that they want their children to be taught their faith (which might be possible outside school) but that the values which secular schools are promoting are incompatible with the values of their religion.

We may think of this as an issue arising within a plural society; and that is a correct perception, but *not* because a plural society is a multicultural and multifaith one, still less because it is a multiracial one.[1] For a plural society is not necessarily any of those things. Too often the idea of diversity of belief and values is associated with the existence in a society of many different cultural, religious and ethnic groups. It is worth remembering that England was a plural society in terms of religious belief long before the large-scale immigration of (mainly) the third quarter of the twentieth century. And even if it had not been plural in that respect, if there had been only one denomination of one religion in England, there could still have been both belief and unbelief, and the differences in interpretation and significance of moral values which that difference may bring in its train. There are multiple influences on people's values in the late twentieth century, quite apart from large-scale movements of people; if we could identify one country as monocultural, we could still find within its culture sufficient plurality to fuel controversy on issues such as abortion, the treatment of animals, sexual orientation – and our present issue of secular or non-secular schooling. This issue is one on which different views will cut across different religious outlooks, but the most significant difference seems to be between those for whom any adequate upbringing and education independently of a religious framework is inconceivable, and those for whom that is not so.

The issue is a worrying one for people with liberal values, particularly if their own outlook is thoroughly secular (there are, of course, many people with religious beliefs who are also liberals). Liberals who have a secular outlook are well aware that there are many people who differ in this respect and, of course, being liberals, they would defend the right of people in a liberal society to hold and practise their religious beliefs; thus, it would seem very illiberal to suggest that parents should not be allowed to bring up their children within their faith.[2] But liberals are also often uneasy about the existence of schools which are committed to a non-secular education, or uneasy at least about state support for such schools. They may be worried that such schools will inculcate in pupils views which the pupils would not have chosen for themselves or which tend to be divisive in society; or, more positively, they may be impressed by the thought that the citizens of a plural society are more likely to live harmoniously together if they have shared a common schooling together.

There are many ways in which the discussion of these issues could be approached: through ideas of parental rights in the upbringing of children; the dangers of indoctrination; the meaning of autonomy, and so on. But these issues have been much discussed in an educational context. Less often examined is the idea of a secular school: what does it mean to say that a school is secular, and is it desirable that schools should be?

SECULAR SOCIETY

In some respects a school, while artificially hived off from the rest of society, may still be a microcosm of the wider society. That is one reason for looking first at what makes a society secular. Another reason is that, if the surrounding society is secular (and here again it will be Britain which I have in mind as my main example), then schools, whether they are themselves secular or not, have to prepare pupils for membership in a secular society.

Whether a society is secular is a matter of degree: we can speak of the secularization of society as a gradual process, and there will hardly be an identifiable point at which a society becomes secular. Secularization involves various changes, but I take it, as does Hirst,[3] that they are linked by 'a decay in the use of religious concepts and beliefs'. But the degree to which a society is secular is not simply a quantitative matter of the extent to which religious concepts are used; it has to do also with the relative position within the society of religious and non-religious thinking.

A lot of thinking goes on in our society which is thoroughly secular, in the sense that it involves no distinctively religious concepts or beliefs at all. This will be true, for instance, of the thinking of the great majority of mathematicians, scientists and engineers within their professional role, and it is true also of a lot of the everyday thinking of a great many people within our society. In this sense much of the thinking of most people is secular, whether or not those persons have religious beliefs. Take a scientist who is a Christian. The person's thinking as a scientist, in doing experiments, writing up the results, reading articles, and (if they are an academic) teaching, may be qualitatively indistinguishable from that of an atheist. However, there will be other contexts – during church services, for instance – in which their thinking is radically different from the atheist's.

There may, then, be a degree of compartmentalization in their life. An important feature of a secular society is that it allows and facilitates this kind of compartmentalization.

It's also the case, though, that the boundaries between compartments are not the same for everyone. There are many contexts which for some people call for the use of religious concepts, while for others they do not. Among them could be (in contemporary Britain) celebrating Christmas; discussing some public moral issue; consoling a dying relative; and everyday domestic conversation. Perhaps, then, the degree of secularization of a society is a matter not only of the extent to which it allows compartmentalization but also of the relative prominence of three sorts of context: those (such as doing maths or shopping at the supermarket) which would be generally acknowledged to call for no religious thinking; those, such as religious worship, which would be widely acknowledged, even by those who do not themselves participate, to call for such thinking; and those which are viewed in different ways by different people.

A related difference is the extent to which different contexts are seen as part of the public life of the society or part of the private life of individuals. The proportion of the population using religious concepts and holding religious beliefs is in itself a far less important measure of secularization than the extent to which such beliefs enter into the public life of the society. At a theoretical extreme, we could imagine a society in which everyone holds religious beliefs, but that all of these are kept private – they do not enter into interpersonal discourse at all. (We would have to imagine some way in which people acquire these beliefs: perhaps parents initiate children into them, but apart from that it is simply not done to mention them.) In such a society there could be, quantitatively, a good deal of religious thinking; but in an important sense the society would be secular, because social discourse would be secular.

Clearly that example rests on a most impoverished view of religion. Sharing the faith with others, coming together to celebrate and to worship, is a central element of at least most religions. But there is a sense in which, even given this, religion can still be a private matter. It is possible to know someone, at work say, without ever knowing whether that person has a religious faith or not: for if he or she does, it may be practised, not strictly in private, but with like-minded others on the appropriate days. One aspect of secularization, then, is that the expression of religious beliefs, both in speech and in ritual, can become marginalized from the mainstream life of the society; and, related to this, that there are many people, whose own thought is predominantly secular, who assume, until there is evidence to the contrary, that the same goes for everyone they encounter.

There are many of us – this again being part of what it is for the society to be secular – who are comfortable with this situation. In academic discussions about education it is often the case either that religious claims do not enter in, or that if they do, they are treated hypothetically only. It may happen in some educational institutions that after a whole series of seminars in which religious claims have been simply bracketed out, apparently by common consent, it becomes apparent that there is at least one member of the group whose own thinking is by no means thoroughly secular, for whom his or her belief is relevant to the issues discussed, but who has – in effect, albeit unintentionally – not been allowed to bring this belief into the discussion. Of course, this would not be true of all institutions: there may be others in which the reverse is nearer the truth, and it is significant that in a secular society institutions of both kinds can exist.

So far I've said nothing about law and politics in a secular society, but clearly there must be some connection. A country like Britain which has a constitutional, though largely symbolic, link between Church and state can still be a secular society, but this could hardly be the case if it had a law enforcing church attendance. Arguments about Sunday opening of shops and pubs are partly (but only partly) about whether the law is out of step with the secularization of society; as are arguments about compulsory religious assemblies in schools. But a more central issue is whether law and national policy are made on secular *grounds* or not. In a democratic society government policy and law will be responsive to popular thinking (though not necessarily determined by it, as the debate over capital punishment shows), and so, if people's thinking about the issues of the day proceeds largely in non-religious terms, we should expect that the reasons which influence government thinking and politicians' voting will be largely non-religious too. But at the same time there are substantial numbers of people whose thinking is religiously based, especially on moral questions, as we've seen. For them it would be natural that questions of the law on capital punishment, abortion, the age of consent for homosexual intercourse, and many other issues should be influenced or even based on considerations which are central to their religious beliefs.

Should such considerations come into law and policy, or not? There is one school of thought which argues that in a liberal and democratic society, the only considerations which should influence public policy and law are those which any citizen could recognize the force of – and that means non-religious considerations. For instance, in debate about whether all businesses should be free to trade on Sundays, the argument that this could exploit workers is a secular argument. Any citizen, whether Christian, of another faith or of no faith, can understand this argument and debate whether it is a strong one. While Christians may also have quite different reasons for opposing Sunday trading, for the school of thought I'm considering, it should only be the arguments accessible to all that come into the public debate.

In a democracy, though, it is hard to see why any kind of argument should be ruled out in advance, or indeed how that could be done in practice. If an argument is irrelevant or inconsistent or unpersuasive, ideally, this will emerge in the course of the debate (provided also that no point of view is held immune from criticism). I say 'ideally', because there is an ideal at work here: the ideal of free and open discussion in which all voices can be listened to.[4] In practice there are many constraints on open discussion. For instance, people whose own thinking is entirely secular may, without repressing non-secular points of view, not really listen to them. This may be simply a matter of settled habits of thought or a lack of understanding, but it can also show a lack of respect and equal opportunity for the people whose voices don't get heard on matters which may be of central importance to them. And in some cases, where links are made in the listener's mind between a person's religion and their ethnicity, it can amount to a form of racism.

So long as religious positions on issues with moral import can be heard in public debate, it is at least possible that their entry will modify the outcome. The outcome in any case is not, in the real world, likely to be a consensus on one view of what's right or good. What may, however, be achievable is an agreement for practical purposes about what ought to be done.[5] And in the process of reaching that pragmatic agreement, there is no reason to assume that religious points of view must entirely give way to secular ones. The entry of non-secular views into the debate does at least make it more possible for secular thinkers to appreciate the force which the other points of view have for those who adhere to them. Secular thinkers may pragmatically be willing to make some accommodation to the views of religious thinkers; movement need not be all one way (as it would be, by default, if religious viewpoints were to remain only in the private realm). The suggestion is not that secular and religious thinkers will meet halfway on the truth of their respective world-views, but that they may indeed meet halfway on practical proposals. Though there is not space here to spell out the possibilities – on issues such as abortion law, or the limitations of freedom of speech and the legal recognition of blasphemy – there is, as I suggested in discussing compromise, nothing incoherent in the idea of a practical accommodation.

THE SECULAR SCHOOL

What makes a school secular? I would suggest first that it's not primarily a matter of what kind of religious education, if any, goes on in the school. It's conceivable that the timetable of two schools could be identical except that in one a couple of periods a week are devoted to comparative religion and in another the same time is set aside for the teaching of the Bible or the Qur'an. But it's unlikely, in practice, that there would be only this difference. If we assume that the first school is secular and the second not, we would expect to find other differences; and I suggest that it is in these differences, rather than in the content and approach to particular bits of the curriculum, that we need to look for the distinction between the secular and the non-secular. I suggest, in fact, that we can apply the ideas about thinking and about policy-making which came up in discussing what makes a society secular.

We can look, then, at the extent to which the life of the school is compartmentalized into areas in which any use of religious concepts and beliefs, perhaps even any mention of them, would be thought inappropriate, and areas in which it will be expected. We may find that in many schools religious concepts will be mentioned in religious education lessons, and sometimes (but by no means always, whatever English law says) in assemblies, but otherwise hardly at all. Whereas in some other schools religious language and assumptions might be constantly coming up in the life of the school, at least outside of lessons, in the interaction between pupils and pupils, staff and staff, staff and pupils, staff and parents. So how far a school is secular will have a lot to do with the extent to which religious concepts are used right across the life of the school, and the attitudes adopted regarding their use. As with the wider society, the proportion of pupils or staff holding religious beliefs is not in itself the major factor, for such beliefs may to a greater or lesser extent be treated as private and so, for practical purposes, marginalized.

The issues about the debate and policy-making in the wider society can also be raised in relation to decision-making in the school. We could imagine all the gradations, from important decisions made exclusively by a headteacher who claims to be following divine guidance, to conventions by which any distinctively religious claims are disqualified from entering into decision-making contexts (so that, for instance, Jewish objections to plans for a special event on a Saturday would have to be wrapped up in some ostensibly secular language). The fact that the wider society is largely secular does not directly determine the secularity of schools: both secular and non-secular schools are possible within the same society. So we must move to asking how far and in what ways it is desirable that schools should be secular.

One argument is the often-heard appeal to the importance of tolerance and hence of understanding: that a democratic polity requires tolerance of different points of view and lifestyles, and that tolerance in turn can rest most firmly on understanding. This is certainly an argument for teaching everyone about the variety of religions within their own society. The argument needs to be made not only as a matter of interpersonal morality but as a matter also of the preparation of citizens to take part in democratic decision-making; and I've suggested that this decision-making should not be confined to purely secular considerations.

Now for the majority of students in state schools, if they have had the equivalent of political education or citizenship education, understanding the terms of *secular* discussion ought not to be a problem. Almost the whole of their education will have been conducted in secular terms. And this will apply to them whether they are themselves from a religious or a non-religious background. Those who may well, as things stand, have problems are children from non-religious backgrounds. They may have little understanding of the contributions to discussion which are expressed in religious terms, or make religious assumptions; and their very lack of understanding will create an imbalance between secular and non-secular points of view, so that in effect the secular will be privileged and the religious marginalized. A certain sort of religious education, then, can be defended as a part of citizenship education, even apart from any other grounds.

There are implications here for the whole ethos and organization of the school. If pupils are being prepared for citizenship in a society which, while secular, is also plural and multifaith, then in any context of school life, and not only in religious education, any input that has a religious dimension will need to be taken seriously rather than dismissed as irrelevant. What this means in practice may differ, depending on whether the context is one of decision-making; or of a curricular area where the relevance of religious belief would be quite widely recognized, such as personal and social education; or in subjects such as science, where the making of a point on religious grounds will be at least unconventional.[6] But in general it is likely to be true that to argue with a view, if it can be done with understanding and without being patronizing, is to accord greater respect to the holder of the view than simply ignoring it. The point, though, will be not only to accord respect to religious beliefs but also to prepare pupils whose own thinking may be thoroughly secular for their participation in public life which will not be *exclusively* secular.

SHOULD THERE BE SEPARATE RELIGIOUS SCHOOLS?

So far I have been talking about ways in which a school which is not dedicated to one faith, or to any, should nevertheless not be *completely* secular. But how do these considerations bear on the debate about whether separate schools, dedicated to one faith, should be supported and funded by the state within a predominantly secular society?

If any school can do the job of preparing people to participate as citizens in a democratic, plural and not exclusively secular society, it will to that extent be fulfilling an important role. And in this respect, religious schools may be *better* placed to carry out such a preparation than the average secular school. For no school which covers a broad spectrum of forms of enquiry including, for instance, science and mathematics (as required by the National Curriculum for England and Wales) can fail to expose its pupils to a good deal of secular thinking. So far as the secular/non-secular dimension is concerned, it is only the secular school which can expose its pupils to one sort of thinking only; and the possibility of this should be seen as a risk rather than a merit of such schools. On the other hand, there is the question of the actual range of substantive positions that are taken within the dimensions of religious and non-religious thinking. While a non-secular school cannot avoid exposing its pupils to some secular thinking, it can, whether deliberately or inadvertently, avoid exposing them to, for instance, some of the particular moral views, say on homosexuality or abortion, that are taken by many people within a secular viewpoint; or if it does not avoid exposure to those views, it may restrict genuine understanding of them. In this direction lies the major danger of the non-secular school within a plural society.

There remains force, too, in the familiar arguments for the benefits of educating children from different backgrounds together, if they are to become citizens who can share in the public life of a society into which all citizens can enter on equal terms, regardless of differences in religion, race, gender, class and other categorizations. In arguing that separate religious schools may after all be justified, McLaughlin[7] has stressed that his arguments support a particular kind of religious school, namely one which is promoting autonomy through upbringing in a particular religion. I would want to say that if we argue for keeping schools as far as possible mixed – in religion or lack of it, as well as in other respects – on grounds of tolerance and cohesion between different groups, our arguments will support only a particular kind of mixed school, namely one which prepares all its pupils to participate in a democratic society in which public discussion is not exclusively secular. And it may be that the more the ordinary state school succeeds in taking non-secular thinking seriously, the less reluctance there may be on the part of many members of religious minorities to send their children there.

If a secular school were taken to be a school which excluded any mention of religious conceptions and beliefs both from its curriculum and from its extracurricular affairs, I would argue that *no* state schools ought to be secular. Of course, the notion of a secular school is not usually understood in such an exclusive sense. Most proponents of secular schools intend rather that state schools should not be committed to bringing up children within one faith, nor to maintaining the superiority of a religious over a non-religious world-view. That most schools in our society should be secular in this thinner sense, while the society as a whole is predominantly secular, I would agree, though I would also maintain that such schools should not privilege the secular to the extent of marginalizing in advance the voice of the non-secular within public debate. And as for whether all schools supported by the state should be secular even in this thinner sense, that seems to me to be an open question still which needs further debate (debate which could not, without prejudicing its outcome, exclude religious considerations from the start). There are many practical issues to be looked at, but so far as the principle goes, if proponents of religious schools could show that such schools can achieve all that secular schools achieve and more, the onus would be on those who argue that there should only be secular schools within the state system to show why.

NOTES

1. For the sake of clarity it is worth trying to maintain the distinction between 'plural' and 'pluralist'. Whether a society is plural – meaning that it contains a diversity of values, beliefs, etc. – is a matter of fact. We can if we wish pick out the kind of diversity we are talking about by referring to plurality of values, of cultures, and so on. But to say that a society is pluralist is to say that it has adopted – perhaps in practice, perhaps officially, or perhaps only as an ideal – the position that different values, cultures, etc. have a right to exist alongside one another without discrimination. It's possible, then, for a society to be plural without being pluralist – South Africa under apartheid was a clear case – and while most societies in the modern world are to some degree plural, perhaps none has fully realized pluralism.
2. This issue has been debated from time to time in the *Journal of Philosophy of Education*. See, for instance, the contributions made in one 1984 issue by Bridges, Hobson and McLaughlin.
3. Hirst (1974), p. 1.
4. In theoretical discourse this notion has been articulated by the German social theorist Jurgen Habermas (mentioned in Chapter 7) in his idea of an ideal speech situation. See Haydon (1994c) for more on Habermas in the context of the present argument, and McCarthy (1978, pp. 291–310) for an accessible treatment of the idea of the ideal speech situation.

5. See Chapter 5; and Benhabib (1992), p. 9.
6. Suppose that in a science lesson a pupil raised an objection from a religious perspective to an orthodox scientific account of evolution or cosmology. Many teachers might want to dismiss this as 'not science'; but there is not, on the face of it, anything *logically* inappropriate about mentioning God as part of an account of the origins of the universe or of life. Even if, for practical reasons, such accounts are not followed up and discussed within a lesson labelled 'science', a school ought surely to see that they can be followed up somewhere within the curriculum.
7. McLaughlin (1987, 1992).

Further reading

Since this chapter was written, a very useful volume of articles has appeared in a special issue of the *Journal of Philosophy of Education*. See Tamir (ed.) (1995).

Part V
Values education

Only after seeing something of the variety and complexity of values can we come back to thinking about moral education or values education as specific aims within education.

Between these two terms 'moral education' and 'values education' there is not, so far as I can see, any firm or systematic distinction made in actual usage. The tendency is for 'values education' to be the broader notion, recognizing the ways in which values are involved in issues, say, of personal lifestyle, religion, citizenship, politics and the environment. There will, then, be large areas of overlap between values education and such curricular concerns as citizenship education, health education and environmental education (or the currently less favoured but also overlapping concerns of 'political education' and 'peace education'). These related areas will contain bodies of knowledge and skills which are specific to each of them, but it is still, arguably, moral values which lie at their heart. The term 'values education' is not normally used, to my knowledge, to include, for instance, education concerning aesthetic values (which is why I can discuss values education here though I have barely touched on aesthetic values in this book). I have the impression that in recent years the term has been more widely used in Scotland than in England. This may change with the formation, in 1995, of the Values Education Council covering the UK: see Appendix.

The term 'moral education' perhaps tends to be used in a narrower sense, and certainly it *could* be used to denote initiation into 'morality', in the sense in which I treated it in Part III; in which case the overlap between moral education and areas such as citizenship education or environmental education will be smaller. But nothing in Part V turns on a distinction between moral education and values education, and most of what I say will be equally relevant under either label.

To some people, the term 'values education' might seem equivalent to 'the transmission of values'; the burden of Part V is that it is not equivalent at all. In Chapter 11 I look at how we can interpret the idea of the transmission of values, and at some of the problems with it; and, recalling the questions about aims in education which I raised at the end of Part I, I ask what it is in the area of values which schools are best placed to do. I suggest that the major and distinctive contribution of schools will be in promoting knowledge and understanding and discussion. In Chapter 12 I go on to argue that where values are concerned this contribution is a large one, and very much needed.

CHAPTER 11

Values education: teachers as transmitters?

THE TRANSMISSION OF VALUES

I have often encountered – perhaps most frequently in texts by sociologists about education – the idea that education transmits values. This is not so much a particular approach to values education – since it says nothing specific about what processes might be involved – as merely a way of talking about it, and one which turns out to be rather unhelpful. The notion of transmission suggests a rather passive picture of what is going on. A transmitter, after all, does not originate anything itself: it has information fed into it in some form, which it then sends out, coded electromagnetically, to be picked up by a receiver – which is equally passive. But even if that is not the analogy intended by the use of the word, I still think we shall find that the notion of transmission is not a very helpful one for teachers who are considering their role as regards values.

One reason why teachers might not like the idea of transmitting values is that, with its associations of passivity on the part of the receiver, it could suggest indoctrination. I want to look only briefly at this idea before moving on, because I do not think that this constitutes the main reason why the idea of transmission of values is unsatisfactory. I don't want to take up space here examining the notion of indoctrination (I've already mentioned it in Chapter 2, and it has been pretty thoroughly analysed in other places).[1] Suffice it to say, by 'indoctrination', I mean roughly any process which leaves people accepting certain ideas which they are incapable of subjecting to any rational assessment. I'll assume that you think – as I do – that indoctrinating people is a bad thing to do. (If you do think this, it will be because of certain values you accept, perhaps values to do with rationality and independence of mind. Not everyone, however, will necessarily acknowledge these values; and some people may well think that indoctrination of *certain* ideas is both good and necessary.) I want to suggest that the likelihood of teachers indoctrinating pupils in moral ideas is actually quite low. That is because the extent of teachers' influence over their pupils is limited, and will have to compete with other influences in the children's lives.[2] Of course, teachers who want to promote their pupils' ability to think for themselves and to think rationally will avoid indoctrination more effectively by encouraging their pupils to ask questions and to consider whatever values the teacher may be hoping to get across.

In general, transmitting some content through teaching does not necessarily constitute indoctrination. Talk of transmission need imply only that the teacher is initially in possession of some content (X) that the pupil does not have, and that it is his or her aim to ensure that the pupil possesses it too. If X is, say, the fact that an atomic bomb was dropped on Hiroshima in 1945, then if you tell this to someone who didn't already know it, and the person takes it in, you have transmitted that bit of information. There need be no indoctrination here. And while the content will often be more complex than a statement of fact, the teacher may also have other aims besides wanting the pupils to be able to reproduce a statement of fact: they may reckon that they have not succeeded unless the pupils are not only able to repeat the information but are able to demonstrate understanding of it, back it up with evidence, argue a case for it, and so on. Clearly in many parts of the school curriculum transmission is an important and legitimate part of what a teacher does.

So if there is a problem about transmission *of values*, it must be something about values themselves that creates the problem. In fact I can see several possible problems: that what would count as transmitting a value, if the idea makes sense at all, will be quite a complex matter; that the precise content to be transmitted may be indeterminate; and that the values of a society can't be transmitted as a whole if there are inconsistent values within the society. Think of a teacher who holds certain beliefs about the importance of, say, telling the truth, and who always tells the truth herself, or, if she doesn't, tends to feel guilty about not doing so. (Remember that in Chapter 3 we spoke of people's values in terms of what they care about or what they consider is important.) I suppose we can say, for a start, that she will have transmitted this value to her pupils if they develop the same, or similar, attitude towards truth-telling.[3] Again, there need be no indoctrination here: it may well be the case afterwards that while the students have adopted truthfulness as a value of their own, they are at the same time able to defend it with reasons and think about its limits; such an outcome would hardly amount to indoctrination.

It is still not easy to see, in relation to values, what process would count as transmission. In the case of items of knowledge which we can identify as 'facts', we do know that, whatever its shortcomings, telling people something *can* work as one method of transmission. It *is* possible to tell people that the chemical formula of water is H_2O, or that the Battle of Hastings was fought in 1066, and simply telling *can* constitute successful transmission. When it comes to values, the picture is much less clear. Even apart from moral values, can a love of science or enthusiasm for history be transmitted? Possibly, but certainly not just by telling people that science and history are good (interesting, exciting, important) things. It's likely that the teacher's example will have more to do with what is transmitted than the fact of simple telling. But once we begin to talk about the teacher's example we are speaking of something which will by no means have the same, or any, predictable effect on each pupil; and for that reason, too, the terminology of 'transmission' begins to look misplaced.

But perhaps a more important difference between the transmission of information and the transmission of values is that the first can be much more clear-cut. In the case of a chemical formula, for instance, you may know *exactly* what it is you're trying to get across.[4] Values are certainly not like that. The fact that values are very often not at all clear-cut (they have a degree of indeterminacy) is one reason why the transmission model is a difficult one to work with.

Another reason why the transmission model of moral education is at least inadequate is the fact of the diversity of values in a plural society. This does not mean that transmission of values as such, is impossible; what it does show, however, is that there cannot be a common moral education which consists of the transmission of *all* the moral values held in the society (unless we are content to recognize that some of these values are inconsistent with each other). So if there is to be transmission of values it will necessarily involve some selection, but the idea of transmission itself tells us nothing about how this selection is to be made.

The suggestion is sometimes made that people get together to discover which values they do in fact share, and that whatever values are agreed on are the ones that should be transmitted. The idea is that a common core of values would then emerge. This might well be so, providing the values in question are characterized rather broadly, and in terms of their content, rather than any agreed sense of their underlying interpretation or the grounds for them. Notions, for instance, such as 'respect for persons' and 'toleration of religious differences' would probably figure on an agreed list. As Chapter 1 suggested, the cross-cultural agreement would not necessarily survive the effort to flesh out the ideas in concrete detail.

But suppose that in fact one generation within society had sufficient agreement, not merely on a set of labels but on a determinate interpretation of certain values. At that point another problem arises: I would argue that to transmit certain values as fixed – when in fact these values may be open to a variety of interpretations – is to be undemocratic.[5] Democracy is partly to do with people working out for themselves and among themselves the values that they are to live by. For one generation to try to fix the values that the next generation will live by has at least some analogies with a colonial power trying to determine the values which the indigenous inhabitants of another part of the world will follow (perhaps we could label this 'generational imperialism').

To sum up, if the content of a set of values is too indeterminate, there will be nothing definite to transmit; on the other hand, if the content is tightened up too much, then this would put constraints on the next generation which can hardly be justified within the terms of the values which a democratic society surely has to subscribe to. So there appear to be a number of problems with the notion of values education as the transmission of values. But it may be that these problems only appear because in the discussion about transmission we have so far no details of what the transmission of values actually consists of: the whole way of talking is just too abstract. Recently, many writers on moral education have been attracted by an idea which might provide one concrete interpretation of the transmission of values: that idea is the development of virtues.

DEVELOPING VIRTUES

In Chapter 3 I pointed out that many of the values which appear in lists, such as the one outlined by John Patten, contain the kind of personal qualities which we can speak of as virtues. In Chapter 5 I referred to two different conceptions of virtues, distinguished primarily by the interpretation of the motivation underlying the possession of a certain value. In one conception (which we could associate more with the Kantian understanding of morality), having a particular virtue is largely a matter of being able to control one's amoral or immoral inclinations by deliberately following a moral imperative. In the other conception (associated particularly with Aristotle), having a certain virtue involves exhibiting appropriate inclinations in the first place (or rather, as second nature, because they have to be acquired), so that one does not have to make a deliberate moral effort to overcome counter-inclinations.[6] It is a more Aristotelian conception that recent writers have had in mind when they have spoken of the development of virtues as an educational aim. And it may be that the major reason for favouring this approach has been the sense that moral education, whatever else it does, should make a difference to how people behave, to how they live, even to what kind of people they are. Talk of virtue does capture this sense of the difference that moral education should make.

A virtue (following roughly Aristotle's conception) is a complex state involving desire, feelings and even perception. The compassionate person, for instance, is likely to notice that someone is suffering (though this could also be true of the sadistic person); but the compassionate person will be distressed by other people's suffering, will want to help, and will in fact do so. I shall not go into more detail here about the nature of virtues, because other treatments of the topic, within an educational context, are readily available.[7] The idea of virtues is an important one, and the concept of the development of virtues might provide a way of interpreting what it is to transmit a value. But before we conclude that the development of virtues gives us a complete and satisfactory notion of moral education, I want (swimming somewhat against the tide of recent discussions, at least among philosophers of education) to raise some awkward questions about the idea.

First, despite recent attention given to the development of virtues as an educational aim, it is by no means clear how the aim is to be pursued or how far it can be achieved. Too often there are only rather vague references to the ethos of the school, the example set by teachers, and the good character of teachers themselves. And these may be relatively small influences among all the influences in a child's life. Since, in speaking of the development of virtues, we are speaking of a person developing a certain 'mind-set' which is more than just cognitive, which also involves some of the person's deepest desires and feelings, we have to wonder how much teachers can do. In fact, the Aristotelian account of the development of virtues has it that initially the main consideration is that people are brought up in the right habits of action. Here again, the influence of a school is limited compared with all the rest of a child's familial and social environment.

Still, it may be possible that schools can do something significant towards the development of virtues (I refer you to other writers on this).[8] In any case, even a modest influence in a desirable direction may be a lot better than none, and we would hardly embark on any approach to moral education if we had to have a guarantee that the results aimed at in every case would be achieved.

My second query is rather different. By its nature, the possession of a virtue runs fairly deep within a person. The advocates of virtues, as against more rationalistic approaches to moral education, see this as a great advantage: too much theorizing about moral education, they tell us, has been concerned only with how people think about the question, 'what should I do?'; the real issue is what *kind* of person should I be? But it is possible to turn this point round and wonder what authority schools (that is, state-run publicly financed schools) have to try to turn children into certain kinds of people.[9] I shall say nothing here about the influences of families or indeed of religious or other communities; perhaps it is appropriate for parents to do all they can to bring up their children as the kind of people they (the parents) want them to be (or perhaps not).[10] I am only raising the question of whether *schools* should be doing this.

That brings us to the question of selection, which is really the same question already raised about the transmission model. The deeper our influence over people is, the more important it surely is to see that this influence is desirable. Modern virtue theorists like to refer to Aristotle on the general nature of virtues, but they usually do not follow him all the way on his particular list of the virtues which are to be cultivated. And we do indeed find that different qualities are treated as virtues within different traditions.[11] For Aristotle, for instance, a kind of pride was a major virtue, and humility was not on his list at all; for Jesus, about three centuries later and less than a thousand miles away, it was almost the reverse. Within a modern plural society there will be at least some difference in the virtues which are favoured within various cultures, either because there will be quite different items on different people's lists (think of the references already made in Chapter 1 to obedience and in Chapter 4 to honour), or different weight put on the same virtue, or different interpretations given to what is nominally the same virtue.

But suppose the problem of selection can be solved. It is also true that however successfully the development of virtues could be carried out, it would not do the whole of the task which a modern society can call on education to perform where values are concerned. For society's concern is not only with the motivation and behaviour of individuals; a modern society also faces moral issues which somehow have to be tackled on behalf of the society as a whole (issues like freedom of speech, censorship, abortion, genetic engineering, capital punishment and many others). However virtuous people may be, they still have to think about questions of this sort, and the possession of virtues does not guarantee an agreed answer (or any answer) to them.

If the development of virtues is to be a viable model even for some aspects of moral education in a heterogeneous society, I think the virtues in question have to be interpreted in quite a conceptually rich way. Let me illustrate what I mean, by first contrasting two different virtues without making any assumptions about the cultural setting in which they might be exercised. Compassion, or at least something very like it, is a quality which we could imagine being displayed by a creature without language or self-consciousness: for all we can tell, the feelings and the motivation to help which are involved in human compassion may be essentially the same as those experienced by one ape or elephant towards another. But contrast this with justice (the quality of the just person, which was one of Aristotle's major virtues, one of the cardinal virtues of the Western tradition, and for Hume, as we saw in Chapter 7, an artificial rather than natural virtue). To be a just person one has to be aware of the claims of others, to be able to make comparisons between different claims and sometimes, at least, to be able to adjudicate between them. One can't be just without having and using a conception of justice; so there is no way that someone could be unthinkingly just.

Now I would suggest that the more complex the cultural setting, the less possible or desirable it is for any virtue to be possessed in an unreflective way. Compassion, for instance, might be unproblematically a virtue within an isolated group, where its exercise would always be a matter of immediate face-to-face response to another. But in the modern world we can be aware of the sufferings of people thousands of miles from us. Are we then moved in the same way? The unreflectively compassionate person would probably not be moved by the mere knowledge that other people were suffering, but might be moved by the sight of their suffering, perhaps on television. But is it reasonable to be moved only by suffering directly seen; is it even just (for compassion and justice do not always coincide)? In the modern world, the compassionate person needs to *think* to know what to do.

A number of writers who have discussed the role of public education in a liberal society have emphasized the importance of certain virtues, including qualities such as a sense of justice, tolerance, respect for the opinions of others, and so on.[12] Now these are clearly qualities which require a good deal of thought for their exercise. The interesting upshot is that when we are thinking about the moral education that schools should be responsible for in a modern, plural society, it may be that seeking to develop virtues in people, and enabling and encouraging them to think in certain ways about moral issues, may not be so far apart after all. While it may be that an approach which emphasizes the cognitive side has too little influence on motivation (one of the complaints which advocates of the virtues approach have made against more rationalistic approaches), it's also the case that concentrating on the idea of virtues doesn't allow us to neglect the cognitive side.

SHOULD LIBERAL TEACHERS TRANSMIT LIBERAL VALUES?

As I've said more than once, many people in teaching, or those thinking of going into teaching, are liberal-minded people: they are for diversity, independence of thought, tolerance and individual freedom of choice; and they are against imposing their values on others. They hold liberal values, and they may hope that their pupils will come to hold equally liberal values. So they would have some reason to try to transmit these liberal values; but should they be worried that in doing this they might be illegitimately imposing their own values? And if they are worried about that, does this mean that they should scrupulously try to be neutral on matters of values? The question is more than a quibble. The difficulties, for instance, which we looked at in Chapter 10 about secular and non-secular schools arise partly because there are many parents who feel that secular state schools are going too far in transmitting distinctively liberal values, which are not the values they, the parents, wish their children to hold.

Let me pose the question again, then, and follow it up with particular reference to the notion of tolerance which we have already looked at in Chapter 5. Because they hold values such as autonomy of thought and freedom of choice, liberal teachers will not wish to inculcate specific points of view. At the same time, because they are liberals, they must hope to see the continuation of the kind of society in which it is possible for their values to be realized. And that will be a society which at the very least does not discourage people from thinking for themselves – in other words, it must be a tolerant society. But it can't be a tolerant society if enough of its individual members are not themselves, and to a sufficient degree, tolerant of diversity. So liberal teachers will want to promote the value of tolerance, and in doing so, of course, they can't be neutral between tolerance and intolerance (just as they will not be neutral between rational argument and resort to force, and so on).[13]

But at this point they may be challenged. If they think (as many teachers do) that they ought not to promote allegiance to specific moral positions or particular lifestyles – that it is not for them to try to turn their pupils into vegetarians or believers in women's right to choose an abortion – then should they also think that they ought *not* to try to turn pupils into people who will value tolerance? For that is just as much a moral value, and one not shared by everyone; indeed, it may be more far-reaching in its effects on people's lives just because it is more general. If education seems to be preaching toleration as one of the highest of virtues in its own right, it could well be charged with being, politically and religiously, sectarian.

What liberal educators must try to do in response to such a challenge is to distinguish between encouraging people to show tolerance towards diversity and persuading people that tolerance is an ideal in itself; it may be quite enough that people appreciate the more pragmatic reasons for tolerance. More generally, liberal educators need to distinguish between the liberal values that are necessary to maintaining a plural society (not because a plural society is necessarily the ideal, but because it is inescapably the kind of society we have) and the values that are themselves marks of a specifically liberal response to moral issues.

We can distinguish between a liberal society and a liberal morality. A liberal society leaves people free to hold different moral outlooks and different sets of beliefs, and within some limits to practise different ways of life (the limits are set mainly by the need to constrain people from causing harm to others). If there is a sense, then, in which being a liberal is itself to have a particular moral outlook, this liberal moral outlook will be only one among those which a liberal society must accommodate. And we clearly can recognize this narrower sense in which certain people have liberal moral views. The liberal characteristically puts a lot of weight on individuals' freedom to choose their own lifestyle and to come to their own beliefs: a lot of weight, that is, on individual autonomy. The liberal sets store by the kind of life in which individuals choose their own goals and their own way towards them ('I did it my way' could be their anthem).[14] This underlying value characteristically leads to the liberal holding certain moral and political positions rather than others: so that we know roughly what is meant by a 'liberal' position on the morality of, say, abortion or homosexuality. And in education the liberal puts relatively more weight on the importance of enabling people to think for themselves and choose their own way of life, rather than on inculcating a particular set of values or a traditional lifestyle. In this sense, then, to be a liberal is itself to have a certain sort of moral outlook.

But we have to say now that being a liberal, in this sense, is not a qualification for being a member of a liberal society. Indeed, a society which tried to exclude anyone who was not a liberal in their moral outlook would be a markedly *illiberal* society. It would have no place for those who believe that abortion is murder or that homosexuality is sin, or for those who see education simply as a matter of transmitting a traditional way of thinking and of living. A liberal society, then, has to be one in which liberals and non-liberals can live together. It will hardly be surprising if this requirement generates problems, if not paradoxes. The liberal educator has to promote the values that are necessary to living in a liberal society, but stop short of promoting a liberal set of moral beliefs or lifestyle.[15]

Take, for instance, the value of compromise which we looked at in Chapter 5. Should schools try to foster a willingness to compromise? Yes, but they should not foster it as an absolute value (it would perhaps be rather paradoxical in any case to hold the uncompromising position that refusal to compromise is always wrong). I suggest that in a plural society it is not the business of publicly supported schools to inculcate (even if such inculcation were possible, which I doubt) either the idea that certain specific values must never be compromised, or the idea that compromise must always be the best outcome. But what schools can try to do is to help pupils realize the extent to which individual decisions often involve a compromise between values; to ensure that pupils are aware of the different attitudes towards compromise that exist within the society, depending on the significance that people's values have for them; and to encourage pupils to explore these different attitudes, enabling them to make the distinctions (such as the distinction, vital in a liberal society, between law and morality) which allow them to avoid an oversimple view of the ways in which compromise is or is not acceptable.

Consider, too, the value we looked at in Chapter 9 – namely, the readiness to resolve conflict without resort to violence. I said then that there are ways in which schools can and should promote the skills of non-violent conflict resolution and the willingness to use them. But I did not say that schools should, even if they could, commit themselves to promoting the belief that violence must never be used. For that itself would be a highly controversial position, implying that the absence of violence is such an overriding value that it must never be jeopardized for the sake of any other value. (Peace and the avoidance of violence are high on my own scale of values, but not absolutes.) Not only would it be controversial, it would also mean adopting a non-neutral position between different cultural and religious traditions: an ethic of non-violence is far stronger in some traditions, such as Buddhism, than in others. For the liberal thinker, the chances are that even a commitment to peace will not be held in an uncompromising way.

It is partly because values such as tolerance and willingness to compromise are not ones that can be applied unthinkingly (because people need to be able to decide when they should not compromise, and what they should not be tolerant of) that liberal educators are committed to enabling people to think for themselves. But if educators leave people with the conviction that the only worthwhile kind of life is one in which the individual establishes all his or her goals and standards, taking nothing as given, and works out a particular route to achieving them – in effect, treating life almost as something to be rationally designed – then the educators have gone too far towards promoting a rather partisan view of how to live one's life. Just where the line is to be drawn between the responsibilities for their pupils' values which educators in a plural society must take on, and the partisan commitments which they must hold back from promoting, will probably be a matter for continual debate and modification in such a society.

WHAT CAN SCHOOLS DO BEST?

At the end of Chapter 2 I proposed a number of questions which we can ask about any aims proposed for education. It is time to raise these questions again, with reference particularly now to the idea of the transmission of values, and with a view to possible alternative approaches to values education.

1. *Is the aim for something of positive value?*

We can't say that the transmission of values from one generation to the next will always be of positive value, since it must make a difference which values are being transmitted. If a whole society was imbued with racist values, it might be much better if these were not transmitted, so that the society could, if this were possible, make something like a fresh start.[16] But if we assume that the values in question are positive in themselves, then the transmission of them will itself be of value.

2. *Is it something that can feasibly be realized or at least promoted through formal education?*

After the arguments of this chapter, we have to be cautious here. No doubt *to some degree* values can be transmitted, and are transmitted, through formal education. It does not follow, however, that the values actually transmitted through schooling are the ones which we might wish to see transmitted. De-schoolers and other critics of schools have long argued that values such as docility and reliance on the authority of others are actually transmitted in schools, regardless of the stated intentions of the staff. If moral education had to be a matter of a school deciding which values it wished to transmit and deliberately setting about this, then, given all the other influences on young persons within society, I do not think we could be very confident of success.

3. *Is what is aimed at something that can be seen as both good for individuals and good for society, or at least as not merely benefiting the few at the expense of many others, or the majority at severe cost to a few?*

Here again it will make a lot of difference which values are being transmitted. The example of racist values given earlier shows that certain values can hold sway in a society at the expense of part of the population. There may be other quite different examples: some critics of educational selection, for instance, would argue that the values associated with academic excellence benefit a minority at the expense of a majority. I suppose it ought to be, above all, the values associated with the ideas of justice and equality that should be to the benefit of all, at the expense of none. But we can hardly aim merely at the transmission of these values, because to a considerable degree our society (any modern, plural society) still has to work out what the demands of justice and equality entail in practice.

4. *Are the aims of broad relevance rather than narrowly specific?*

Here we should remember the problem mentioned in the first section of this chapter – trying to transmit too narrow a version of certain values. Can we say, in detail, what values will be of most importance in, say, the mid twenty-first century? The aim of broader relevance would be to enable each generation to think through, and if necessary to rethink, its values.

5. *Is what is aimed at something which would not come about anyway, independently of formal education? Is it something that teachers and schools are particularly well placed to promote?*

We need to be cautious here, too. If, suddenly, we didn't have schools for, say, a decade, would society fall apart morally? Would nothing of the moral values of society be transmitted? I doubt it. At least, I think we can say that if we were to set out with a clean slate to devise the best method we could of transmitting values from one generation to another, schools as we know them would probably not be what we would come up with.

6. *Is it something which it is important for everyone to have (achieve, be exposed to, etc.)?*

Here the answer seems to be both yes and no. Maybe, as I've suggested from time to time, there are some values, a sort of common core of morality, which ought to be passed on to everyone. But the more richly we fill in our picture of morality the less possible it will be to say, in a plural society, that everyone should have it (and consequently, less reason for using the resources offered by compulsory schooling to achieve it). It's more arguable that what everyone needs in a plural society is the ability to think and talk about values.

7. *Is it something which has a justified place in education because of its sheer importance, regardless of the other considerations above?*

I suggested in Chapter 2 that conceivably we might judge one aim (for example, avoiding global disaster) so important that we could justifiably put all our efforts into attempting to achieve it. Some people may think that the dangers of moral breakdown of society are such that all possible efforts, in schooling and in any other way, should be devoted to avoiding such breakdown. We ought not to be too easily persuaded by that. Suppose we did try to gear schooling above all to transmitting the values which would prevent moral breakdown (assuming, of course, that we knew which values these were and how to transmit them). We would still need to ask ourselves: how great a danger is there of moral breakdown anyway?[17] If the danger is great, is it likely that anything schools can do will prevent it? If the danger is not great, aren't there many other things that schools would be better employed in doing? As we saw in Chapter 2, there are many other values which education is concerned with; if the transmission of moral values were at the expense of science and arts, humanities and technology, would we be better off in the end?

8. *Can the aim be pursued without violating any moral values in the process?*

I have suggested that the transmission of values, so far as we can make sense of the idea at all, need not involve indoctrination. Yet so long as we think in terms of the transmission of values, there is the danger that our concentration will be on whether a certain end result is achieved – whether the values we want to transmit are in fact received at the other end. And if that is what we are concentrating on, the danger of using morally illegitimate means will never be far behind.

Given all these questions, to my mind the value of even thinking in terms of 'the transmission of values' is, at best, unproven. There is a strong case, I suggest, for concentrating on what schools can do best, which is I suspect, even given the important recognition of ethos and example, to teach things of a broadly cognitive nature. Schools may or may not lead to people being different kinds of people, but we should have some confidence at least that they *can*, and sometimes do, lead people to a knowledge and understanding which, without formal schooling, they probably would not have developed. If this is a valid point about schools in general, then its validity is not altered when it is values we have in mind.

My argument is that in a plural society there is a greater need than ever for people, not just to have values but to have an understanding of values – their own and other people's. Given compulsory schooling, we do in fact have the possibility of promoting a greater breadth and depth of understanding about values than any society perhaps so far has achieved (for in a more homogeneous society, in which most values are widely shared, these values are also likely to go relatively unquestioned, and so there will be less depth of reflection).[18] So, with respect to those who would like to see teachers primarily as transmitters of values or developers of virtues, I shall turn back, in the next chapter, to the idea that moral education is, after all, a matter above all of *education*, involving knowledge and understanding and rational thought.[19]

NOTES

1. The classic collection is Snook (ed.) (1972).
2. There may be greater room for worry about indoctrination in the particular context of religious or moral instruction within a school which is itself dedicated to one religion; see Chapter 10.
3. To be accurate, we must also be supposing, if we are to speak of the teacher transmitting this value, that the pupils would not have come to hold this value were it not for the influence of this teacher; and that is something which it would be very difficult in practice to be sure of.
4. I am not suggesting that this is a model for good education; far from it. Student teachers should not be misled by the idea that before a lesson they must have a plan which makes explicit in detail everything that pupils will learn as a result of the lesson; some learning may be quite serendipitous.
5. See Haydon (1993b).
6. Aristotle's own account is his work known as the *Nicomachean Ethics* (often published in translation just as *Ethics*), Books 2 and 3. There have to be more complex accounts of some of the virtues we have names for, such as temperance and courage, because we could not speak of temperance or courage at all if the person concerned didn't in some sense recognize a temptation or a danger respectively. The temperate person, for instance, does refrain from indulging certain inclinations; but, roughly, in one account he or she takes some positive pleasure in that self-restraint, whereas in the other there might be only reluctance.
7. Carr (1991); Tobin (1986, 1989); White (1996). virtues?
8. Ibid.
9. See Bereiter (1974).
10. See the debate referred to in note 2 to Chapter 10
11. See MacIntyre (1981), chapter 16 on the variety of lists of virtues in different cultures and historical periods.
12. See, for example, Gutmann (1989); Galston (1989); Macedo (1990); White (1996).
13. While I am putting parts of my argument here in terms of neutrality, I shall not take the space to explore that notion specifically. Ways in which teachers could be neutral on questions of values, and whether they should be, are discussed in Norman (1975); Warnock (1975); Bailey (1975).
14. The title of the popular song was used in the title of an article on

autonomy and education by Richard Norman (1994). On autonomy, see also Chapter 12, note 1.

15. The American political philosopher John Rawls, who has been influential in liberal thinking since the early 1970s, has in his recent work clearly distinguished between 'political liberalism' and liberalism as a comprehensive doctrine. See Rawls (1993).

16. This is not entirely unrealistic; it could be argued, for instance, in the case of Germany or Japan after the Second World War that these societies did to some degree make a fresh start, in that some of the values which had found expression in militarism were not transmitted to rising generations. More morally ambivalent examples are provided by some of the ex-communist societies of Eastern Europe, where there may be both positive and negative facets to the fact that the values of communism are being transmitted much less than they were before the 1990s.

17. What would count as the moral breakdown of a society? One famous example, but concerning a very different society, is what happened to the Ik, as reported in Turnbull (1973). The Ik were an East African tribe displaced from their traditional hunting grounds into barren mountainous territory. Turnbull, an anthropologist, describes the virtual disappearance of altruistic behaviour and customary norms in the face of the sheer precariousness of survival.

18. See Haydon (1995a).

19. For the assumptions about 'education' I am making here, see Chapter 2, notes 3 and 4 and the text to those notes.

CHAPTER 12

Values education: teachers as educators

THINKING FOR ONESELF?

Historically, the idea that moral education is about the transmission of a given set of values is perhaps the most venerable. But having concentrated on that notion in Chapter 11, I want now to look at approaches to moral education which assign a large role to rational thought and understanding.

At first sight the approach which lies at the opposite end of the spectrum from the simple transmission model is the hands-off 'policy', which in effect eschews any involvement of formal education in people's values at all. (Some liberal-minded people are attracted to this idea, but it is difficult to sustain it for long.) It can at least be said for this approach that in avoiding the transmission of anything in particular it avoids deliberate indoctrination and recognizes the diversity of values in modern society; but it only does that in a passive way. It does not help people to cope with the diversity. In so far as its message is one of 'do your own thing', it may even by increasing diversity at an individual level, make harmony within a society less likely. It does nothing, for instance, to prevent people from growing up with racist values and the disposition to pursue them through violence. (You may object at this point that the hands-off aproach to individual values ought to be coupled with the promotion of tolerance; but then that is no longer a hands-off approach, since it is trying to influence people's values.)

I said that 'at first sight' it appears to lie at the opposite end to the transmission model, because so far as the end result for the individual goes the hands-off approach may not be so far from the transmission of particular values after all. Individuals may grow up with one conviction or another, or with no clear values at all, but it doesn't follow, simply because formal education has taken a hands-off approach, that people have made up their own mind about their values. Their values will certainly have been influenced in one way or another by factors in their upbringing and environment, factors which they may themselves be unaware of. They will, perhaps unwittingly, have received some values even if no one has set out to transmit them. Their values will not necessarily be ones they have freely endorsed, any more than if someone had set out deliberately to indoctrinate them.

The hands-off approach has not, I suspect, recommended itself to many teachers who have tried to think through their position on values; for even if teachers want to avoid inculcating substantive moral values, they do mostly believe that certain things are important, including people's ability to think for themselves – in other words, independence of thought or, in one of its aspects, autonomy.[1] In effect I have just argued that autonomy is not well served by the hands-off approach. It requires, rather, that people make their decisions with some measure of understanding and with a degree of rationality, rather than with no reason or with irrelevant reasons. Many educators, then, have favoured an approach which encourages people to *think* about their values. Indeed to many teachers such an approach may seem obviously right, but it still needs defending, partly because the value of people thinking for themselves is not a value which everyone in contemporary societies accepts; there are groups which do not have a tradition of encouraging reflection about their own values. We will have to see whether encouraging people to reflect on their values can be justified to people who do not share *this* value; and we may in the end have to rely on arguments of a pragmatic kind concerning the great importance of reflection about values within a plural democratic society.

There is room, too, for different conceptions of what is involved in encouraging people to reflect on their values. One that was popularized in the USA is 'Values Clarification', by which individuals are encouraged to identify and reflect on their own values.[2] This certainly goes beyond the hands-off approach, for rather than saying that values are not the business of education, it entails a great deal of explicit attention to values. And I think we can agree that it is important for individuals to be clear about their own values – both the content of their values and the significance the values have for them – because without this kind of self-understanding, discussion between people holding different values is unlikely to be much more than a stand-off between conflicting positions, and the participants may be at cross-purposes without realizing it. Notice that there is no implication here that the significance and explanation of an individual's values are to be found solely within that individual. If one's central values have been assimilated from a particular tradition, then to understand that (and to have some depth of understanding of one's own tradition) will itself be an important part of understanding one's own values.

Here I am concerned, not with the specific programmes promoted under 'Values Clarification' but with the idea that the *only* educational approach to values might be enabling and encouraging individuals to be clear about their own values. This approach in itself will be trying *not* to influence pupils towards holding certain values rather than others. It does not entail, for instance, that the teacher should express disapproval of expressions of racist values; proponents of values clarification may well expect that such values would not survive sincere reflection. But if that turns out to be true, it will not be because clarification in itself will undermine racist values (there is not necessarily anything unclear about such values) but because

rification may bring with it a degree of critique of the individual's
ilues.

One kind of critique which a person may undertake of their own values
(which formal education is well placed to help people with) involves seeing
whether they all fit together consistently. A useful notion here is that of
'reflective equilibrium', which was named, though probably not invented,
by the American political philosopher John Rawls.[3] People's values can
come with any degree of abstractness or concreteness, generality or speci-
ficity: anything, say, from the most abstract appeals to respect for persons
and toleration, to the most concrete opinions that a particular sort of
behaviour is or is not acceptable. Rawls suggests that I can seek coherence
between all my values by moving backward and forward between the
particular and the general; where I become aware of inconsistency I can
modify my ideas at either level, changing what seems more peripheral and
holding more tightly to what appears central or fixed, until I arrive (if I
ever do) at a point where all my views hold together: this is the point of
reflective equilibrium.

If individuals have been able to reflect on and if necessary modify their
moral views, to the point where they are fully aware of them and can say
that they all hang together, then that will certainly constitute a pretty thorough clarification.[4] And it could enable them in the process to overcome
any inner conflict which they may have been feeling as a result of discrep-
ancies between their values. Of course, it may be that few people, moral
philosophers included, ever achieve a completely self-consistent set of
moral values; nevertheless, the idea of reflective equilibrium (not necessarily under that name) may be one that education can promote, and in so
doing make a contribution towards enabling people to have a greater self-
understanding about their own values.

THINKING THE RIGHT WAY?

This kind of awareness of his or her own values and moral beliefs is likely
to lead the individual at some point to ask 'which views are right?' and
'how can I know?' (The question is particularly likely to arise where inconsistencies emerge. But even if someone has been brought up with a
completely consistent set of values, rooted perhaps in a unified tradition of
thought, it is still in principle possible to ask whether there is any way of
showing that the beliefs involved are right.) Here we come back to the
question I considered in Chapter 3 and again in Chapter 7: whether there is
some right way of thinking about moral questions which can lead to determinate answers. There have been a number of approaches to moral
education, proposed especially by philosophers, which, while retaining the
idea that individuals should think for themselves about values and come to
their own conclusions, have also stressed that the individuals' thinking
should be rational, and have gone on to say something more specific about
what distinguishes rational from irrational thinking in the field of values.
One of these philosophers of education in Britain, John Wilson, suggests
that there are ways of thinking morally – amounting, in Wilson's own word,
to a methodology – which can be taught quite specifically in timetabled

lessons.[5] In the USA, Kohlberg (see Chapter 6), basing his approach to moral education on his research into developmental stages, argued that while it was not possible directly to teach people to think in the way that his own arguments most favoured, it was possible to provide people with 'cognitive stimulation' to their own thinking so that they would progress more rapidly and further along the developmental ladder that culminates in Stage Six (see page 70).

These rationalistic approaches claim to eschew the inculcation of partisan positions on substantive issues; instead, they leave individuals free to come to their own conclusions. But at the same time, they want to see individuals reasoning in a way which, if followed through consistently, will lead to certain results rather than others. Hare, in many articles, has supported substantive positions on the basis of the form of critical moral thinking which he advocates, and he has also claimed that, with sufficient time and information, different people applying the same method would converge on the same answers.[6] Kohlberg seems to have taken a similar view: he argued, for instance, that a Stage Six reasoner would be opposed to capital punishment.[7]

What this illustrates (regardless of your own views on capital punishment) is that if a form of moral education, rather than telling people what to believe on particular issues, encourages or teaches them to think about moral issues in a certain way, this does not mean it is neutral with regard to the particular issues. That should not by itself be a reason for rejecting this kind of approach to moral education. After all, *if* there is such a thing as a right, or uniquely rational, way of thinking about moral issues, we would surely want people to be able to think in that way, and we should also expect that it will lead people to certain answers rather than others. In line with my argument in the last section of Chapter 7, we can say that if people did the thinking appropriately, the answers they came to *would* be the right answers (or they would be so far as it is humanly possible to attain them); but we would be enabling people to come to the answers for themselves rather than imposing them.[8]

But before we look at what such a way of thinking might involve, I need to say more in reply to critics who would reject the idea that there can be such a thing at all. To use yet again the distinction between content and significance of moral positions, it's clear that the approaches advocated by writers such as Kohlberg, Wilson and Hare are not neutral on the *significance* of moral ideas – on conceptions of what moral values are and how they work. In the first place, of course, to encourage people to believe that they must think about moral questions so as to come to their own decisions is already to go against a view which would expect people to defer to the authority of their elders or of their scriptures.[9] But among those who would not dispute that people need to be able to do their own thinking, there are still, as we saw in Chapter 6, different conceptions of the kind of thinking this should involve. In particular, we looked there at the distinction between the 'justice orientation' and the 'care orientation'. It's worth repeating that the proponents of the care orientation are not advocating an unthinking or unreflective approach to life, but that they do have a different understanding of the kind of thinking that is appropriate. The justice orientation requires the ability to take what its advocates might call an objective, rational view of a situation, which involves in turn a degree of detachment from the situation; whereas the care orientation does not attempt any detachment, but responds to the perceived situation from within, in all its concrete reality. This distinction was developed initially in response to the recognition that the kind of thinking which Kohlberg argued for revolved around the conception of justice; and on the face of it, any approach which suggests there is a rational methodology (Wilson's phrase) that can be followed in dealing with moral questions is aligning itself with the justice orientation rather than the care orientation.

So it may seem that we have to settle the question of whether to promote the care orientation or the justice orientation before we can usefully say any more about 'methodologies' of moral thinking. In Chapter 7 I argued, in effect, that the justice orientation should not be dispensed with; now I want to argue that quite apart from any arguments for the intrinsic superiority of one way of thinking or the other, there are good reasons for education to concern itself with both. One reason is the kind of liberal concern we have encountered before, that we should always be careful about promoting a specific way of thinking when there are defensible alternatives. A concern with the educational development of the individual as one who is capable of thinking autonomously would suggest that having both orientations available is a more desirable goal. And since the evidence suggests that most people are capable, with prompting, of taking either perspective, the educational task here may be not so much one of actually teaching anything as of giving practice in contexts in which people can themselves reflect on the ways in which they are thinking.[10]

Another reason why it may be desirable for any individual to be able to work within either orientation is that the different orientations may be appropriate to different sorts of situation. The majority of academic discussion has focused on interpersonal moral problems rather than on broader political issues. Feminist writings have persuasively argued that in many ways the personal is political: political issues of power and domination, writ large at the level of the whole society, penetrate even to the closest personal relationships. What is less clear is how far the political on the large scale can be approached through ways of thinking which seem to have their home in the personal. While an individual woman faced with the decision to have an abortion or not may well find, as we saw in Chapter 6, that thinking in terms of rights seems quite alien and inappropriate, whereas thinking in terms of relationships and responsibilities comes naturally, the political question – which is still at the same time a moral question – of what the law on abortion should be for a whole society seems to call much more naturally for the abstractions of rights and justice.

It might be said in response that what seems to be naturally called for is a function of the way the large-scale political realm has been shaped, predominantly by men, through the justice and rights orientation. And it is as clear in the large-scale realm as it was in the fable of the moles and the porcupine that appeals to justice are not necessarily a road to harmony. The similarities between the analogy of the moles and the porcupine and that of two ethnic or religious groups fighting for control over a single territory, each claiming to have justice on its side, may be more than merely accidental. On the other hand, there are many situations in which appeals in the language of the care orientation, especially if addressed by outside observers to those actually involved, and if not at least coupled with a recognition of evident injustice, would sound very hollow and perhaps patronizing.[11] In any case, if there are to be laws and general policies at all (and perhaps they could be avoided only in the most thoroughly devolved and anarchistic society of small and largely self-sufficient face-to-face communities), they have to be framed in general terms and cannot be designed so as to be always responsive to the nuances of particular and individual circumstances. The challenge, on the large-scale political level, is to design institutions in such a way that legislation and policy-making is sensitive to the values represented by the orientation of caring. And this only reinforces the point that citizens of a democracy should have access to both orientations, and should be able to move from one to the other.

A further reason why it is desirable for individuals to be able to work within either perspective is that understanding of the values of others will thus be increased. However much a person tends to work within the justice orientation, he (or, less often, she) will come across people whose focus is that of caring; and vice versa. And when we take into account the point already stressed, that understanding is necessary across cultures, the need for people not to be confined within one way of thinking becomes all the clearer.

We can quite legitimately, then, see it as part of the role of values education to give people an acquaintance with systematic ways of thinking about moral questions, without implying that this is, or should be, all there is to the moral life. But what might such ways of thinking be? Any likely candidates, I think, will involve the idea of *universalizability*, though not necessarily under that label (Kohlberg speaks more of reversibility, a closely related notion).[12]

The underlying idea, which we've encountered before in referring to Kant's ethics, is that the perspective of morality is in a sense an impartial perspective. If something is right for me to do when I am in this position (perhaps standing to benefit from some course of action), and you are in that position (perhaps standing to lose), then (unless there are any special considerations which rightly make a difference) the same thing would be right for you to do if the positions were reversed. This means that, when I am contemplating an action which I know will make someone else worse off, there is always a challenge I can put to myself (or which others could put to me): namely, 'I think it is all right for a person in this position (which happens at the moment to be my position) to act this way towards someone in that position (which happens at the moment to be your position).' Now I try to imagine what it would be like to be in the other person's position, on the receiving end. I know I wouldn't like it, but I might just try to shrug off that realization. I then have to ask myself, recognizing what it is like to be on the receiving end, 'Am I really prepared to endorse this as a moral position: am I really prepared to stick to the idea that it is all right for a person in this position (which could be anyone) to act like this towards a person in that position (which could, at least in my imagination, be me)?' It is not a matter only of being aware of what one would or wouldn't like if one were in the other person's shoes, but of trying to be consistent in one's own thinking – and the capacity to do that, and to be concerned about doing it, is also something which education has to promote.[13]

Notice, now, that to think in this way is not, after all, to commit all the faults which critics have seen as the vices of the justice perspective. It does not mean that I try to put myself in some privileged detached position, nor that I set up very simple general rules which I hold to rigidly. On the contrary, it demands that I think myself into what it is like to be each of the people affected by what I might do, in this concrete situation; and in a matter of personal relationships that may involve all the awareness and sensitivity that any advocate of the care orientation could call for. But it also demands that I make the effort to distance myself from what might be only my own inclinations or prejudices.

THINKING WITH CONTENT: KNOWLEDGE AND UNDERSTANDING

So far in this chapter I have looked at ways in which education may enable and encourage people to think for themselves, both in understanding their own values and in thinking about what they are to do. There is also a large role for education in promoting knowledge and understanding, both about values in general and about the values of others within a plural society in particular. The field here is large, so I shall not try to give a comprehensive review of it, but only to illustrate its importance.

First, as I mentioned in Chapter 8, there is a role for the study of values, and of morality in particular, from the perspectives, for instance, of sociology and psychology as well as from that of philosophy (which has provided the basis for much of the argument of this book). Perhaps as an explicit and systematic study this might come in only at the upper levels of secondary schools, but there is much that could be done at earlier ages if teachers had sufficient relevant knowledge themselves. Second, and more specifically, there is understanding of the particular varieties of moral outlook which are important within one's own society. The need for know-ledge *about* people's values adds importantly to the liberal emphasis on rational autonomy. The liberal aim that individuals should be able to make up their own minds on questions of values, and to make their own choice of ways of life, does require some knowledge and understanding of the poss-ible values and ways of life that are available, but only to the extent that the possibilities are real options for the individual concerned. But in a plural society, I would argue, it is important for people to have knowledge and understanding of ways of life which are lived and values which are held by others in one's society, even if they are not live options for oneself. An example will illustrate the point. A teenage girl, brought up in a family with progressive liberal views about equality of the sexes, will not, so far as her own freedom of choice is concerned, need any knowledge of what it is like to be a girl brought up within a strict Muslim tradition which expects conformity to a differentiation of male and female roles; for that kind of life, founded as it is in a wider social and religious context, is simply not an option for her. But if the educational aim is not (or not only) that each should choose for herself, but that each should have some understanding of the lives of others in the same society, then the girl will need some understanding of the Muslim standpoint.

Promoting knowledge and understanding relevant to life in a plural society is readily compatible, as an aim, with the aim of promoting tolerance which we looked at in Chapter 11. It is not *necessarily* true that in understanding more about someone's beliefs or their reasons for acting as they do, you are more likely to be tolerant of them; but on the whole this is likely to be the case. Here again the significance of toleration is larger than it would be if the moral autonomy of the individual were the only aim. The autonomously choosing individual needs to have tolerance of a range of moral standpoints only in the sense that the person must be able to entertain different possibilities in an unprejudiced way, while deciding which one to adopt. Once the person has made their decision, it will not be inconsistent if they reject intolerantly, when they are held by others, the values which the person has rejected for themself. (Those who have made a 'leap of faith' into a religious commitment are not necessarily going to be tolerant afterwards of those who have not made a similar leap.)

In addition to the hope that individuals are less likely to act intolerantly towards each other if they have a greater knowledge and understanding of each other's positions, the argument for educating people about the variety of values operating within their own society is that such understanding is necessary to participation as a citizen in a democratic and plural society.[14] As an illustration, take the Salman Rushdie affair, where so many liberals found their notions of tolerance and respect for other cultures severely strained. As we saw at the end of Chapter 4, the liberal tendency was to interpret the objections to *The Satanic Verses* as claims that Muslims had been offended by it. Liberals were also aware that, even if it were possible to interpret offence as a kind of harm, it was difficult to fit the notion of blasphemy under the notion of offence to persons (since blasphemy, if it is an offence to anyone, would seem to be an offence to God; but then it would be hard to interpret the offence as harm, since this would involve the idea that God, a perfect being, can be harmed).

Yet liberals may still have been working with the wrong conceptual scheme even in thinking in terms of blasphemy. At least one British Muslim commentator has pointed out that Muslim objectors to *The Satanic Verses* tended to use the terminology of honour and dignity rather than that of blasphemy. And he distinguishes between *izzat*, the form of honour associated with the social standing or respectability of a family, and *ghairat*:

> while the former is about the respect others accord to one, the latter is about the quality of one's pride or love. While *izzat* is something to be maintained, *ghairat* is something to be tested. ... *The Satanic Verses* is for some Muslims a challenge to demonstrate their attachment to and love for their faith; their *imani ghairat*.[15]

Now I hope there will be some readers of this book who will not only recognize the concepts Modood is using here but may be able to assess for themselves the interpretation he puts on them. But almost certainly to many readers these concepts will be quite new. And that, of course, illustrates the point – that understanding differences over values in a plural society requires a great deal of knowledge. And the only way that such knowledge is likely to be acquired by substantial numbers is through formal education. Remember, too, that the kind of knowledge involved is not something that could be put across just as information, partly because, as so often, it involves a difference not just in the content of moral views but in the significance of moral concepts to the people who hold them. In effect, we could say there is a further kind of moral perspective or orientation in operation here: instead of asking, 'Are my rights, or anyone else's, violated by this? Is it just?' one asks, 'Is my honour and that of my family and my religion maintained?' And little understanding of a moral perspective will be possible without the ability to some degree to appreciate what it is like to see things from that perspective on the inside.

The educational task, then, is a challenging one, but at least it is clear that it *is* an educational task. To progress even in understanding the points I quoted from Modood, I need more than just information; I need some further explanations and I need examples. I need to think about these and see where they do or do not relate to anything that is within my experience. In doing this I shall be exercising some imagination, and also critical reflection: the two are complementary. If this kind of process doesn't count as educational, what does?[16]

THINKING WITH OTHERS: DISCUSSION AND DIALOGUE

Most teachers will recognize that discussion in the classroom can be a useful means towards a variety of educational ends. But before looking further at discussion within the context of formal education, it is worth stressing that, where values education is concerned, discussion is much more than a means to an end. That people should, throughout their lives, and in personal as well as public contexts, be willing and able to turn to discussion of their differences rather than stand-off or conflict, is itself one of the most important aims for values education. But rather than simply issue a plea for discussion, I want to stress that there is an ideal of reasoned discussion that is more difficult to achieve, and less commonly realized, than may be thought at first sight. Discussion may have a variety of aims, and the aim with which it is undertaken can make a difference to how it is pursued.[17]

At one end of the spectrum, what passes for discussion may be no more than an exchange of differing points of view. If this happens in a classroom, it may fulfil at least one learning aim: it can make people aware of the variety of views that exist among a group that may be relatively homogeneous. And if this awareness comes about within a context of amicable interpersonal relations, then some contribution may have been made towards tolerance also. But this will be a limited achievement and too low an aim for education if it does not lead on to something more searching. It can, too, lead to pupils taking a dismissive view of discussion about moral issues ('Oh no, not abortion/sexuality/treatment of animals again!').

If there is to be discussion which is more than an exchange of views, the first difference will be to give reasons for the views put forward. Where pupils are encouraged to think through the reasons for their views, so that they can defend them, this will have some educational value by helping people to clarify their own values: and may take them further in understanding others' points of view than the superficial exchange of opinions. But this is still a limited aim; and if discussion at this level is set up as debate, it can even be counterproductive from the point of view of promoting tolerance and reducing conflict. For it is characteristic of debate that two opposing sides are set against each other, and that each sets out to undermine the credibility of the other. This presupposes that the important differences can be assigned to just two camps (an appropriately military metaphor), and that a satisfactory outcome consists in one position winning: in which case a satisfactory outcome for all concerned is ruled out from the start.

To establish the superiority of one's own point of view is by no means the only possible aim of participants in a discussion; in fact there is a sense in which someone who tries to do this is not really engaging in discussion at all, since it presupposes that his or her own views cannot be altered. But where a person does not make this presupposition, discussion can be a way of testing their own views: others may point out inconsistencies or bring up counter-evidence which they might not have thought of.

Another possible aim which can be shared by all participants in a discussion is to establish the truth about some matter. Some writers have characterized discussion, as distinct from debate, by just this mutually shared aim.[18] Thinking of the aim of moral discussion in this way, though, does raise difficulties. For anyone who does not think that there is, ultimately, a truth to be discovered on moral questions would on this basis be debarred from participation in moral discussion (and though there are extreme forms of subjectivism or relativism – see Chapter 3 – which imply theoretically that no rational discussion about values is possible, the fact that such discussion does go on counts against those theories). But on the other hand, if an objective truth exists, in the first of the senses I distinguished in Chapter 3 – a truth which is independent of what anyone thinks on the matter – then even if all the participants come to agreement, that won't guarantee that they have found the truth.

Actually, there is at least one kind of context in which we would be able to say that agreement does itself guarantee that the answer found is right. Borrowing from Habermas's communicative ethics,[19] we can imagine a situation in which a dispute is seen, by all those involved, as a matter of conflict of interests. If a context of dialogue could be realized in which all whose interests were affected were free to put forward proposed solutions, and equally free to raise any objections they had to proposed solutions, then any solution that emerged at the end to which no one had any further objection would constitute an answer to which there *was* no objection (since this solution would have survived all the objections of all those involved). And if we can say that there is no objection to a certain proposal, we can surely say that this *is* right. In such a case, it would not be that there is, already, a right answer which the discussion may or may not discover, but rather that any answer which emerges unscathed at the end of the discussion is by that very fact shown to be right.

But real discussions do not take place in ideal conditions or with unlimited time; and many moral issues are ones in which some of the interests at stake are not directly represented in the discussion, and in which at least some of the participants may not see the problem in terms of *interests* at all (see Chapter 9 for examples). For that reason, the idea that discussion must be aiming at the truth is not, in practice, a very helpful one. But we do not have to accept that there are only two possibilities, that *either* there is a truth which reasoned discussion will lead rational people to agree on, *or* there can be no reasoned discussion of values. Another possibility is that participants in a discussion seek a practical accommodation about what is to be done, while not necessarily trying to persuade each other of the truth of their respective positions. Though discussion in this sense is not aiming at truth, it is by no means irrational or non-rational. Just as in the search for truth, it requires understanding and articulation of the views of each participant, and the exploration of possibilities and objections.

It may be illuminating here to think again of the difference between the justice and care perspectives. As I pointed out in Chapter 6, the justice perspective tends to set up difficult situations as conflicts of rights. If this perspective is assumed from the beginning, it may lend itself to the kind of debate in which each party is out to win. Or even if the parties do engage in a genuine discussion seeking a common solution, they may assume that the solution must be one of two given alternatives. As viewed from the justice orientation, the issue between the moles and the porcupine posed the question, who had right on their side? Whereas viewed from the perspective of the care orientation, the question is a practical one: what, in the actual circumstances, given the different points of view and interests, is the best thing to be done? It is more likely that the moles and the porcupine would agree on the latter issue (especially if they have not been schooled to assume a bipolar view of discussion) rather than the former. All that was said in Chapter 5 about compromise is, of course, relevant here. To be able and willing to engage in discussion towards a practical accommodation is, I suggest, an important skill and disposition for citizens of a plural society, and is one that can be practised in schools, through discussion rather than bipolar debate.

Earlier I stressed the importance of knowledge and understanding of the variety of moral outlooks within one's society. Just as discussion may help to promote that kind of knowledge and understanding, so the possession of some of that knowledge and understanding may help to make particular discussions more productive. But any reasoned discussion is unlikely to happen if the conditions are not appropriate for it. It is accepted that discussion needs some ground rules; but I would like to add two further conditions to this. First, that different sorts of ground rules are appropriate to, indeed are partly what constitute, different kinds of discussion; and second, that ground rules need not themselves be sacrosanct. Within a classroom, the ground rules may initially have to be laid down by the teacher. But it would be part of the teacher's aim that pupils should recognize the point of the ground rules for themselves, and they are more likely to do this if they themselves have a hand in setting them up. Some flexibility can be allowed, then: pupils may suggest rules for themselves and gain the experience of discussion within different frameworks of rules, reflecting on why some discussions seem to lead nowhere while others may achieve a resolution which leaves everyone feeling that they have gained something.

What the teacher needs is not so much an authoritative set of rules which he or she will lay down, as a repertoire of the sorts of rules which it has been established make for constructive discussion. A good deal has been written about ground rules for rational discussion in general, and I shall not add to it here.[20] I would just like to add that there is a philosophical tradition which provides many examples of rules which may be relevant in discussion of moral issues in particular. Some of them derive from the characteristic features of moral values which I mentioned in Chapter 3. Thus, given an expression of a moral position, questions can be asked such as 'Does the person putting this view forward see it as an expression of personal preference?'; 'Are they taking other people's interests into account?'; 'Do they want to say that everyone should act in accordance with their view?'; and (a familiar challenge) 'What if everyone did that?' The last example shows that we are not talking here about the kind of rule that can be mechanically applied in substantiating some positions and filtering out others; nor about rules that cannot themselves be challenged. To the question, 'What if everyone did that?' it will sometimes seem appropriate to reply, 'not everyone will'. But when would that response be appropriate and when simply an evasion? This itself is something that can be discussed,[21] as can the question of whether moral positions must be universalizable in any case (which would be denied by some advocates of the care orientation). These matters have been explored (but not resolved) by moral philosophers, but they do not need technical terminology or special knowledge, and there is no inherent reason why an ability to think about such matters should not be part of the education of everyone in a plural society.

Discussion of values requires more than formal ground rules; it also requires some conceptual clarification to be brought to bear on the range of possible positions. Philosophers and others have divided up and classified the various kinds of moral position and argument in many ways, some of which I've used in this book: for example, the distinctions between the justice and care orientations, and between consequentialist approaches (which hold that what matters is the promotion of the best consequences overall) and approaches which maintain that some kinds of action are required or ruled out independently of their consequences.[22] The value of such distinctions is not that people should be able to play an academic game of pigeon-holing other people's views, but rather that to be able to locate someone's position within a conceptual scheme is an important part of understanding it. Debates over abortion or capital punishment, for instance, often reach deadlock because participants are arguing from conflicting assumptions, some holding that the decision should be made in terms of desired consequences, others seeking to apply an absolute principle about the taking of life. To overcome the deadlock, may require standing back and looking at the general issue between the conflicting assumptions.

One further point about the conduct of discussion: don't be afraid of the use of explicitly moral language. As I said at the end of Chapter 7, to state a view that some course of action is morally wrong, and to give reasons for the view, is not to condemn the person holding a contrary view. Where else, if not in discussion in school, will people learn that it *is* possible to have reasoned discussion about morality; that to say 'that's wrong' or 'this is what you ought to do' need not be an expression of personal preference or an uncritical adherence to tradition? If that kind of language is not used, in the context of a reasoned discussion, then, as I argued in Chapter 7, we can't be sure even that morality will survive.[23]

NOTES

1. I say one of its aspects, because autonomy is not just a matter of being able to think for oneself; it may also include being able to act on the results of one's thinking. If someone, through their own thinking, has come to certain firm convictions, then what we call having the strength of one's conviction will also be an aspect of that person's autonomy. There are many discussions of autonomy, both generally and in the context of education: see, for example, Callan (1988); Dworkin (1988); Lindley (1986).
2. See Kirschenbaum and Simon (eds) (1973). For a comment, see Pring (1984), pp. 75–6.
3. Rawls (1972), p. 20.
4. Rawls would claim that it constitutes a justification of them too, and the only kind of justification we can have, but that claim raises large issues which I shall avoid here.
5. See Wilson (1975, 1990), chapter 10.
6. Hare (1992); and for the argument about convergence (1981), chapter 12.
7. Kohlberg (1981), chapter 7.
8. So far we have been assuming that the right kind of thinking is something which individuals could do for themselves; but as we saw at the end of Chapter 7, we should not neglect the possibility that the right kind of thinking has to be a shared, collective process. This possibility will be relevant again in the final section of this chapter.
9. What thinkers such as Hare, Wilson and Kohlberg would probably say to this is that the attitude of relying on authority is not one of morality at all (in that they are influenced by the tradition which runs from Kant, as we saw in Chapter 7). So far as *morality* is concerned (they would probably claim), they are not being partisan, but rather talking about a way of thinking which as a matter of language and logic is the right way of thinking about moral questions. That does not mean they are inculcating acceptance of a particular set of answers to moral questions, any more than the teacher of maths is inculcating acceptance of a set of answers to calculations.
10. The evidence also suggests that the distinction between the two

perspectives will often not be, in practice, as clear-cut as it seemed to be in the story of the moles and the porcupine (which is why I used that rather artificial story, to bring out the distinction in the first place). Having made the distinction, we are likely often to be able to recognize elements of both perspectives in someone's thinking on a given occasion. See also Dancy (1992).

11. See Wingfield and Haste (1987) for an investigation in which the different orientations were revealed in a political context. I would like to thank Helen Haste for helping me in following up the implications of the justice/care debate.

12. Kohlberg (1981), chapter 5.

13. It is Richard Hare, many of whose writings are specifically concerned with values education, who has given the most thorough and careful articulation of the idea I am trying to get across here. Philosophically, it owes a lot of Kant. My own attempt at an informal, non-technical presentation may not convey the power which (I agree with Hare) this way of thinking, taken seriously, may have. It is, of course, related to the everyday appeals, 'What if everyone did that?' or 'How would you feel if he did that to you?', but it is necessary to think through more carefully what is involved in that sort of appeal, if people are not to be able to shrug it off with a simple 'So what?' See Hare (1981, 1992), chapters 9–11.

14. See Haydon (1995a).

15. Modood (1992), pp. 72–3.

16. A good deal more reflection would be possible on the relation between moral orientation and cultural traditions, and such reflection could be helpful for any teachers trying to work out the content of relevant syllabuses. I lack the anthropological and sociological knowledge to fill in any detail here, but the following would be worth exploring: is it the case, for instance, that the strong orientation of some Asian communities towards the importance of familial relations means that the care orientation would be more at home there? Or does the absoluteness with which questions of family honour are viewed in some cultures mean that an orientation in terms of honour is closer to that of justice? What sort of relationship is there between the justice and care orientations and different religious cultures? One might see a justice orientation as being very strong in Judaism and Islam, while some developments of Christianity (e.g. the situation ethics of Fletcher (1966)) look more akin to an orientation of caring.

17. I intend the remarks that follow to apply to primary as much as to secondary schooling. Of course, the vocabulary and the complexity of arguments may change as pupils become older, but (within schooling) it's never too early to get people into the habit of asking for and giving reasons for what they say; indeed, if they don't get into this habit early, the level of vocabulary and complexity of arguments they exhibit later may still be very limited.

18. See Bridges (1979); Wilson (1990).

19. Habermas (1990b); and see Chapter 7, notes 16 to 19.

20. See Bridges (1979); Habermas (1990a); Haydon (1993b).

21. Here, particularly, an acquaintance with Hare's arguments would be helpful.
22. See also Chapter 9.
23. See also Chapter 8.

Further reading

For a variety of approaches to moral education see Carr (1991), Cochrane *et al.* (1979), Cowney and Kelly (1978), Jarrett (1991), Noddings (1992), Peters (1981), Sandin (1992) and Straughan (1988a). On the role of discussion in tackling prejudice in a plural society see Jones, M. (1977).

Part VI
Values in the teaching profession

The teaching profession – if indeed it is a profession, which some would question – has not paid the explicit and systematic attention to values which one might expect a profession to pay. This seems to be true whether we are thinking of the preparation of teachers for their role in values education, or of the part that any teacher may play in discussing and deciding on the issues of values which concern the profession collectively. This is, no doubt, a sweeping generalization, and one large and honourable exception to it exists in the area of equal opportunities, where the profession has often been ahead of public or political opinion.

In this concluding section I am concerned to look ahead, in broad terms, at what could and ought to happen. I do not have detailed prescriptions, and in the case of equal opportunities in particular, I am not attempting to add to an already large literature, except to note an interesting link between recognition of equal opportunities and the education of teachers themselves in knowledge and understanding of values.

CHAPTER 13

Valuing teachers

EDUCATING THE EDUCATORS

If I am right, in my argument in Chapter 12, about the amount of know-ledge and understanding that schools can and should contribute to values education, then there is a lot of knowledge and understanding about values that teachers themselves need to acquire. One response to this point could be to suggest that values education should be treated as a subject in its own right, and that specialist teachers should be trained to teach it.[1] This would have the advantage of fitting the kind of pattern (especially for secondary education) that we have become used to, but it would have strong disadvantages too, not least the burden of having to add a new subject to curricular provision right through the system. Besides, there are other candidates as additional school subjects already in the field, one of which, indeed, I would put in a plea for, partly because it is so relevant to values education. I mean philosophy.

There is already a movement – established for some years in the USA and in Australia, and gaining ground in Britain – for the teaching of philosophy in schools, at all ages and stages from early primary to A level.[2] Philosophy is not only about asking the deep and difficult questions; it is also concerned with the way one approaches questions, whether they are of cosmic importance or merely worrying to the individual. It is a way of approaching questions which tries to be as clear as possible about the concepts being used; which makes careful distinctions so as to avoid confusion and cross-purposes; which tries to be aware of alternatives to the ways of thinking one is familiar with; which looks for underlying prin-ciples and asks whether they can be justified. Philosophy does have its own established body of theories and texts, like any other subject, and it is perfectly possible for these to be studied by school students. But it is also possible to raise and discuss the questions of philosophy without advance or specialized knowledge of theories and texts, which is the method that is being employed in primary schools, often through the use of stories and picture books.

One of the concerns of philosophy has always been the understanding of values and morality. Much of what I have been doing in this book is, I hope, recognizable as philosophy to readers who know something of the subject; but it is also important that I didn't have to label it as philosophy on the cover. That might have put some people off; but if you came to the book unaware that it was philosophy, I hope you will see that the subject need not be esoteric. Of course, if people were introduced[3] to philosophical discussion from an early age, no one would think of the subject as esoteric.

So, if there is to be an addition to the curriculum, and one which would be very relevant to values education, it should be philosophy. That will, like other subjects, create a place for trained specialists. But whether philosophy becomes established as a school subject or not, *all* teachers need to be able to contribute to values education (or, at the very least, be able to think about other issues involving values which education inevitably raises).

All teachers, then, need a good deal of knowledge and understanding about values. This will include (if the proposal is not too immodest) an ability to work with the kinds of ideas and distinctions presented in this book. On the other hand, while it might be good for sales if I claimed that teachers could get everything they need from a book like this, I certainly don't want to make that claim. Teachers need the opportunity to reflect on such ideas, to discuss them, to try them out in practice.

In the old style of teacher education (I'm thinking now of Britain of the mid to late 1980s) the obvious suggestion would have been to build some new content into initial training courses. But even assuming that this would have been effective, it is not an option now, as teachers are getting their training more and more on the job. New teachers, and those teachers in schools who are responsible for the training of new teachers, may have to do a lot for themselves (in-service education may, of course, have a lot to contribute as well). What I want to stress here, though, whatever the institutional context, is that opportunities both for individual reflection and for discussion between teachers are essential. In Chapter 12 I emphasized discussion as part of the educational process; but how will teachers be able to facilitate and take part in educational discussion about values if they have not had the experience of engaging in such discussion themselves? What teachers need, after all, is not passively to assimilate the kinds of ideas mooted in this book – any more than pupils need that. Pupils and their teachers need to be able to use these ideas, which means making sense of them in relation to the ideas one already has. Teachers, in facilitating discussion, should start from where the pupils are; indeed, the teachers themselves, in learning to teach about values, will also be starting from where they are, with values of their own.

People may go into teaching for all sorts of reasons, but it would be surprising if most people who have chosen to enter teaching did not bring with them some concern for the value of knowledge, understanding and skills, and some concern for the well-being and future prospects of children. Often these values have been developed over many years; people entering into teacher education are not, after all, naïve or uneducated. In many countries, to an increasing extent, they are already graduates when they decide to go into teaching, and a surprising number of them have not come directly from school through higher education to teacher education;

they may have varied experience of working in other jobs, living in other countries, bringing up their own children, and more. To say to such people, in effect, 'These are the values you are going to transmit, and this is how to do it' (even supposing the techniques existed) would be patronizing. Where teachers are seen essentially as technicians delivering a predetermined content – even where that content is supposed to consist of values – the strategy may fail if we try to get them to transmit values they themselves do not necessarily want to endorse; and in any case it will surely fail to build positively on the enthusiasms, commitments and understandings which teachers already bring to their task.

To stress that teachers come into teaching with some of their values already formed is not to say that they should simply be left to get on with the job of values education – far from it. That people entering teaching have values of their own does not necessarily mean that they have thought a lot about them, that they can readily articulate and defend them, or that they will know how to respond when encountering others with contrary values. In all these respects, the educators may themselves need educating. But, as in education generally, what is needed here is not the importing of something quite new, but a linking into the concerns already there. While student and new teachers will usually be anxious about their classroom experience, and eager for practical advice, this does not prevent many of them from reflecting on the system they are entering, and asking how well it is serving young people.

On matters like this, as well as on everyday classroom concerns, both new and established teachers ought to be able from time to time to sit back, observe from the outside, and reflect, discuss, revise and clarify their own views. For new teachers especially, at least some of this should be done with others who are at the same stage, and not just with experienced teachers who may be rather more set in their ways and their views, and rather less prone to the same worries.

The moves in Britain away from university-based teacher education toward school-based training were motivated partly by a rather inaccurate perception that the universities and colleges were too much concerned with theory. But in school-based training the danger is that there will be too little space for reflecting, and for the kind of illumination which good theory can bring. That is not to say that new teachers should be subjected to seminar after seminar, in which the agenda is something as open as 'Let's talk about education' or 'Let's talk about values'. For one thing, given a shared interest in and concern about education, this can lead too easily to an apparent agreement, whereas what may be more worthwhile is to look at differences. For though there may perhaps be a greater degree of consensus on certain values among teachers than among the population as a whole, it may too easily be assumed that the consensus extends more widely than it actually does.

TEACHERS, VALUES AND EQUAL OPPORTUNITIES

The fact that our society is a plural one means not only that teachers will be working in a context in which pupils and their parents have different perspectives on questions of values but also that the values of teachers themselves will reflect this plurality. (It is true, certainly, that not enough recruits to teaching are being drawn from some sectors of society, particularly the ethnic minorities; but a considerable diversity of religious, cultural, political and ethical perspectives can still be represented in an institution of teacher education or in a school, even if not in proportion to their strength in the wider society.)

Because of this diversity in society, policies for equal opportunities are vital within education. This is not a matter of political fashion; the central reason for concern – itself an expression of values, of course – is that it is wrong for anybody's education, career or other life prospects to be hampered because the person happens to fit into a category which is viewed by much of society in a prejudiced, intolerant or, as many people with disabilities could testify, a patronizing way. And it would be inconsistent, a bad example and unjust to new teachers themselves if this same central value, which ought to be realized in the education of pupils, were not also realized within the professional education of teachers.

One reason why it is difficult to put into practice even the best of intentions in the area of equal opportunities also explains why this is itself a fruitful area to focus on in encouraging new teachers to think about values: namely, that the issues – once one moves beyond superficial albeit important slogans – are by no means clear-cut. This is partly because people's values, including the values of teachers, differ where equal opportunities are concerned. If this is not recognized, one of the dangers (a danger of not preparing teachers as well as they ought to be prepared for their encounters with their pupils' developing values, and a danger of being unjust to new teachers themselves) is that too much of what matters to some of the individuals in teaching will be overlooked. I know from experience as a tutor within initial teacher education that a consensus can too readily be assumed among tutors and new teachers: 'Yes, of course, we are all anti-racist and anti-sexist here'. And as I mentioned in Chapter 10, there is a widespread tendency in our secular society either to think in altogether non-religious terms, or, at most, to maintain that a person's religion is a private matter.

But if all discussion is conducted in such terms, is due respect being shown to those persons – perhaps one or two in a seminar group – who do not agree? When the secular liberal consensus extends, for instance, to gay and lesbian rights, what of those who are still uneasy on this? My point here is not to express dissent from the liberal consensus, within which a person's sexual orientation seems no stronger a ground for discriminating against them than skin colour or regional accent. My point is rather that there are many people outside this consensus who, from sincerely held religiously based conviction, would not see these cases as at all equivalent. Not to let their voice be heard is to discriminate against them on account, indirectly at least, of their religion. Of course, it may be that in other institutions, perhaps some with a strong religious base, the positions are reversed, and it is individuals whose sexual orientation is different from that of the majority who feel unable to speak in the face of a conservative consensus.

In teacher education, as much as anywhere, the fact that our society is far from homogeneous in its values is inescapable. There are additional reasons here why we should hope that the teaching profession will itself be multiethnic, multicultural and multifaith. One reason is the general equal opportunities consideration that nobody entering the teaching profession – or any other occupation – should be faced with special barriers because of their culture, religion or ethnic origin. A second reason, often mentioned, is that young people from ethnic minorities should have suitable role models. The third reason, less often noticed, is that teachers should have the chance among themselves, in their professional interaction, to discuss and conduct dialogue across different points of view and on the basis of different kinds of experience.

Whatever their background, teachers have to respond to diversity of values among the people they are teaching and among parents, some of whom may hold values with which the teacher profoundly disagrees. At the same time, teachers have to educate people in such a way that they will themselves be able to cope with conflicts of values within the society. If teachers are not able to face openly and with tolerance their own differences in values, they will hardly be able to help others to do so. This means that discussion between teachers, in which their own differences are honestly explored, ought to be an essential part of the expectations which the profession has of itself. And such discussion may very well grow out of teachers' collective attempt to handle the particular issues that come up in a school, rather than out of more abstract discussions about values in general.

Some of the most productive discussions may themselves arise from the attempt to make an equal opportunities policy work. While student teachers should be expected to follow the equal opportunities policies of the schools in which they are working, this does not mean that they cannot view such policies critically. (A similar point applies to the schools' policies for Personal and Social Education.) On the contrary, they should be encouraged to look at such policies, discuss the principles behind them and their operation, and in the process express their own values and explore their areas of consensus and disagreement. The opportunity to do this in a structured way should be made available; this means both a sufficient allocation of time and the availability of suitable facilitators, whether drawn from school or university staff. Meanwhile university and college departments of education (if they survive in Britain in anything like their present form) could give more prominence to research and teaching about the role of values in education, and especially to the still rather underexplored area of culturally and religiously based differences in values within our society. And student teachers should be made aware that more systematic study of values is possible and that, though what can be done in initial teacher education is limited, there are further possibilities during in-service education.

VALUES AND PROFESSIONAL STANDING

It is sometimes said that one mark of a profession is its shared possession of a body of expertise and knowledge, such as the medical knowledge of doctors or the legal knowledge of solicitors.[4] The claims of teachers to professional status based on this criterion have proved somewhat controversial. There are those who will argue that, apart from relevant knowledge of the subjects being taught, there is no body of expert knowledge of 'teaching' equivalent to medicine or the law. There may be skills, as the current emphasis on competence models of training seems to assume, but the professional model in question speaks not of skills *per se* but of skills rooted in specialized and theoretically articulated knowledge. If in the case of teachers the idea of skills or competences, to be learned on the job, is detached from the notion of a body of expert knowledge and theory, then teachers are being seen more as technicians.

A second mark of a profession sometimes proposed is that it controls its own professional education. This is not at the moment the case for teaching in Britain, or indeed in many other countries. Of course, a profession will have a stronger case for controlling its own professional education to the extent that it has a collective sense of what that education should involve and what form it should take. But currently in Britain there is perhaps hardly a stronger shared sense of this within the profession than there is among the public at large.

A third possible mark of a profession is one that is perhaps influential among the general public, and for that reason often not clearly articulated. It is the sense, mentioned in Chapter 1, that a professional, if anything, maintains perhaps rather higher than ordinary ethical standards. It's true that this expectation is often accompanied by a good deal of suspicion about certain professionals. In some cases their members may be seen as out to get power, status and income for themselves. That kind of charge could be made to stick, perhaps, against a minority of lawyers or certain medical consultants with private practices; it would seem merely laughable in relation to nurses or the average schoolteacher. In some people's eyes it may be that the very lack of prestige and high income makes the professional status of teachers or nurses dubious. But for others, the same factors will tell in favour of these groups, for there is the idea that the true professional is motivated by concerns other than income and status. In particular, it may be thought that the professional is motivated, at least in part, by altruistic concerns, and by the same token has to respect high ethical ideals.

But just what kind of demand does this idea make on teachers? Does it mean that teachers must be paragons of virtue? A good footballer or a good basketball player is not necessarily a good person. Must a good teacher be a good person? Some would say that anyone who is not a thoroughly good person cannot be a good teacher. And some might suggest that if we could rely on teachers being good persons, little more would have to be said about the role of teachers in values education.[5]

I have already argued that, so far as values education goes, it is certainly not sufficient that teachers be good persons: there is a lot that they need to be able to teach. Is it even necessary that they be good persons? One could overstate the answer to this question in either of two directions. On the one hand, if we say that a teacher must be a thoroughly good person in all respects, we need some standard by which to evaluate this goodness; and any such standard will be controversial. The more content we build into a conception of a thoroughly good person, the more it will be, in a plural society, some people's conception rather than everybody's; and besides, the higher we set the standards, the more difficult it will be to find enough teachers who would measure up to it. (I am not even entering here into the weighty problem of how any standard of morality or character could actually be applied within selection and professional education.)

On the other hand, if we were to say that all that can be required of teachers is that they have the necessary skills and competences, and that no moral demands are placed on them at all, we would be demanding less than is commonly expected of the members of other professions. Recognizing the large and potentially very damaging influence that the members of other professions can exercise on the layperson, the general public can reasonably ask that they respect certain ethical standards. In the same way, recognizing the potential influence for good or ill that teachers can exercise towards pupils, such an expectation is equally reasonable.

Some professions have responded to such public expectations, as well as to their own internal concerns, by formulating and promulgating a code of ethics. This has not happened in teaching. Nor is there an established field, or even a recognized label, that can be set alongside the expanding academic concerns of legal ethics, business ethics and health-care ethics. This must be partly because teaching does not have the professional mechanisms through which such issues could be addressed. In the absence, for instance, of something like a General Teaching Council,[6] there is no professional body which could establish any agreed ethical standards. Yet teaching is certainly in something of a Catch-22 situation here: until it is seen, both from within and from outside, to have more of the marks by which high-status professions are distinguished, there will not be sufficient motivation for the establishment of such a professional body.

It's doubtful, though, whether the possession of a code of ethics as such is the major factor in the public perception of a profession's ethical standing. The general public is unlikely to know the details of such codes, and may not even know of their existence. Its moral expectations of the professions may have more to do with the sense, mentioned above, of what it is that motivates the professional: a sense that the professional is committed to certain ethical concerns. What might these concerns be?

Here it may be helpful too to look to a kind of answer which, in essence, has existed at least since Plato: namely, that each profession has a particular goal, something of value which its practitioners aim at, and that this goal, or this recognized kind of *good*, is both what gives the profession its unity and what distinguishes it from others. In the case of medicine – perhaps the most clear-cut case – the goal is health, or at least life rather than death: the professionals are expected to have a shared commitment to this goal. In the case of law the goal, arguably, would be justice. In the case of the ministry within religious communities, the goal has been claimed to be salvation.[7]

Pursuing the example of medicine a bit further, it's important to recognize first that there are other professions besides medicine that are concerned with health, and that they will not all be concerned with it in the same way – nurses, for instance, may see themselves as concerned with the relief of suffering and the comfort of the whole person rather than with the curing of disease. But for our purposes here, I shall assume the overriding goal of medicine to be the curing of disease, and ask how such a goal is meant to function. For one thing, it provides the *raison d'être* for the profession as a whole: because the cure of disease is widely recognized as a goal worth aiming at, it is seen as good that there is a profession devoted to it.[8] There may be a sense too that this goal is aimed at for its own sake. The medical profession does not primarily, for instance, serve the goals of a flourishing economy, even though it is true that by curing people's diseases it will often enable them to return to work or to work more productively; essentially, the profession aims at the restoration of health as a worthwhile end in its own right. The goal is also one that can be shared across national boundaries, and this is part of what constitutes the identity of a profession whose members can identify themselves as such, independently of where in the world they work. By reference to this shared goal, for instance, it is possible for doctors in any part of the world to criticize the actions of those who put their medical expertise at the disposal of partisan political goals (as in Nazi Germany or, for psychiatry, the Soviet Union at one time).

All this may be to some degree idealistic, but we need not deny that ideals may have some force for at least some professionals. What, now, of teaching? Is there a central, shared good which will stand for teaching as health does for the health-care professions and (arguably) justice for the law and salvation for the ministry? The obvious answer is 'education'. And perhaps this answer will work, if there can be a clear enough shared understanding of what education is. Teachers could then see themselves, and be seen publicly, as committed to the pursuit of education. This implicit commitment would form the basis for professional ethics, providing teachers with a reason why they should resist calls – whether from parents, industry or government – to serve ends, such as indoctrination or narrow technical training, which would be incompatible with the good of education; and it could be the source also of the standards which individual teachers would know they must not fall short of despite the day-to-day pressures of the job.

While this is a possible model, we can't avoid asking whether teachers actually share a conception of what constitutes the good of education. There is a conception available: it would be roughly the liberal conception once articulated by philosophers such as Richard Peters, and seen as being of value for its own sake rather than for any extrinsic end. The problem is that neither teachers nor the wider public may agree that the central and overriding goal to which they must be committed is education in this sense. My arguments in Chapter 2 suggested that there are many aims which could legitimately be pursued by schools. In some contexts, perhaps in a developing economy dependent on subsistence farming where the productivity of its land must be improved to avert the danger of famine, education in the full-blown liberal sense might seem at best a long-term goal for everyone, at worst an unnecessary luxury. At least there would be room for debate; and so there is, even in Britain and the USA.

The difference in this respect between teaching and what I called the most clear-cut case, medicine, may, after all, be only one of degree. Even within the medical profession there is room for debate about how its goals are to be conceived, about how health is to be defined and even, as some of the controversy over euthanasia shows, over what counts as life. A shared sense of values in a profession like medicine will not be entirely a matter of agreeing on the specification of goals; it will be partly also the recognition of the importance of the debate and the willingness and capacity to engage in it. That is what much of medical ethics is about: not handing down answers but equipping professionals to handle the questions. (This is perhaps even more true of nursing ethics, where the goals in question never even seemed clear-cut.)

I suggest we should say the same for teaching. Teachers will not necessarily share a unified sense of what it is they are aiming at, or of what the standards are which they should apply to themselves. But part of what distinguishes the teaching profession from the general public, and part of what could give it a well-deserved standing, ought to be, not that the profession is a repository of society's values which its members transmit but that the professionals do engage in the debate and that they are rather better equipped to engage in it than the general public.

NOTES

1. This response would fit well with John Wilson's advocacy of the teaching of the methodology of morality (see Chapter 12). It should be said that Wilson does not see this as the sole approach to moral education in schools. See Wilson (1972) and (1990), part 4.
2. For readers wishing to follow up the possibilities of philosophy in schools, addresses may be more useful than publications. See under 'SAPERE' in the Appendix.
3. 'Introduced' may be misleading. Advocates of philosophy with children have pointed out that young children naturally tend to ask the kinds of questions which adults may label as 'philosophical'. See Matthews (1980); Lipman (1991); White (1992).
4. Some of the marks of a profession may be realized, for teaching, in some countries but not in others. My remarks here apply, as often, to Britain, and to England and Wales more particularly. For discussion of how far teaching is a profession, see Downie (1990); Langford (1978); Pring (1993).
5. See Carr (1991), pp. 256ff. Carr would not fully endorse this suggestion.
6. The case for a General Teaching Council has been argued for over many years by Baroness Warnock; see, for example, Warnock (1994).
7. The argument here is made by Koehn (1994). Some passages in the present section are also in my review of Koehn's book in *Journal of Philosophy of Education*, **30** (2), 1996.
8. But see Illich (1976) for a contrary view.

Afterword: Next steps

As I anticipated in the preface, many questions in this book have been far from fully answered. Even where there have been answers, I am not sure that they are all consistent with each other. In a book intended (as this was not) to be an academic treatise proposing a theory of values, inconsistency would be a serious flaw. In a book intended (as this was) to encourage readers to think their own way through the issues, without oversimplifying them, it may be no bad thing that the arguments reflect the plurality and ambivalence which exist, not just within society, but within many of us individually. It's desirable, I suggest, that the teaching profession itself should reflect this plurality. Even if it is a good thing that every individual teacher should have a consistent set of values (a matter on which I have not actually given an argument either way), it does not follow that every teacher should have the same set.

In concluding this book, I am conscious of how much I have not discussed, examined or explained fully enough. But when so little attention is generally paid in the professional education of teachers to the explicit consideration of values, one can only hope that even a limited and flawed contribution will be helpful.

There are several directions in which the issues in this book could be followed up. One could delve more deeply into moral philosophy, setting out more fully and discussing more thoroughly the interpretations of moral values which I have only been able to touch on. That itself could be another book. But for readers who wish to follow up the moral philosophy for themselves, the notes and references in this book will serve as a guide.

The same issues could be pursued outwards, as it were, into broader social and political concerns. I have consciously said very little, beyond brief discussions of pluralism, liberalism and the secular society, about distinctively political questions; there is nothing, for instance, about competing theories of justice and of democracy, or about the rights and responsibilities of the citizen *vis-à-vis* the state, or about the currently influential notions of individualism and communitarianism. That could provide the material for yet *another* book. Then again, individual teachers could follow up the issues raised in this book for themselves, through further reading or in-service courses (if they can get any time or funding for such courses). And they can join organizations devoted to shared concerns (see Appendix).

Finally, and perhaps most important of all, teachers and others involved in the planning and implementation of the work of schools can continue to tackle these issues, as they always have, in the face of all the difficulties, adopting a collective approach to the issues and becoming as clear as they can in their own discussions about what they are trying to do and how to do it.

Appendix

There are many organizations in the UK devoted to various aspects of the teaching and promotion of values in education. A selection of these organizations is given below:

British Humanist Association
47 Theobalds Road
London WC1X 8SP

Centre for Citizenship Studies in Education
University of Leicester
Queens Building
Northampton NN2 6AF

Children's Rights Office
235 Shaftesbury Avenue
London WC2H 8EL

Citizenship Foundation
63 Charterhouse Street
London EC1M 6HJ

Impact
University of North London
116/220 Holloway
London N7 8DB

Gordon Cook Foundation
Hilton Place
Aberdeen
Scotland AB9 1FA

Journal of Moral Education
The Mere
Upton Park
Slough SL1 2DG

National Association for Pastoral Care in Education
Education Department
University of Warwick
Coventry CV4 7AL

Norham Foundation
University of Wolverhampton
West Midlands WV1 1SB

Rimscue Centre
Rolle Faculty of Education
Exmouth
Devon EX8 2AT

Steiner Schools Fellowship
Kidbrooke Park
Forest Row
East Sussex RH18 5JB

Unicef (UK) Education Department
55 Lincoln's Inn Fields
London WC2A 3NB

Values and Visions Project
The Development Education Project
c/o Manchester Metropolitan University
801 Wilmslow Road
Manchester M29 2QR

Values Education Council
University of Central England
Edgbaston
West Midlands B15 3TN

TACADE
Furness House
Trafford Road
Salford M5 2XJ

Human Values Foundation
92 Culford Road
London N1 4HN

Centre for the Study of Human Relations
University of Nottingham
Nottingham NG7 2RD

Trust for the Study of Adolescence
23 New Road
Brighton
East Sussex BN1 1WZ

Among organizations concerned with philosophy in schools is SAPERE, which can be contacted via:

The Secretary
Stammerham North
Christ's Hospital
Horsham
RH13 7NF

Bibliography

Almond, B. and Wilson, B. (eds) (1988) *Values: A Symposium.* Atlantic Highlands, NJ: Humanities Press.

Aristotle (1954) *Ethics.* Oxford: Oxford University Press (World's Classics edition; there are many other translations available).

Baier, A. (1985) *Postures of the Mind.* London: Methuen.

Bailey, C. (1975) 'Neutrality and rationality in teaching'. In Bridges, D. and Scrimshaw, P. (eds), *Values and Authority in Schools.* London: Hodder & Stoughton.

Barrow, R. (1981) *The Philosophy of Schooling.* Brighton: Harvester Wheatsheaf.

Benhabib, S. (1992) *Situating the Self.* Cambridge: Polity Press.

Benjamin, M. (1990) *Splitting the Difference: Compromise and Integrity in Ethics and Politics.* Lawrence, KS: University Press of Kansas.

Bereiter, C. (1974) *Must We Educate?* Englewood Cliffs, NJ: Prentice-Hall.

Berger, P. (1983) 'On the obsolescence of the concept of honour'. In Hauerwas, S. and Macintyre, A., *Revisions: Changing Perspectives in Moral Philosophy.* Notre Dame, ID: University of Notre Dame Press.

Berlin, I. (1969) *Four Essays on Liberty.* Oxford: Oxford University Press.

Blackburn, S. (1984) *Spreading the Word.* Oxford: Oxford University Press.

Blackburn, S. (1993) *Essays in Quasi-Realism.* Oxford: Oxford University Press.

Bottery, M. (1990) *The Morality of the School.* London: Cassell.

Bridges, D. (1979) *Education, Democracy and Discussion.* Windsor: NFER-NELSON.

Bridges, D. (1984) 'Non-paternalistic arguments in support of parents' rights'. *Journal of Philosophy of Education,* **18** (1).

Bridges, D. (1996) 'Competence-based education or training: progress or villainy?' *Journal of Philosophy of Education,* **30** (3).

Brown, S. (1975) *Philosophers Discuss Education*. London: Macmillan.

Callan, E. (1988) *Autonomy and Schooling*. Kingston/Montreal: McGill-Queen's University Press.

Carr, D. (1991) *Educating the Virtues*. London: Routledge.

Carr, D. (1995) 'Towards a distinctive conception of spiritual education'. *Oxford Review of Education*, **21** (1).

Carruthers, P. (1992) *The Animals Issue*. Cambridge: Cambridge University Press.

Clark, S.R.L. (1977) *The Moral Status of Animals*. Oxford: Oxford University Press.

Cochrane, D., Hamm, C. and Kazepides, A. (eds) (1979) *The Domain of Moral Education*. New York: Paulist Press.

Cupitt, D. (1980) *Taking Leave of God*. London: SCM Press.

Dancy, J. (1992) 'Caring about justice'. *Philosophy*, 67, 262.

Dawkins, R. (1976) *The Selfish Gene*. Oxford: Oxford University Press.

Day, J. (1989) 'Compromise'. *Philosophy*, 4, 250.

Dewey, J. (1916) *Democracy and Education*. New York: Free Press.

Downey, M. and Kelly, A.V. (1978) *Moral Education: Theory and Practice*. London: Harper & Row.

Downie, R. (1990) 'Professions and professionalism'. *Journal of Philosophy of Education*, **24** (2).

Downie, R. and Telfer, E. (1969) *Respect for Persons*. London: Allen & Unwin.

Dworkin, G. (1988) *Autonomy in Theory and Practice*. Cambridge: Cambridge University Press.

Dworkin, R. (1993) *Life's Dominion: An Argument about Abortion and Euthanasia*. New York: HarperCollins.

Fletcher, J. (1966) *Situation Ethics*. London: SCM Press.

Foot, P. (1978) *Virtues and Vices*. Oxford: Blackwell.

Freeman, A. (1993) *God in Us: A Case for Christian Humanism*. London: SCM Press.

Frey, R.G. (1980) *Interests and Rights: The Case Against Animals*. Oxford: Oxford University Press.

Galston, W. (1989) 'Civic education in the liberal state'. In Rosenblum, N. (ed.) (1989).

Galston, W. (1991) *Liberal Purposes: Goods, Virtues and Diversity in the Liberal State*. Cambridge: Cambridge University Press.

Garforth, F.W. (1985) *Aims, Values and Education*. Hull: Christygate Press.

Gilligan, C. (1982) *In a Different Voice: Psychological Theory and Women's Development*. Cambridge, MA: Harvard University Press.

Gilligan, C., Ward, J. and Taylor, J. (1988) *Mapping the Moral Domain*. Cambridge, MA: Harvard University Press.

Gutmann, A. (1989) 'Undemocratic education'. In Rosenblum, N. (ed.) (1989).

Habermas, J. (1976) *Legitimation Crisis*. London: Heinemann.

Habermas, J. (1990a) 'Discourse ethics: notes on a program of philosophical justification'. In Benhabib, S. and Dallmayr, F. (1990) *The Communicative Ethics Controversy*. Cambridge, MA: MIT Press.

Habermas, J. (1990b) *Moral Consciousness and Communicative Action*. Cambridge: Polity Press.

Halstead, M. (1992) 'Ethical dimensions of controversial events in moral education'. In Taylor, M. and Leicester, M. (eds) (1992).

Hampshire, S. (1983) *Morality and Conflict*. Oxford: Blackwell.

Hare, R.M. (1981) *Moral Thinking*. Oxford: Oxford University Press.

Hare, R.M. (1992) *Essays on Religion and Education*. Oxford: Oxford University Press.

Hare, R.M. (1993) *Essays on Bioethics*. Oxford: Oxford University Press.

Hart, H.L.A. (1961) *The Concept of Law*. Oxford: Oxford University Press.

Haydon, G. (1977) 'The "right to education" and compulsory schooling'. *Educational Philosophy and Theory*, **9** (1).

Haydon, G. (ed.) (1987) *Education for a Pluralist Society: Philosophical Perspectives on the Swann Report*. London: Institute of Education.

Haydon, G. (1992) 'Teaching education for values education: is there a way forward under current constraints?' *Australian Journal of Teacher Education*, **17** (1).

Haydon, G. (1993a) 'Moral education and the child's right to an open future'. *The International Journal of Children's Rights*, **1** (1).

Haydon, G. (1993b) 'Values education in a democratic society'. *Studies in Philosophy and Education*, **12** (1).

Haydon, G. (1993c) *Education and the Crisis in Values: Should We Be Philosophical about It?* London: Institute of Education.

Haydon, G. (1994a) 'Moral education'. *Philosophy Now*, 8.

Haydon, G. (1994b) 'Order and ritual are never enough'. *Observer*, 13 March.

Haydon, G. (1994c) 'Conceptions of the secular in society, polity and schools'. *Journal of Philosophy of Education*, **28** (1).

Haydon, G. (1995a) 'Thick or thin? The cognitive content of education in a plural democracy'. *Journal of Moral Education*, **24** (1).

Haydon, G. (1995b) 'Aims in education'. In Turner, T., Leask, M. and Capel, S. (eds), *Learning to Teach in Secondary Schools*. London: Routledge.

Haydon, G. (1996a) 'Educational aims and the question of priorities'. In Lidstone, J. (ed.), *Education for Natural Disaster Reduction: Handbook for Teachers* (publication sponsored by the International Council of Scientific Unions: Committee on the Teaching of Science).

Haydon, G. (1996b) 'Values in the education of teachers: the importance of recognizing diversity'. In Selmes, C. (ed.), *Values Education and Teacher Education*. National Association for Values in Education and Training.

Hicks, D. (1988) *Education for Peace*. London: Routledge.

Hirst, P. (1974) *Moral Education in a Secular Society*. London: University of London Press.

Hobbes, T. (1968) *Leviathan*. Harmondsworth: Penguin (first published 1651).

Hobson, P. (1984) 'Some reflections on parents' rights in the upbringing of their children'. *Journal of Philosophy of Education*, **18** (1).

Hume, D. (1888) *A Treatise of Human Nature*. Oxford: Oxford University Press (Selby-Bigg edition; first published 1739, and frequently republished).

Illich, I. (1973) *Deschooling Society*. Harmondsworth: Penguin.

Illich, I. (1976) *Limits to Medicine*. London: Boyars.

Jarrett, J.L. (1991) *The Teaching of Values: Caring and Appreciation*. London: Routledge.

Jones, M. (1977) 'Prejudice'. In Haydon, G. (ed.) (1987).

Jones, R. (1980) 'An aspect of moral education'. *Journal of Philosophy of Education*, **14** (1).

Kant, I. (1785) *Groundwork of the Metaphysic of Morals*. Translated in Paton, H. (1948) *The Moral Law*. London: Hutchison.

Kant, I. (1927) 'On a supposed right to tell lies from benevolent motives'. In Abbott, T. *Kant's Critique of Pure Reason and Other Works on the Theory of Ethics*. London: Longman (first published 1797).

Kirschenbaum, H. and Simon, S. (eds) (1973) *Readings in Values Clarification*. Minneapolis: Winston Press.

Koehn, D. (1994) *The Ground of Professional Ethics*. London: Routledge.

Kohlberg, L. (1981) *The Philosophy of Moral Development*. San Francisco: Harper & Row.

Kymlicka, W. (1990) *Contemporary Political Philosophy*. Oxford: Oxford University Press.

Langford, G. (1978) *Teaching as a Profession*. Manchester: Manchester University Press.

Lindley, R. (1986) *Autonomy*. Basingstoke: Macmillan.

Lipman, M. (1991) *Thinking in Education*. Cambridge, MA: Harvard University Press.

Lukes, S. (1985) *Marxism and Morality*. Oxford: Oxford University Press.

Lyons, N. (1988) 'Two perspectives: on self, relationships, and morality'. In Gilligan *et al.* (1988).

McCarthy, T. (1978) *The Critical Theory of Jurgen Habermas*. London: Hutchison.

Macedo, S. (1990) *Liberal Virtues: Citizenship, Virtue and Community in Liberal Constitutionalism*. Oxford: Oxford University Press.

MacIntyre, A. (1967) *A Short History of Ethics*. London: Routledge.

MacIntyre, A. (1981) *After Virtue: A Study on Moral Theory*. London: Duckworth.

Mackie, J. (1977) *Ethics: Inventing Right and Wrong*. Harmondsworth: Penguin.

McLaughlin, T. (1984) 'Parental rights and the religious upbringing of children'. *Journal of Philosophy of Education*, **18** (1).

McLaughlin, T. (1987) ' "Education for All" and religious schools'. In Haydon, G. (ed.) (1987).

McLaughlin, T. (1992) 'The ethics of separate schools'. In Taylor, M. and Leicester, M. (1992).

McNaughton, D. (1988) *Moral Vision: An Introduction to Ethics*. Oxford: Blackwell.

Matthews, G. (1980) *Philosophy and the Young Child.* Cambridge, MA: Harvard University Press.

Mendus, S. (1989) *Toleration and the Limits of Liberalism.* Basingstoke: Macmillan.

Meyers, D. (1987) 'The socialized individual and individual autonomy'. In Kittay, E. and Meyers, D., *Women and Moral Theory.* Totowa, NJ: Rowman & Littlefield.

Midgley, M. (1979a) *Beast and Man.* Brighton: Harvester Wheatsheaf.

Midgley, M. (1979b) 'Gene-juggling'. *Philosophy,* 54, 210.

Midgley, M. (1991) *Can't We Make Moral Judgements?* Bristol: Bristol Press.

Milgram, S. (1974) *Obedience to Authority.* London: Tavistock.

Mill, J.S. (1962a) *An Essay on Liberty.* In Warnock, M. (ed.), *Utilitarianism.* London: Fontana (first published 1859; many other editions available).

Mill, J.S. (1962b) *Utilitarianism.* In Warnock, M. (ed.) *Utilitarianism.* London: Fontana (first published 1861; many other editions available).

Modood, T. (1992) *Not Easy Being British.* Stoke-on-Trent: Trentham Books.

Mott-Thornton, K. (1996) 'Experience, critical realism and the schooling of spirituality' In Best, R. (ed.), *Education, Spirituality and the Whole Child.* London: Cassell.

Nagel, T. (1986) *The View from Nowhere.* New York/Oxford: Oxford University Press.

Nagel, T. (1991) *Equality and Partiality.* New York/Oxford: Oxford University Press.

National Curriculum Council (1993) *Spiritual and Moral Development: A Discussion Paper.* York: NCC (reissued by SCAA, 1995).

Noddings, N. (1984) *Caring: A Feminine Approach to Ethics and Moral Education.* Berkeley, CA: University of California Press.

Noddings, N. (1992) *The Challenge to Care in Schools: An Alternative Approach to Education.* New York: Teachers College Press.

Norman, R. (1975) 'The neutral teacher?' In Brown, S. (ed.) (1975).

Norman, R. (1983) *The Moral Philosophers.* Oxford: Oxford University Press.

Norman, R. (1994) ' "I did it my way": some thoughts on autonomy'. *Journal of Philosophy of Education,* **28** (1).

Oakley, J. (1992) *Morality and the Emotions.* Cambridge: Cambridge University Press.

O'Hear, P. and White, J.P. (1991) *A National Curriculum for All: Laying the Foundations for Success.* London: Institute of Public Policy Research.

Peters, R.S. (1966) *Ethics and Education.* London: Allen & Unwin.

Peters, R.S. (1981) *Moral Development and Moral Education.* London: Allen & Unwin.

Phillips, M. (1996) *All Must Have Prizes.* London: Little, Brown.

Plato (1955) *The Republic.* Harmondsworth: Penguin (many other translations available).

Pring, R. (1984) *Personal and Social Education in the Curriculum.* London: Hodder & Stoughton.

Pring, R. (1993) 'Is teaching a profession?' Paper given at annual conference of the Philosophy of Education Society of Great Britain.

Raphael, D. (1988) 'The intolerable'. In Mendus, S. (ed.), *Justifying Toleration: Conceptual and Historical Perspectives*. Cambridge: Cambridge University Press.

Rawls, J. (1972) *A Theory of Justice*. Oxford: Oxford University Press.

Rawls, J. (1993) *Political Liberalism*. New York: Columbia University Press.

Robinson, J.A.T. (1963) *Honest to God*. London: SCM Press.

Rosenblum, N. (ed.) (1989) *Liberalism and the Moral Life*. Cambridge, MA: Harvard University Press.

Ross, W.D. (1930) *The Right and the Good*. Oxford: Oxford University Press.

Ross, W.D. (1939) *The Foundations of Ethics*. Oxford: Oxford University Press.

Sandin, R. (1992) *The Rehabilitation of Virtue*. New York: Praeger.

Scanlon, T. (1982) 'Contractualism and utilitarianism'. In Sen, A. and Williams, B. (eds) (1982).

Schama, S. (1995) *Landscape and Memory*. London: HarperCollins.

Schon, D. (1983) *The Reflective Practitioner*. London: Temple Smith.

Sen, A. and Williams, B. (eds) (1982) *Utilitarianism and Beyond*. Cambridge: Cambridge University Press.

Singer, P. (1973) *Democracy and Disobedience*. Oxford: Oxford University Press.

Singer, P. (1976) *Animal Liberation*. London: Jonathan Cape.

Singer, P. (1981) *The Expanding Circle: Ethics and Sociobiology*. Oxford: Oxford University Press.

Smart, J. and Williams, B. (1973) *Utilitarianism: For and Against*. Cambridge: Cambridge University Press.

Snook, I. (ed.) (1972) *Concepts of Indoctrination*. London: Routledge.

Snook, I. and Lankshear, C. (1979) *Education and Rights*. Melbourne: Melbourne University Press.

Straughan, R. (1982) *I Ought To But ... A Philosophical Approach to the Problem of Weakness of Will in Education*. Windsor: NFER-NELSON.

Straughan, R. (1988a) *Can We Teach Children To Be Good? Basic Issues in Moral, Personal and Social Education*. Milton Keynes: Open University Press.

Straughan, R. (1988b) *Beliefs, Behaviour and Education*. London: Cassell.

Tamir, Y. (ed.) (1995) *Democratic Education in the Multicultural State*. Special issue of *Journal of Philosophy of Education*, **29** (2).

Taylor, C. (1982) 'The diversity of goods'. In Sen, A. and Williams, B. (eds) (1982).

Taylor, M. and Leicester, M. (1992) *Ethics, Ethnicity and Education*. London: Kogan Page.

Tobin, B. (1986) 'Development in virtues'. *Journal of Philosophy of Education*, **20** (2).

Tobin, B. (1989) 'An Aristotelian theory of moral development'. *Journal of Philosophy of Education*, **23** (2).

Tombs, D. (1995) ' "Shame" as a neglected value in schooling'. *Journal of Philosophy of Education*, **29** (1).

Turnbull, C. (1973) *The Mountain People*. London: Jonathan Cape.

von Furer-Haimendorf, C. (1967) *Morals and Merit: A Study of Values and Social Controls in South Asian Societies*. London: Weidenfeld & Nicolson.

Waldron, J. (ed.) (1984) *Theories of Rights*. Oxford: Oxford University Press.

Waldron, J. (1993) *Liberal Rights*. Cambridge: Cambridge University Press.

Walsh, P. (1993) *Education and Meaning: Philosophy in Practice*. London: Cassell.

Warnock, G. (1971) *The Object of Morality*. London: Methuen.

Warnock, M. (1975) 'The neutral teacher'. In Brown, S. (1975).

Warnock, M. (1994) 'Educational obligations of the state'. In Haldane, J. (ed.), *Education, Values and the State*. St Andrews: Centre for Philosophy and Public Affairs.

White, J.P. (1982) *The Aims of Education Restated*. London: Routledge.

White, J.P. (1990) *Education and the Good Life*. London: Kogan Page.

White, J.P. (1992) 'The roots of philosophy' in Griffiths, A.P. (ed.) *The Impulse to Philosophise*. Cambridge: Cambridge University Press.

White, J.P. (1995) *Education and Personal Well-Being in a Secular Universe*. (Inaugural lecture) London: Institute of Education.

White, P. (1996) *Civic Virtues and Public Schooling: Educating Citizens for a Democratic Society*. New York: Teachers College Press.

Williams, B. (1976) *Morality: An Introduction to Ethics*. Cambridge: Cambridge University Press.

Williams, B. (1981) 'Conflict of values'. In *Moral Luck*. Cambridge: Cambridge University Press.

Williams, B. (1985) *Ethics and the Limits of Philosophy*. London: Fontana.

Wilson, J. (1972) *Practical Methods of Moral Education*. London: Heinemann.

Wilson, J. (1975) 'Moral education and the curriculum'. In Taylor, M. (ed.), *Progress and Problems in Moral Education*. Windsor: NFER-NELSON.

Wilson, J. (1987) *A Preface to Morality*. Basingstoke: Macmillan.

Wilson, J. (1990) *A New Introduction to Moral Education*. London: Cassell.

Wingfield, L. and Haste, H. (1987) 'Connectedness and separateness: cognitive style or moral orientation?' *Journal of Moral Education*, **16** (3).

Wringe, C. (1981) *Children's Rights*. London: Routledge.

Wringe, C. (1988) *Understanding Educational Aims*. London: Unwin Hyman.

INDEX